PHILADELPHIA PRESIDENTIAL CONVENTIONS

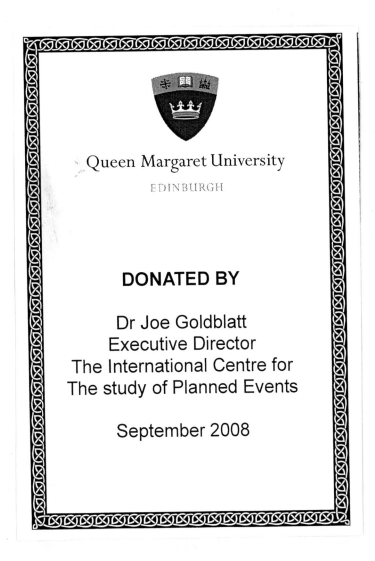

Books by R. Craig Sautter

The Power of the Ballot
> (staff project of the Citizenship Education Department,
> National Urban League)

Expresslanes Through the Inevitable City (poetry)

Smart Schools, Smart Kids (with Sally Reed and Edward B. Fiske)

Floyd Dell: Essays from the Friday Literary Review 1909-1913

Wicked City: Chicago from Kenna to Capone
> (with Curt Johnson)

Who Got In?
> College Bound's National Admissions Trends Survey
> (editions 1986-2000)

Inside the Wigwam: Chicago Presidential Conventions 1860-1996
> (with Edward M. Burke)

PHILADELPHIA PRESIDENTIAL CONVENTIONS

R. CRAIG SAUTTER

december press

A special issue of December Magazine,
comprising vol. 41 nos. 1 and 2, 2000

ISBN 0-913204-37-4
Library of Congress Catalog Card Number: 99-075049

Manufactured in the United States of America

Photo credits will be found on p. 344

Published by December Press
Box 302, Highland Park, Illinois 60035
(847) 940-4122

Distributed by Independent Publishers Group (IPG)
(312) 337-0747

For my wife, Sally Reed, for her generosity,
kindness, and deep spirit; with great love.

And in memory of my father,
Robert Underwood Sautter,
who first took me to Independence
Hall and taught me the meaning
of intellectual freedom.

—R.C.S.

Contents

Acknowledgments

I wish to gratefully acknowledge the assistance and support of several people in the development and production of this book: particularly, Curt Johnson, my publisher, for editing and sage guidance; Sally Reed, for editing; Chris Sautter; Ted Sautter; Alan Goddard; Bob Connelly; Tom Legge; Marc Davis; Kenan Heise; David Justice; and Weldon and Shirley Rougeau, and Kathryn King, all for valuable suggestions and support; also members of the Blue Heron Club.

Thanks also for resources and assistance: The Historical Society of Pennsylvania, especially Dr. Daniel N. Rolph and Bruce Sherer; The Library Company of Philadelphia, especially Sarah J. Weatherwax and Erika Piola; Greta Greenberger, Director, (Philadelphia) City Hall Tours and The Foundation for Architecture; The Minnesota Historical Society; The DePaul University Library; The Chicago Public Library, especially Commissioner Mary A. Dempsey and Marta G. O'Neill; The Chicago Historical Society; The Museum of Broadcast Communications, Chicago.

ILLUSTRATIONS

Preface

Philadelphia is America's original convention city. Beginning in 1774 with the First Continental Congress in which representatives from the 13 Colonies convened in Carpenters' Hall to put the British Crown on notice that America would no longer succumb to the tyranny of the "Intolerable Acts," the City of Brotherly Love has served as a revered meeting place for political representatives of the American people. Philadelphia became America's most important convention city when a year later the Second Continental Congress met in the Quaker City's State House (later renamed Independence Hall) and in 1776 proclaimed America's independence and freedom. From Philadelphia, Jefferson's immortal declaration, "We hold these truths to be self evident, that all men are created equal, that they are endowed by their Creator with certain unalienable Rights, that among these are Life, Liberty, and the pursuit of Happiness," first rang out to inspire a nation to revolution and self-definition, words which in subsequent years have transformed many of the world's political systems and served as the model for the United Nations' Universal Declaration of Human Rights, applicable to all men and women everywhere.

And it was from Philadelphia in 1787, that the Constitutional Convention reformulated the United States of America as a functional political entity regulated by a federal Constitution that has endured to this day, and is presided over by a President, Congress, and Supreme Court, all of which sat in their second session in Independence Hall and nearby buildings, after removing from New York, and remaining until the new capital city of Washington D. C. was ready for government use in 1800. To Philadelphia came the first President of the United States, George Washington, whose Continental Army had vanquished the British redcoats, and who had been president of the Constitutional Convention, before presiding over the affairs of the new nation alongside the Congress and Supreme Court.

In 1791, Congress, meeting in Philadelphia's State House, enacted James Madison's Bill of Rights, which continues to protect individuals against the excesses of government, and extends to all citizens the right to gather in peaceful assembly; to speak, write, and publish freely their thoughts; to worship without interference; to obtain a fair trial; and to be protected against unreasonable searches and seizures.

Ever since those early days of historic import, Philadelphia has continued to play a prominent role as a convention city. Among other events, Philadelphia hosted the first National Negro Convention of 1830;

was the site of the founding of the American Anti-Slavery Movement in 1833; and was the location of the Anti-Slavery Convention of American Women, which met with the Pennsylvania Anti-Slavery Society in 1838.

The historic red-brick city has also been a popular location for political parties to hold their Presidential nominating conventions, to proclaim their national platforms, and to rally their followers for the nation's quadrennial Presidential elections. Philadelphia places third on the list of most Presidential nominating conventions, with nine before 2000, among which were some of the most important and exciting in U.S. political history. Partly because of its geographic centrality, Chicago has attracted the most major-party Presidential nominating conventions with 25, followed by Baltimore which is geographically closer to Washington D. C. than Philadelphia, with 11, most of which were held during the first years of convention history.

Since 1848, Philadelphia has hosted five Republican, two Democratic, one Whig, and one Progressive party conventions to nominate candidates to become President of the United States. In July 2000, when the Republicans return after a hiatus of 52 years, Philadelphia welcomes its tenth Presidential nominating convention, and because of its heritage of freedom, is likely to host many more in years to come.

The U.S. Constitution makes no provision for political parties. Indeed, it was the fervent hope of the founding fathers that there would be no need for parties at all, which they saw as divisive "factions," likely to bring hatred and turmoil to the Republic. They were wrong. Instead, the two-party system has provided long-term stability to the United States. Notwithstanding the founders' desires, political parties emerged on the American landscape by the 1796 Presidential election to marshal support among like-thinking legislators as they confronted the ever-changing social and economic problems that faced the nation. Parties helped them to effectively legislate solutions. Parties were also essential for mobilizing support for those positions at election time. In 1896, 13 candidates received votes for President in the Electoral College. By 1800, parties had helped to reduce that number to five. Viable parties further narrowed the choices in subsequent elections, thus avoiding a fracturing of the popular vote that would have produced a parade of weak, minority-vote Presidents.

Just as the Constitution makes no provision for political parties, it does not mention the practice of Presidential nominating conventions. At first, none of the political parties held national nominating conventions. Instead, Presidential candidates were nominated by secret congressional caucuses, and those nominations were given to the acknowledged party leaders in Congress. Philadelphia was an important meeting place for three of the early congressional caucuses. In May 1796, Federalist party leaders secretly met in Philadelphia to nominate John

Adams, of Massachusetts, and Thomas Pinckney, of South Carolina, for President and Vice President.

The American people did not actually vote for President in the early Presidential elections. Rather, in most cases, state legislatures or state and district conventions elected Electors to vote in the Electoral College. Those Electors reflected the power of the political parties in their respective states. In the fall of 1796, John Adams won the Presidential vote in the Electoral College with 71 votes. But his opponent, Anti-Federalist, Thomas Jefferson, of Virginia, attracted the second most votes, with 68, and became Vice President, instead of Adams' running-mate, Pinckney, who finished third with 59 votes. Thus began the tradition in which the Vice President had little to do with the affairs of state; Jefferson was virtually exiled from the Adams administration, with which he had little sympathy.

In May of 1800, the Democrat/Republican party congressional caucus met in secret in Philadelphia to nominate Thomas Jefferson for President and Aaron Burr, of New York, for Vice President. That same month the Federalists secretly convened in Philadelphia to renominate John Adams for President, and Charles Cotesworth Pinckney, of South Carolina, for Vice President. In the fall election, Jefferson and Burr each attracted 73 Electoral votes, while President Adams came in third with 65 votes, thus throwing the contest to the House of Representatives. A Federalist conspiracy to give the election to Burr over Jefferson was avoided. Jefferson became President when his bitter enemy Alexander Hamilton persuaded Federalist congressmen not to pervert the process. In 1804, the Twelfth Amendment to the U. S. Constitution was enacted to avoid the discomfort of forming a government of political opponents who disagreed over philosophy and policy, and to make clear which candidate was intended for the Presidency and which for the Vice Presidency.

By 1824, voters in the westward-expanding American democracy rebelled against the secrecy of the congressional caucus system, and Andrew Jackson, of Tennessee, was nominated by state legislatures which had more direct ties with the people. Not until 1831 did a political party hold a public national Presidential nominating convention. In that year the anti-Masonic party staged the first Presidential nominating convention in New York to nominate William Wirt, of Virginia. Later in 1831, the National Republican party held its convention in Baltimore to nominate Henry Clay, of Kentucky. The Democrats also met in Baltimore in May 1832 to renominate Andrew Jackson, who then defeated Clay and Wirt in the general election, which by that time was mostly determined by the popular vote of white males, with or without property. "The Democracy" returned to Baltimore for its next five Presidential nominating conventions, and has been holding conventions every four years ever since, making it the oldest continuing political party in the world.

The Presidential nominating conventions held in Philadelphia over a 100-year period running from 1848 to 1948 have marked some remarkable moments in U. S. political history. The Whigs of 1848 were the first party to hold a Presidential convention in Philadelphia, nominating two men who would become President over the next four years (Taylor and Fillmore). In 1856, the anti-slavery crusaders who had recently formed the Republican party came to Philadelphia, the citadel of freedom, to nominate their first candidate, a young national hero and bold adventurer (Fremont), and to declare their intention to bring to trial the sitting President (Pierce) for crimes against humanity, should they win. In 1872, the Republicans returned to Philadelphia as a triumphant and powerful party to renominate the victorious general of the Civil War (Grant), and to declare their determination to quell the Ku Klux Klan in the South.

One hundred years ago, in 1900, the Republicans once more traveled to Philadelphia to renominate the "most popular President since Lincoln," and to celebrate America's new global power. Again, the convention nominated two men who would become President during the next four-year term (McKinley and T. Roosevelt). In 1936, the Democrat party arrived in Philadelphia for the first time to nominate a candidate (F. Roosevelt) who proclaimed that the people of the United States, who were just beginning to emerge from devastating economic depression, had a "Rendezvous with Destiny."

In 1940, the Republican party assembled in Philadelphia as the world peered into the abyss of global war, and enthusiastically nominated a candidate who had never held public office, who had no campaign staff or funds, and who had only declared his intention to seek the nomination two months before the convention (Willkie), in what was aptly called the "Miracle in Philadelphia." Finally, in 1948, when World War II had ended in total Allied victory, Philadelphia played host not to one, or two, but three national Presidential conventions, the only triple convention site in American history.

Philadelphia Presidential Conventions tells the stories of those first nine conventions, profiles the men who sought the Presidency, outlines the issues of import to the nation during each era, captures some of the masterful oratory and excitement of each event, and recounts the national elections that followed the conventions.

In the year 2000, as another national convention arrives in Philadelphia, many observers complain that Presidential nominating conventions have become obsolete. For the past few convention years, it has been, perhaps, more accurate to call these party assemblies ratifying conventions rather than nominating conventions. For while it is true that a formal nomination is extended to and accepted by the winning candidate at the national party conventions, in most cases the meetings are the culmination of a nominating process that has taken candidates through the state primaries where members of their parties have passed their own direct verdict upon the aspirants' fitness for the nation's highest office. Not since 1952, has the nomination fight gone more than one ballot on the convention floor, although as late as the 1968 Democratic National Convention in Chicago, the volatile issue of war or peace made the process and outcome uncertain until the vote was actually taken.

But looking backward, it can be pointed out that many conventions before 1952 were also decided on the first ballot and still had historical significance. In fact, 32 of the 57 Presidential conventions held by the Democrats and Republicans before 1952 were determined on the first ballot. (The 1924 Democratic National Convention held in New York City was the most contentious and went 103 ballots before John W. Davis, of West Virginia, won the nomination. But that was before the Democracy, meeting in Philadelphia in 1936, abolished the two-thirds vote rule needed to capture the nomination.)

The fault of not producing more drama over the outcome of the nomination is not so much that of the convention, nor of the primaries, but of the fact that the political parties themselves have not produced many strong national leaders who can compete for the prize, as well as the dominant role that money and the media have come to play in today's campaigns. A spirited three-way race, for example, could still produce a deadlocked situation in which no candidate came to the convention with a clear majority and several ballots might be required before a nominee is chosen.

But even as a ratifying event, today's national Presidential conventions still serve other essential party and public functions, and it would be hard to do without them. Next to nominating a Presidential candidate, the most important task of the convention is to adopt a national platform that defines and declares the ideals and legislative program of the party for the American voter. At no other time is the attention of the nation more fully directed on the parties and their positions on critical issues than during convention week. The attentive citizen is able not only to read the party's platform, but to listen to the debates and the oratory defining and defending those views which, should the party candidate be elevated to the Presidency, will serve as guideposts for legislative action. The democratic purpose of a national election would be diminished without that function.

Finally, the national convention still serves as an important way for the national party to bring together its vastly dispersed geographic members, for party activists to get together face-to-face and to have their spirits lifted, and receive a call to action in defense of a common ideological mission and candidate. It is hard to imagine the parties holding together as national entities without the glue provided by the quadrennial national nominating convention. After all, politics is not primarily entertainment performed for a television public, but is about the serious business of winning power and using that power to guide the nation through the inevitable perils of the next four years.

Whatever the future may hold for the parties and their conventions, the past Presidential nominating conventions examined in this book offer a fascinating glimpse into the history of the political parties as they developed and changed over time. In their convention annals is written the political history of the nation. These Presidential conventions provide snapshots of the parties and the country as they confronted the large issues of each era. Here are portraits of the personalities and passions of an America bygone which is the foundation of the America of today. In these stories are etched pictures of the great men who became or almost became President of the United States of America.

Here too are eloquent expressions of the highest political ideals of each epoch exuberantly projected through the passionate speeches of great orators and statesmen. (It is particularly fascinating to recall the speeches of the early convention orators who were called to the rostrum by popular demand of fellow delegates on the convention floor and who without prepared speeches or teleprompters swayed the emotions of their listeners with expression of the highest ideals of their parties.) Here is not only the record of political contests and celebrations, but reflections of the aspirations and fears of the American people as they prepared to pick their national leaders. Overlooked by many historians, and denigrated by many contemporary commentators, the Presidential nominating convention has been and continues to be one of the greatest of our democratic institutions, and one of the fullest expressions of our freedoms first declared in Philadelphia.

The 1848 Whig Convention: "Old Rough and Ready"

Convention-at-a-Glance

Event: 1848 Whig National Convention
Date: June 7-9, 1848
Location: Lower saloon of the Philadelphia Museum Building, also known as the Chinese Museum, N. E. corner of Ninth and Sansom Streets
Philadelphia Mayor: John Swift, Whig
Philadelphia's Population: 408,672 (1850)
Convention President: John M. Morehead, North Carolina
Number of Delegates: 279
Number Needed to Nominate: 140
Candidates for Nomination: Henry Clay, Kentucky; John M. Clayton, Delaware; General Winfield Scott, Virginia; Major General Zachary Taylor, Louisiana; Senator Daniel Webster, New Hampshire
Presidential Nominee: Major General Zachary Taylor
Age at Nomination: 63
Number of Ballots: Four
Vice Presidential Nominee: Millard Fillmore, New York
Largest Audience: 15,000
Platform Positions: The convention adopted no platform, but Whigs stood for preservation of the Union, dedication to patriotism, promotion of the protective tariff, a national bank, and internal infrastructure improvements, peace, no new territories through war, no executive patronage.
Campaign Slogan: "Old Rough and Ready"

1

Zachary Taylor
1848 Whig Presidential Nominee

Millard Fillmore
1848 Whig Vice Presidential
Nominee

1848

The 1848 Whig Convention: "Old Rough and Ready"

In Europe, 1848 was a dramatic year of democratic revolution that violently swept across the continent, country by country, throwing out or attempting to throw out decaying and repressive institutions of royalty and aristocracy. The United States, too, was undergoing tumultuous transformation, but instead of revolutionary change, 1848 marked another quadrennial election year for the young nation.

President James Knox Polk, of Tennessee, the eleventh President of the United States, a Democrat and a disciple of President Andrew Jackson, added more territory to the nation in his term than any other President since Jefferson. In the spirit of westward expansion, Polk had pushed for the annexation of Texas and at his urging Congress declared war against Mexico on May 13, 1846. Polk alleged that Mexican troops had crossed the Rio Grande and killed U.S. soldiers in an act of invasion.

But when President Polk introduced legislation to appropriate two million dollars to pay for negotiations to end the Mexican conflict, a young Democratic congressman from Pennsylvania, David Wilmot, introduced a provision to Polk's bill that insisted "neither slavery nor involuntary servitude shall ever exist" in the new southwestern territories. The proviso was modeled after a section in the Northwest Ordinance, which had forbidden slavery in those territories. The Wilmot Proviso passed in the House of Representatives, but the Senate adjourned before action could be taken on it. President Polk was angered by the young congressman's intervention and vowed to veto the "Wilmot Proviso" if it ever reached his desk. During the 1847 session of Congress, the Wilmot Proviso again passed the House, but John Caldwell Calhoun, of South Carolina, who advocated the spread of slavery into the new territories led a fight to defeat it in the Senate. The Wilmot Proviso sharpened the sectional divisions over the slavery issue, and a decade later its author would be among the founders of the Republican party.

3

The Mexican War split the nation. Northern "Conscience" Whigs who opposed slavery also resisted Polk's war for fear that it was a pretense to spread the hated institution into the new territories. Abraham Lincoln, "the lonely Whig from Illinois," rose on the floor of the House of Representatives demanding that President Polk name the "exact spot" where the Mexican invasion had taken place and American blood had been shed. Had it really been on American soil as Polk contended? Or had the battle taken place on Mexican soil as a pretense for war? Southern "Cotton" Whigs and Southern Democrats both embraced the conflict, since they anticipated that the slave-holding territory of the nation would be expanded when the war ended.

One national hero to emerge from the controversial war was Major General Zachary Taylor, of Louisiana, who despite reluctance to march on the Mexican army on his own initiative before the war, had taken up the sword when attacked. On May 8, 1846, at Palo Alto, Taylor's troops came under cannon fire by Mexican General Mariano Arista. With superior artillery, Taylor won the brief encounter and drove Arista's forces into retreat. The Mexican soldiers regrouped on higher ground where Taylor's artillery was ineffective. The next day a more bloody hand-to-hand battle raged at Resaca de la Palma, and Taylor's troops chased the Mexican forces back across the Rio Grande. Three times as many casualties were suffered by Mexican soldiers as by U.S. troops and Taylor's home base, Fort Texas, was saved. Overnight, Zachary Taylor became a national hero.

On September 21, "Old Rough and Ready" attacked Mexican troops at Monterrey in house-to-house combat. General Pedro de Ampudia surrendered, then was allowed to retreat. President Polk was outraged that Taylor let Ampudia slip away and transferred most of Taylor's troops to the command of General Winfield Scott. Taylor later said his actions were taken to spare the lives of women and children. But Polk, wanting a short war, made a tactical error of his own in granting the exiled leader Antonio Lopez de Santa Anna safe conduct through a U.S. naval blockade in hopes that he would negotiate a quick peace.

Instead, on February 22, 1847, Santa Anna charged the undermanned Taylor. Outnumbered four to one, Taylor's inexperienced troops halted wave after wave of Mexican attackers in a rugged terrain. Santa Anna retreated after two days of bloody battle, and Taylor was hailed as "the hero of Buena Vista." The general then led his forces into Vera Cruz in March. In September 1847, General Scott took Mexico City against an over-matched but proud opponent who refused to surrender.

The unresolved issue of slavery, which had vexed the nation since its origins, was again driving national events. Not long after the Mexican War ended, Southern Senators such as Calhoun, the first Vice President to resign from office and an ardent advocate of "States' Rights," along with Jefferson Davis, a U.S. Senator from Mississippi who had served with Major General Zachary Taylor at Buena Vista, were already openly organizing a secessionist movement to take Southern states out of the Union, more than a decade before the outbreak of Civil War. The national situation was tense.

Members of the Whig party, who were dedicated above all else to the Union, patriotism, and peace looked for a candidate who could unify their party and stop the Democrats, who seemed committed to territorial expansion at any cost. The Whig party was founded in the 1830s as heir to the National Republican party that grew up in opposition to Andrew Jackson's brand of "Democracy." Spiritually, Whiggery was also the descendent of the conservative Federalists of John Adams and Alexander Hamilton.

Pro-Taylor Whigs in Congress became known as the Palo Alto Club. Another group of Whigs, called the "Young Indians," took up the political battle for General Taylor. The group included Albert T. Burnley, of Louisiana, Alexander C. Bullitt, co-editor of the *New Orleans Picayune*, a Whig organ, Robert Toombs, of Georgia, John C. Pendelton, of Virginia, and Abraham Lincoln, of Illinois. Although Lincoln greatly admired Henry Clay as a statesman, he favored Taylor as a candidate who could help win Whig congressional seats in Illinois. Truman Smith, of Connecticut, who served as the Whig's unofficial national chairman, also admired Clay but was a private supporter of Taylor. Smith said the Whigs could not win the Presidency with "any man from the free states." He noted, "We are a minority party and cannot succeed unless we have a candidate who can command more votes than the party can give him."

Zachary Taylor, who was born in Virginia, had been a fighting man since 1806 but after a 40-year military career was a political novice. He was unschooled, an atrocious speller, stuttered, and could not deliver a coherent speech. But he had native intelligence and his troops were devoted to him. Taylor lived in Baton Rouge and owned a Mississippi plantation with 118 slaves, but was silent about expansion of slavery into the territories. Even though many Whigs were now courting him, the major general had never even cast a vote for President, much less held office. He indicated his Whig preference by declaring in a letter that if he had voted in 1844, "it would have been for Mr. Clay."

When initially approached about becoming President, Taylor replied, "Such an idea has never entered my head, nor is it likely to enter the head of any sane person." But his war record made him "available" to a draft and both the Whigs and Democrats actively sought to make the general their own. "If I ever occupy the White House it must be by the spontaneous move of the people," Taylor advised party boosters. And he asserted that if elected he would be a President "of the nation and not a party." He insisted, "I ask for no favors, and shrink from no responsibilities."

Many Conscience Whigs felt the Taylor boom was an attempt by Cotton Whigs to stampede the nomination. Indeed, the Young Indians wanted the party to endorse Taylor without a national convention as "the People's candidate" or as a "No party" candidate. But Whigs as a whole balked at this strategy. In December 1847, when the Young Indians called a meeting in Washington to nominate the general as an independent, most Whig congressmen angrily refused to attend. The majority of Whigs became insistent that a national convention be held and argued that in order for Taylor to receive the nomination he must declare his Whig convictions, specifically that he was against war and territorial expansion.

When a similar Taylor meeting in January 1848 failed to intimidate Northern Whigs into accepting Taylor or admitting they faced certain defeat in November, party leaders issued the call for a national Whig convention to assemble in Philadelphia on June 7, 1848. Indiana Whig Godlove Orth declared, "I am truly glad to learn that the Whigs of the North take the noble stand of requiring Taylor to pass the ordeal of a national convention and to require an expression of his political opinions. Those opinions must accord with the well-known principles of the party."

Taylor's chief opponent for the Whig nomination was the great orator and Whig leader Henry Clay, of Kentucky. Clay, born in 1777, had been Speaker of the House on three occasions, Secretary of State under John Quincy Adams, and had served a third tour as U.S. Senator from 1831-42. The tall, blond, charismatic leader also had been a candidate for President in 1824, as a National Republican, and as a Whig in 1832 and 1844.

Clay was an early architect of an "American System" of domestic improvements paid for by the federal government, a protective tariff that allowed U.S. commercial interests to develop without foreign dominance, a national bank to fund commercial expansion, and cooperation with South American patriots, positions that would elevate the United States, he said, "to the height to which God and nature destined it."

Clay was sometimes called "the Great Pacificator" because he authored the Missouri Compromise of 1820 which kept sectional interests in balance by admitting Missouri to the Union as a slave state and Maine as a free state, and stipulated that all territory north of the line 36 degrees and 30 minutes would be admitted to the Union as free states, and that those south of the line would be slave states. Although he was a slave-owner, Clay advocated the gradual emancipation of all slaves, and hence was seen as a traitor by many white Southerners. He also opposed the Mexican War, in which his son was killed. Clay had insisted that his party renounce "any wish or desire on our part to acquire any foreign territory whatever, for the purpose of propagating slavery or of introducing slaves from the United States." Such pronouncements weakened his support with the Cotton Whigs. On all questions of principle Clay declared, "I'd rather be right than President."

While Henry Clay was presented as "the embodiment of Whig principles," General Taylor was seen as a non-partisan and popular military hero. Although Clay was a slave-holder, many Northern Whigs who had opposed him in 1844 now saw him as preferable to Taylor who also owned slaves and avowed no Whig principles.

When Clay visited Washington in January of 1848 to argue cases before the Supreme Court, he seemed charming and vigorous, clearly capable of leading the nation. He made the social rounds as well, enchanting Washington society with his charisma. His admirers urged him to try again for the Presidency, convincing him that at long last he could win. He reiterated his opposition to war and to slavery in the territories. Northern congressional Whigs lined up in his favor and promoted an anti-war and anti-acquisition Whig platform. But the situation was fluid. Godlove Orth pointed out, "This Mexican War and its probable termination, and the consequences of such termination will all have an important bearing upon our candidate."

This was the background against which began the fight for delegates to the Philadelphia Whig convention in June. The first battlegrounds were the state and district Whig conventions across the nation. No one could with any sureness accurately predict the outcome. Each state would send delegates to Philadelphia equal to its electoral vote number. The method of selection varied from state to state, however. Since rules were not formally set by the national party, intense maneuvering and intrigue took place in the states between advocates for the various candidates. Most Southern states, along with Indiana, Iowa, and Rhode Island, for example, selected all their delegates at once in one state Whig convention. Several other states picked two delegates statewide and the rest at congressional-level conventions.

Early in 1848, Rhode Island Whiggery declared for Clay. Tennessee favored Clay at the state level, but district conventions meeting in May after the end of the Mexican War went for Taylor. Indiana sent uncommitted delegates who would read the situation of the moment when they arrived in Philadelphia. After intense in-fighting, partisans of Supreme Court Associate Justice John McLean got the upper hand in the Ohio convention, but it sent uncommitted delegates to the national convention.

February 22, 1848, the anniversary of Washington's birthday as well as of Taylor's Buena Vista victory, saw Whig state conventions in Kentucky, North Carolina, and Virginia. Forty delegates were at stake in one day. The Clay and Taylor forces furiously mobilized. But intra-party fighting in Kentucky and North Carolina prevented clear victories by either candidate. Fifteen of 17 Virginia delegates left its convention committed to Taylor. Louisiana Whigs nominated Taylor on their own on the February 22, 1848, anniversary of his Buena Vista victory.

On the same day, Philadelphia Whigs held their "Buena Vista Festival" in the lower saloon (public hall) of the Museum Building, also known as the Chinese Museum, located on the northeast corner of Ninth and Sansom streets. Washington's birthday was, along with the Fourth of July, one of the two days of major patriotic celebration in Philadelphia, where the Revolutionary War General had served most of his two terms as America's first President. Pennsylvania Whigs descended on Philadelphia by the hundreds as a prelude to the national convention in June. Inside the saloon, red, white, and blue bunting decorated the walls. Delegates stood under banners and raised signs declaring "General Taylor Never Surrenders"; "We are for the Union as it is, and for the Union as the will of all the states, legitimately expressed, may hereafter make it."

These Whigs called General Taylor "The man of the People." Toasts also were raised to the party's luminaries, Taylor, Clay, and Major General Winfield Scott. Washington too was lavishly extolled, since Whiggery traced its roots back to the Federalists and their successors, the National Republican party. Women also were saluted as, "The guardian of infancy, the companion of manhood, the solace of age: from the cradle to the grave, the ministering angel of humanity."

On February 23, 1848, President Polk sent the Senate the Treaty of Guadalupe Hidalgo by which Mexico ceded half a million miles of Mexican territory in upper California and New Mexico to the United States in exchange for payment of 15 million dollars. The territory would eventually yield the states of California, Nevada, Utah, Arizona, New Mexico, and portions of Colorado and Wyoming. The treaty was a victory for the beleaguered Democratic administration and robbed the Whigs of peace as a campaign issue.

With Whigs holding 21 of 58 Senate seats (they also controlled the House), and only 19 votes necessary to block the treaty, the Whigs commanded the nation's fate. But the choice Whiggery faced was peace and expansion or the resumption of war. The Whigs opposed both expansion and war. They were caught on the horns of this dilemma. If they rejected the treaty, many Whigs feared that President Polk would take all of Mexico by force. If they endorsed it, they sanctioned territorial expansion and the possible spread of slavery, despite the fact that slavery had been illegal in Mexico.

Whigs in the Senate were divided. New York Whig Nathan Hall lamented, "In truth we have the wolf by the ears and it is doubtful which is most dangerous, to hold or let go." With seven of 21 Whigs voting "No," the Senate confirmed the treaty by a 38 to 14 vote on March 10. (Mexico did not ratify the treaty until May 30, just one week before the Whig's Philadelphia convention.) The party stood denuded of its twin

The Great Whig Convention of 1848, held inside the Museum Building at Ninth and Sansom Streets. The Library Company of Philadelphia.

issues of ending the war and "No Territory." The Democrats were free to campaign on peace, prosperity, and expansion. "The war will have ended, and an immense acquisition of land will be pointed to as the result of Democracy," bemoaned John Defrees. "The land stealing, even among our best Christians, is popular!"

The Philadelphia Buena Vista celebration had been scheduled to show Clay's weakness in a state that he had narrowly failed to carry in 1844. Whig Congressman Joseph Ingersoll, of Philadelphia, had declared on the House floor that Taylor was "a Whig, not indeed an ultra-partisan Whig, but a Whig in principle." But Clay also had plenty of support in Philadelphia and throughout Pennsylvania. Clay's friends hosted a lavish dinner for him the day after the Buena Vista celebration. David Outlaw said the event would put "the Taylor concern into a cocked hat."

However, the Whigs had lost statewide in Pennsylvania in 1847 and held only 37 of the 100 seats in the state assembly. Philadelphia Whigs were concerned as well about the rising power of the Native American party, led by Lewis C. Levin, that was opposed to the influx of immigrants and to Catholics. Clay had declared himself opposed to the Know-Nothings, as the secret society was popularly known. Some Whigs, who sought a coalition with the Native Americans, knew the alliance could not be built on a Clay candidacy. Then to everyone's surprise, when the Keystone State Whig convention convened, General Winfield Scott outdistanced both Clay and Taylor.

In the Empire State, New York *Tribune* editor Horace Greeley, a passionate Whig, was busy promoting Clay, who felt he had lost the Presidency four years earlier because of New York Whig defections. The popular New York State Comptroller, Millard Fillmore, opposed Clay. William Henry Seward and Whig boss Thurlow Weed, editor of the Albany *Evening Journal*, who were normally allied with Greeley, favored Taylor. But with deep Democratic divisions becoming more evident each day, any Whig was expected to carry New York in 1848. New Jersey delegates split between Clay and Taylor. In almost every state Whig convention, the intra-party conflicts became intertwined with selection of committed delegates to the national convention.

But in late winter, Taylor's campaign had been jolted when New York papers printed private letters from General Taylor to several members of the Native American party stating that he was "entirely independent of party considerations." Taylor insulted Whigs with his declaration, "If the Whig party desires... to cast their votes for me, they must do it on their own responsibility without any pledges from me." Angry denunciations from Whig regulars followed. One New York Whig proclaimed, "Unless indeed we have reached a political millennium and the Whig party is to be disbanded," Taylor's letters "ought to put an end to all idea of his nomination by the Whigs." Another moaned, "A

Northern man with Southern principles was bad enough, but a Southern man with no principles may be worse."

Taylor's managers sought to stop the bleeding with new and more favorable letters from the uncontrollable general. Instead, things got worse when Taylor wrote a letter to one Kentucky Democrat that hinted he might accept a draft from either the Democrats or Whigs. Indiana Whig Congressman Caleb Smith wrote, "The man is certainly demented." John Defrees, editor of the *Indiana State Journal*, told a Taylor advocate, "I do not very well see how a national convention, having regard for principle, can nominate him."

On April 12, the always ambitious Clay, fearing the parade might pass him by, boldly announced that he was a candidate for the Whig nomination, a pronouncement that flouted all tradition. He became the first candidate ever to publicly announce his desire for the Presidency. A Presidential contender, it was thought, must show the decorum of disinterest. The country wasn't ready for the change. Clay's move backfired and alienated even Whigs who had favored him. Taylor himself reacted angrily, writing the *Richmond Republican* that he would become an independent candidate if the Whigs nominated Clay.

The general's managers in New Orleans saw a chance to regain momentum with the Whigs. They prepared several letters for Taylor's signature, addressed to Captain John S. Allison, of Kentucky. In a letter dated April 22, 1848, the general at last declared, "I am a Whig, but not an ultra Whig." In concordance with Whig principles, the general also denounced wars of conquest, called for magnanimity toward defeated Mexico, endorsed a weak Presidency and a strong Congress that set tariff and currency policy, and funded internal improvements. As to his campaign, he said, "I trust I will not be again called on to make further explanations." While Taylor's private pronouncements helped reverse his rapid fall, many Northern Whigs still opposed him.

The end of the Mexican War brought the slavery issue to the fore, since now the debate shifted to the status of the newly ceded territories. Northern Whigs sought to impose the Wilmot Proviso. Slavery was an issue that could fatally split the Conscience and Cotton Whigs, and without issues of broader appeal, Henry Clay, a three-time Presidential loser who had trouble appealing beyond his party, looked weaker than he had at the beginning of the year. Indeed, with the nomination of an anti-slavery man like Clay, "the Whig party will be annihilated," said Tennessee Whig Meredith P. Gentry.

But Clay was not giving up the nomination. "He is determined to rule or ruin the party," claimed Robert Toombs after a visit to Ashville, Clay's Kentucky estate. The struggle for delegates to the Philadelphia convention reached a new pitch. Now many Northern Whigs yearned for a Northern candidate who could beat both Clay and Taylor in Philadelphia. Some turned to the other great Whig leader, Senator Daniel Webster, of New Hampshire, who had served in the Senate from 1827 to 1841, before becoming Secretary of State for the first Whig President, William Henry Harrison, and his successor John Tyler, and then returning to the Senate.

Webster had denounced territorial expansion in a stirring speech after the Senate accepted the Mexican treaty. New York publisher Hiram Ketchum put out a pamphlet promoting Webster, entitled, "A Whig from the Start." And he promoted him to other party stalwarts such as Millard Fillmore, of Buffalo. His slogan was "Webster and the free states. Webster and the North." He argued that Webster could draw Northern Democrats as well as Whigs. Webster was supported by the New Hampshire and Massachusetts Whig delegations to the convention.

Other Northern Whigs touted Justice McLean as a compromise candidate. Some Whigs turned to General Winfield Scott, "Old Fuss and Feathers," who unlike Taylor had a Whig record and came from Virginia but did not carry the stigma of being a slave-owner. Like Taylor, he was a military hero of the Mexican War. His campaign gained strength in Indiana, Ohio, Pennsylvania, and New York. At the same time, the prospect of any military figure offended many Whigs such as the Quakers of Pennsylvania, Ohio, and Indiana. As delegates headed for Philadelphia, a party split loomed, with the prospect of Conscience and Cotton Whigs running separate candidates after the convention.

The June 7th gathering neared and thousands of Whigs poured into Philadelphia. They came from the bench and the bar, worked with plough and anvil, lived in mansions and cottages, but shared the Whig conservative ideal of dedication to patriotism. Many arrived on the new Pennsylvania Railroad, chartered in 1846, but whose steam engines were prohibited from entering the city limits. Delegates made their way downtown on horse-drawn omnibuses to the hotels and boarding houses that were packed to capacity. Some stayed at the new American House, across the street from the State House where the Declaration of Independence and the Constitution had been adopted. Others boarded at the Washington House on Chestnut Street above Seventh Street, the Girard House at Chestnut and Ninth Streets, and the La Pierre Hotel on Broad Street between Chestnut and Sansom Streets. New York alone sent 10,000 party members.

But because of the large delegations from other states, many of the Whigs who arrived in town could not even jam into the Philadelphia Museum Building, which had opened in 1838. The lower saloon of the Museum Building, known as the Chinese Museum, had been named by Nathan Dunn, a wealthy Philadelphia merchant who had carried on commerce and lived in the Far East and brought back to the city his collection of oriental art and life-like wax figures of Chinese men and women in costume. Dunn sent his collection to London in 1842 and though the hall had stood empty, it was still called the Chinese Museum and as a matter of course became the city's major meeting place and location for lavish balls.

With the exception of the great hall in Westminister Abbey, it was the largest hall in the western world and could accommodate as many as 15,000 people. Besides the original Continental Congresses and Constitutional Convention, no more imposing assemblage had ever met within the limits of the city than the great Whig Convention of 1848. (The last event staged in the Chinese Museum was the Philadelphia Grand Consolidation Ball and Banquet held on March 11, 1854. Then on July 5, of that year, flames jumped from the National Theatre next door and burned the museum to the ground, along with much of the south side of Chestnut Street. The land was then sold and on the site rose the Continental Hotel, which was later replaced by the massive Benjamin Franklin Hotel.)

When the doors of the Chinese Museum opened, thousands of delegates crowded onto the floor, while thousands of spectators stood in the galleries looking down on the mass of Whigs mingling between the 34 ornate columns on each side of the hall. The Young Indians were working the convention floor for Taylor. Greeley marshaled Clay forces from the office of Mayor John Swift. (The popular and courageous Swift, a Whig, was serving his third non-consecutive term as Philadelphia mayor. In 1838, he had been attacked by a white mob while trying to protect delegates to the Anti-Slavery Convention of American Women and members of the Pennsylvania Anti-Slavery Society as their headquarters at Pennsylvania Hall was burned to the ground. Then during the anti-black riot in the hot summer of 1840, Swift had confronted the white mob moving up Fifth Street that had broken through police lines, and armed with only his cane had dragged away the ringleader and turned him over to police thus saving the lives of many African-Americans.) McLean's effort was coordinated by James E. Harvey and Thomas Dowling. Zachary Taylor was being promoted by his brother, Colonel Joseph Taylor, who was on the convention floor.

The convention apparatus was run by party regulars, several of whom were nominally committed to Clay. John M. Morehead, of North Carolina, was voted convention president. But Thomas Butler King, of Georgia, a Taylor advocate, chaired the Credentials and Rules Committee, which made several rulings among disputed delegations that had sent more delegates than votes permitted by their state's Electoral College strength. And it assigned Taylor delegates to vote for states like Texas that had not sent any delegates. Clay men were locked out of the Louisiana delegation. And the committee voted against the "Unit Rule" that required a delegation to vote entirely as the majority declared. This allowed Taylor to pick up isolated votes in delegations controlled by Clay managers.

When the proceedings began, scores of speeches were made supporting the party and its potential nominees. To shore up Taylor's position, Garnett Duncan, of Louisiana, told delegates that he had seen a letter written by General Taylor to Balie Peyton, of New Orleans, in which he declared in favor of Whig principles, something Whigs reluctant to vote for Taylor were still demanding.

Seeking to discredit Taylor, Lew Campbell, of Ohio, introduced a resolution that the convention only offer its nomination to a Whig who had publicly declared his faith in Whig principles. The chair ruled Campbell's motion out of order. Campbell protested, but the delegates voted to table his protest. One Clay delegate wrote, "The treatment of such a resolution, in the manner it was disposed of by the convention, is virtual dissolution of the Whig party of the Union, by their chosen representatives, and absolves every honest man from being fettered by their decisions."

Lafayette Saunders, also from Taylor's home state of Louisiana, sought to lessen the bitter tension by declaring that the general was not about to launch an independent campaign if he were not nominated by the Whig convention and that Taylor men would support whomever the convention nominated. Discussion and debate of the various candidates lasted a day and a half.

Early Thursday evening, July 8, nominations were formally submitted to the body. The candidates were presented in brief statements. The names of Major General Zachary Taylor, Henry Clay, Senator Daniel Webster, General Winfield Scott, Supreme Court Associate Justice John McLean, and John M. Clayton, of Delaware, were offered from the floor. Sensing little support for McLean, Samuel Galloway, of Ohio, withdrew his name before the balloting began.

After a floor fight over who was actually eligible to vote, 279 delegates were allowed to cast ballots. A majority of 140 votes was required to win the nomination. The South controlled 111 votes, while the North held 168, more than enough to secure the nomination. That meant Clay had a theoretical advantage, if Northern Whigs held together.

The excitement grew as the states cast their voice votes and cheers went up for each candidate. At the end of the first ballot, Taylor took the lead with 111 votes, 85 from the slave states of the South. Despite his lead, Taylor faced a steep challenge to win. Eighty-five percent of the Northern delegates had voted against him. Clay closely trailed Taylor with 97 votes, but only 5 of the 12 Kentucky delegates favored their native son. Clay was in deep trouble. General Scott attracted 43 votes. If his votes had gone to Clay, the Kentuckian would have won on the first ballot. Webster had 22; Clayton drew 4; and Justice McLean received 2 votes, despite the withdrawal of his name.

Clay managers tried to convince delegates that Taylor's strength in the convention was actually illusionary, since the general's base was in states that would vote Democratic in November such as Alabama, Arkansas, Illinois, Maine, Mississippi, Missouri, South Carolina, and Texas. A move by Clay forces to make a deal with Scott's managers was blocked by the false rebuff that Scott would not accept the second spot. Had the truth been told, Scott would have accepted, and Clay could have won on the second round.

On the second ballot, Taylor picked up steam, gaining to 118 votes. Disheartened Clay delegates deserted him and left Clay with only 86. Scott inched forward with 49; Webster held his ground at 22; and Clayton clung to his 4. McLean's support evaporated. Clay's managers angrily demanded a recess until morning, which the convention, deeply split on the nomination, was happy to accord them.

In the interim, the cagey Thurlow Weed, who had master-minded Harrison's "Log Cabin" Presidential campaign victory in 1840, worked on delegates, looking for switches among the camps least able to win. One tactic he used was to appeal to the self-interest of the youngest delegates among them, pointing out that as an old leader with many commitments, Clay was likely to hand out the spoils of victory to older party men. Switch to Taylor, he said, and you will be rewarded. Meanwhile, Clay's Southern support fell under withering pressure to back Taylor, another Southerner but with a real chance to win.

Senator-elect Truman Smith, of Connecticut, the party's unofficial chairman and long a Clay admirer who had reluctantly favored Taylor, feared the entire party would break apart along sectional lines. He spent the evening urging delegates to vote to adjourn the convention altogether until unity could be restored. He was adamantly opposed by the Taylor managers. But they also feared that the convention might conclude that the only hope for party unity rested in a compromise candidate like Scott, who was Southern by birth, but since he was not a slave-holder would be more palatable to Northerners.

On Friday morning, June 9, 1848, the Whig delegates reconvened in the Chinese Museum for the third ballot. Alabama cast its votes for Taylor. Arkansas followed with all but one Clay man voting for Taylor. Then Truman Smith, leader of the Connecticut delegation, took the floor and along with two others switched his vote from Clay to Taylor in an attempt to save the party. The vote set off a loud celebration among Taylor delegates and spectators in the gallery. Smith heard strong denunciations from his Northern colleagues, but his influential vote was crucial as others followed suit. At the end of the pivotal third ballot, General Taylor surged ahead with 133 votes. He needed only seven votes now to claim the prize. Clay tumbled to 74. Webster slipped to 17, while

Scott gained to 54. Clayton clung to a single vote.

The bandwagon was pulling away and delegates jumped to get on board for the fourth ballot when Taylor scored his victory with 171 votes; General Scott, Taylor's commanding officer in the Mexican War, garnered 63 votes. Scott would become the Whig nominee in 1852, during the party's last viable campaign. Taylor had attracted 50 Northern votes since the first ballot. Only 12 of the 26 Pennsylvania delegates voted for Taylor. Clay was reduced to 35 votes and Webster to 13. The party that the two great statesmen had founded and nurtured had abandoned them and their principles for a popular military hero, despite the fact that the Whigs had built their reputation on anti-war stands. Clayton's support vanished in Taylor's fourth-round victory. General Zachary Taylor, a gentle and kind man, was on the road to his greatest victory, the Presidency. His supporters staged a wild demonstration on the floor and in the galleries.

The scene was bittersweet. Many delegates were angry. Whig party unity had been protected, but at the expense of axioms dear to Whiggery. Publisher Greeley called the convention, "a slaughterhouse of Whig principles." Amid the confusion following Taylor's victory, John Collier, of New York, took the floor and announced his support for the Taylor nomination. Then he nominated a Northerner, Millard Fillmore, for the Vice Presidency to balance the ticket and bind up the sectional wounds. Southerners favored Abbott Lawrence, a wealthy Boston textile manufacturer.

But Charles B. Allen, of Massachusetts, was inconsolable over the nomination of a slave-owner. The Bay State "rejected the nominee of the convention, and Massachusetts would spurn the bribe that was offered to her," he thundered, referring to Lawrence. "I say the party of the Whigs is... dissolved." He was answered with "boos" and "hisses."

A member of the Ohio delegation rose to move that Taylor's nomination stand only on condition that he adhere to the Whig's "great fundamental principles: no extension of slavery, no acquisition of foreign territory by conquest, protection of American industry, and opposition to executive patronage." The convention floor was stirred with yells in support and in opposition to the Ohio resolution, but President Morehead ruled it out of order. A young Henry Wilson, of Massachusetts, who would become President Grant's second Vice President, exhorted, "...sir, I will go home, and so help me God, will do all I can to defeat the election of that candidate." The Ohio delegation shouted for Wilson.

George Ashmun, of Massachusetts, who would become a Republican party founder eight years hence, objected that Wilson did not represent Whiggery in his state. Others in Ohio spoke up for Taylor. Then convention President Morehead called for nominations for Vice President. Fourteen names were submitted, including Thomas Ewing, of

Ohio; William Henry Seward and his political enemy, Millard Fillmore, both of New York. The Boston textile manufactuer Abbott Lawrence, a Taylor man, had considerable support North and South. His great wealth could help the party during the coming national canvass.

Daniel Webster's son, Fletcher, spoke of his father's opposition to Lawrence. Weed, Seward's sponsor, worked against Fillmore. The large delegation of Native Americans warned that Seward's pro-Catholic and pro-immigrant sentiments made him unacceptable to them and would sink Whiggery in Pennsylvania. They worked actively to elevate Fillmore, who was sympathetic to their cause and who in 1856 would become their Presidential nominee.

While the arguments raged on the convention floor, the vote was taken. At the end of the first ballot, Fillmore took a slim lead with 115 votes to Lawrence's 109. On the second ballot, several Southerners, attentive to the possible breakup of the party, switched to Fillmore, who was nominated with 173 votes to 83 for Lawrence. The concession seemed to solace many Clay men. Fillmore, who had been an Anti-Mason before he became a Whig and had been a leader in the House of Representatives, also was chosen to help the party win his home state of New York.

Delegate after delegate rose to salute the Taylor and Fillmore ticket. Amidst the cheers, the convention broke up in order to attend a mass ratification meeting in Independence Square, without even adopting an official platform. Daniel Tilden, of Ohio, rose to object, but a Pennsylvania delegate shouted, "Taylor is the only ammunition we need." Then the large convention crowd, those who had failed to gain entry, and many Philadelphians listened to enthusiastic speeches by the likes of Francis R. Shunk, governor of the Pennsylvania commonwealth, William F. Johnston, speaker of the senate, John Sherman, of Ohio, and others.

Taylor was later endorsed by the Native American party in its secret convention. It nominated Henry A. S. Taylor, of Massachusetts, a Know-Nothing as his running mate. In the Whig convention's wake, a bitter Henry Clay wrote, "The Whig party has been overthrown by a mere personal party," and he declared that he would "take no active or partisan agency in the ensuing contest." A political cartoonist friendly to Clay depicted the Whig convention as "The Assassination of the Sage of Ashland." Featured in the drawing were political assassins led by Daniel Webster quoting lines from Shakespeare's "Julius Caesar" while Clay calmly read Horace Greeley's *Tribune*.

Indeed, the fact that Clay was defeated and no platform was adopted offended many Whigs who saw theirs as a party of principles. Some prominent Whigs bolted from the party altogether, the first signs of the party's eventual disintegration eight years later when leading Whigs abandoned it, eventually joining the anti-slavery Republican party.

One tradition of early American political parties was to officially notify the Presidential nominee by letter. This practice allowed the candidate to remain insulated from the rough and tumble of the convention and retain all of the dignity required for the office itself. The candidate would then accept the nomination with a return letter of his own that affirmed the party platform. But the Whig party, which had no platform at all in 1848, was itself running out of steam. Someone failed to affix enough postage to its notification letter, which was thus sent to the Dead Letter Office. People wondered why Taylor failed to respond. Over a month later, Taylor, who was out of public view in Louisiana, paid the postage due and finally received his formal notification. He then retreated in silence for the remainder of the electoral canvass. As a result of the embarrassing mixup, future conventions appointed special notification committees which hand-delivered letters of nomination.

The Democrats had held their convention in May in Baltimore. The Democracy, as the party of Jackson was called, was as deeply divided on the issue of slavery between Northern and Southern delegates as the Whigs had been. President Polk had alienated too many with his war to gain renomination and had declared he would not run again. Taylor's name had even been placed into nomination by an admiring South Carolina delegate.

But Lewis Cass, United States Senator from Michigan, won the two-thirds vote needed for nomination on the fourth ballot. Cass, a corpulent old political hand, was born in Ohio, had been a brigadier general in the War of 1812, served as governor of the Michigan Territory for 18 years, and had acted as President Jackson's Secretary of War and Minister to France. Cass's running mate was William Orlando Butler, of Kentucky, who had served as a major general under Taylor in the Mexican War. He was a gifted orator and a poet.

Cass was an advocate of "popular sovereignty" which called for letting the new states vote on whether they would enter the Union free or slave. That made him a compromise candidate between the party's divisive factions. Cass resigned from the Senate on May 30, 1848, so that he could withdraw from the political turmoil surrounding the campaign made by Democrats on his behalf. In his acceptance letter, written before he vacated Washington, Cass declared his approval of Democratic party positions because they echoed the "principles and compromises of the Constitution." Standing on his public record of 40 years, he noted that his letter "closes my profession of political faith."

Cass's nomination led former President Martin Van Buren (1837-41) to bolt from the party he once had led. Van Buren despised Cass. In Buffalo, in August, the Free Soilers nominated Van Buren, who called for "Free soil and freedom of the public lands to actual settlers." (He had also been nominated by the Free Soilers in Utica in June.) His New York faction was branded the "Barnburners," because, like an old Dutch farmer it deemed to burn the barn down to kill some rats. Charles Francis Adams, son of one President and grandson of another, was Van Buren's running mate.

"Free Soil, Free Speech, Free Labor, and Free Men" the Free Soil party faithful chanted. The Barnburners were mostly old Locofocos who strongly opposed slavery anywhere in the Union. Van Buren's new Free Soil party united the Barnburners, some Conscience Whigs who still opposed Taylor's nomination, as well as veterans of the 1844 Liberty party. The new coalition vowed not to let slavery spread any further on "freedom's sacred soil." Free-soil "stumpers" scattered across the nation to deliver lengthy anti-slavery speeches at every cross-roads, barn, and saw-mill where people would listen.

Cass was a moderate who urged that, "If we are not struck with judicial blindness, we shall cling to the Constitution as the mariner clings to the last plank, when night and the tempest close around him." But when Cass heard that Van Buren had bolted from the Democrats, he knew his election was doomed. He was right.

Still, the ensuing campaign was bitter. One campaign parade in New Orleans resulted in shooting and arson. None of the candidates campaigned for themselves, although Taylor kept up his habit of writing letters, and these caused occasional problems. One anti-Taylor campaign poster featured Major General Zachary Taylor in full uniform perched on top of a large, triangular pile of parched skulls, trophies of his Mexican War campaign. In contrast, Whig posters featured "Old Rough and Ready," dressed in his military blue parade jacket, white parade pants, and formal hat with white plume, bravely mounted astride his horse, "Old Whitey." The image was an ironic one, since Taylor hated his uniform and usually wore old baggy civilian clothes and a straw hat while in battle. The Whigs called their candidate "the People's President."

Everywhere images of the candidates were painted, on snuff boxes, cigar boxes, porcelain mugs and pitchers, whiskey flasks, song books, broadsides, silk ribbons, brass medallions, cameos, pewter-rim buttons, even in needlepoint. The Whigs paraded about with banners of General Taylor circled by the embroidered names of his Mexican victories at Palo Alto, Resaca de la Palma, Buena Vista, and Monterrey.

Taylor's total silence drew bitter Democratic barbs. He was called "two-faced" because in his silence he seemed to court both abolitionists and slave holders. Democrats charged he held to no principles at all, except himself and the commands he issued. The Whigs responded with attacks of their own on Cass, who they claimed was a land speculator who had cheated the government out of over $64,000 during his government service. And they mocked his meager military record. Abraham Lincoln said he hoped that he would never be a Democratic candidate for fear they would make "fun of me, as they have of General Cass, by attempting to write me into a military hero." One Whig slogan ran, "And he who still for Cass can be; He is a Cass without the C." The Democrats countered with the slogan of "Principles Not Men!"

Congress had passed legislation in 1845 setting uniform procedures for selecting Presidential electors, thus creating a need for simultaneous campaigns in the various states. So the Democracy formed the first Democratic National Committee in Washington to coordinate its 1848 state campaigns. The DNC produced a "Democratic Textbook" for local campaigners to follow as they spoke in favor of the national ticket.

Passions ran high throughout the fall and over 70 percent of eligible white male voters, and countless ineligible "floaters," turned out in November. On election day, Whig Taylor attracted 1,360,967 votes to 1,222,342 for Democrat Cass from voters in 30 states. The spoiler was Free Soil candidate Van Buren who polled 291,263. In the Electoral College, the vote was equally close, with Taylor cornering 163 electors; Cass 127. Former President Van Buren, who held the balance of power in New York, swung its 36 votes to Taylor, but received no electoral votes himself. Before New York was counted, Cass and Taylor were tied at 127. Pennsylvania proved equally crucial to Taylor's victory. The Whigs won Philadelphia by 10,000 votes, enough to swing the state and the nation. Taylor was President, but Whig principles had been sacrificed. Horace Greeley called Taylor's election, a Pyrrhic victory in which the Whigs were "at once triumphant and undone."

After his election, "Old Zach" declared "I shall continue to devote all my energies to the public good, looking for my reward to consciousness of pure motives, and to the final verdict of impartial history." Facing a Democratic plurality in the House of Representatives and a Democratic majority in the Senate, a Congress where feuding legislators carried pistols and fistfights broke out, President Taylor resisted all efforts to spread slavery to the new territories, thus justifying the confidence Whigs had placed in his candidacy.

Two unanticipated and fortunate minor by-products of the election came when Nathaniel Hawthorne was ousted from his job in a post-election patronage sweep. The young writer spent his free time composing *The Scarlet Letter*. In New York, a Democratic paper dismissed Walt Whitman, who then went to work on *Leaves of Grass*.

Two years after the election, on July 9, 1850, President Taylor died in office of typhus fever, and was replaced by his Whig Vice President, Millard Fillmore.

The 1856 Republican National Convention: Birth of a Party

Convention-at-a-Glance

Event: First Republican National Convention
Date: June 17-19, 1856
Location: Musical Fund Hall, 808 Locust Street
Philadelphia Mayor: Richard Vaux, Democrat
Philadelphia's Population: 565,529 (1860)
Convention President: Henry S. Lane, Indiana
Number of Delegates: 558
Number Needed to Nominate: A majority
Candidates for Nomination: Nathaniel Banks, Massachusetts; Salmon Portland Chase, Ohio; John Charles Fremont, California; Supreme Court Justice John McLean, Ohio; Senator William Henry Seward, New York
Presidential Nominee: John Charles Fremont
Age at Nomination: 43
Number of Ballots: Two (one informal, one formal ballot)
Vice Presidential Nominee: William Lewis Dayton, New Jersey
Largest Audience: Several thousand
Platform Positions: Restoration of the Missouri Compromise; prohibition of slavery and bigamy from the territories; immediate admission of Kansas to the Union as a free state; opposition to admitting Cuba to the Union because of its practice of slavery; federal funding of internal public improvements; a transcontinental railroad
Campaign Slogan: Free Soil, Free Speech, Free Men, Fremont
Campaign Song: "Champion of Freedom"

**John Charles Fremont
1856 Republican Presidential
Nominee**

1856

The 1856 Republican National Convention: Birth of a Party

In the spring of 1856, two Presidential nominating conventions were convened in Philadelphia, America's original convention city, and from them came two nominees, seeking the highest office in the land. One nominee was a former United States President running with a political party which had grown out of a secret society. The other was a young explorer and daring national hero who was nominated by a new populist party that had burst upon the national scene. A third national party on the ballot was in its death throes. And the fourth party, the one that had dominated the Presidency for much of the previous two decades, abandoned the sitting President of the United States in favor of a former Secretary of State, a statesman who hailed from Pennsylvania. The nation was in a state of crisis and the people of the United States looked to the November election to resolve the deadly rift that already threatened disunion and civil war.

The national crisis was "Bloody Kansas." On January 23, 1854, Democratic Senator Stephen Arnold Douglas, of Illinois, chairman of the Committee on Territories, called for division of the Nebraska Territory into two states that would "be received into the Union, with or without slavery, as their constitutions may prescribe at the time of their admission." His "simple solution" to the slave status of the new states was a repudiation and repeal of the Missouri Compromise of 1820 that had forbidden the extension of slavery north of latitude 36 degrees and 30 minutes. Crafted by Whig Senators Daniel Webster and Henry Clay, the Missouri Compromise had ushered in a generation of relative stability for the young Union founded on the North/South fault line of human bondage.

Douglas promoted his solution of "popular sovereignty," inherited from the 1848 Democratic Presidential nominee Lewis Cass, in hopes of currying favor with Southern Democrats and thereby reenergizing his long-simmering Presidential ambitions. Congress, controlled by

Democrats, passed his "Kansas-Nebraska" bill after two months of acrimonious debate. Southern Democrats enjoyed the seeming paradox of a simple solution that could democratically extend slavery. The decision whether the new states would be free or slave was left to local citizens at the polls. What could be more American?

The Mexican-American War had been waged primarily by Southern Democrats in hopes of expanding the number of slave states in the Southwest. (Mexico itself, from which territory was taken to form new states, had abolished slavery 20 years earlier.) But Whig President Zachary Taylor, a Southerner who had fought in that war, blocked their scheme. With the gold rush in California changing the dynamics of the territory, he accepted the entry of California into the Union in 1850 as a free state and the balance of power in Congress shifted for the first time away from the slave states of the South.

Southern legislators immediately made plans to break Texas into five slave states with ten Southern Senators, and to annex Cuba and Central America as slave states. Until they could enact their scheme, they knew that entry of Kansas as a slave state would restore the old balance. Only two Southern Senators, Sam Houston, of Texas, and Thomas Hart Benton, of Missouri, rose in opposition to the Kansas-Nebraska Act. But abolitionists who had voted for the Free-Soil party in 1848 and 1852, "Conscience Whigs" of the northeast who opposed slavery, and an assortment of anti-Nebraska Democrats in Congress and across the North were appalled by the Kansas-Nebraska Act. Mobs rushed into the streets of Northern cities expressing outrage. Douglas, Congress, and the Democratic President, Franklin Pierce, were denounced in angry speeches made beneath the flare of torches. Senator Douglas remarked that he could travel by train from Boston to Chicago by the light of his own burning effigy. He was booed off a speaker's platform in his own hometown of Chicago and a mob threatened to burn his newspaper building to the ground.

But popular indignation in the North could not stem the flood of homesteaders who raced into Kansas eager to make money from the natural bounty of rich farm lands. Nor could it halt the speculators bent on profits from real estate opportunities and transportation right-of-ways. The nation was pushing west with a frenzy fueled by the discovery of California gold, more gold than existed in the entire U.S. Treasury. Kansas was smack in the middle of the transcontinental route. Abolitionist crusaders from Massachusetts, led by Eli Thayer and his Massachusetts Emigrant Aid Society, and Southern slavers each recruited and funded homesteaders to stake claims in Kansas in preparation for the crucial election of representatives who would craft the state constitution. Farms were purchased and plowed, towns rapidly sprang up.

The Kansas-Nebraska debacle demonstrated the necessity of a

political party to direct the anti-slavery, anti-Democrat vote of the nation. To do just that, a new Republican party was founded on February 28, 1854, in the small, First Congregational Church of Ripon, Wisconsin. "We went in Whigs, Free Soilers, and Democrats," said Alvan E. Bovay. "We came out of it Republicans." Bovay, a Ripon lawyer, had been working with New York *Tribune* editor Horace Greeley along with others since 1852 to bring about an anti-slavery party. Bovay and Greeley gave the party its name, "the only one that will serve all purposes present and future, the only one that will live and last," Bovay declared. The new Republicans felt that the national issues that had defined the old parties 20 years earlier were no longer relevant to the fast-growing nation. Fresh ideas fired the imagination of these men.

Republicans demanded moral and political action against the dominance of the Southern slave states. The Northern men feared that the congressional balance of power that had held slavery in check for the first 78 years of the nation's history, and had isolated it as a "Southern evil," would soon be broken if the Kansas territory entered the Union as a slave state. With a majority in Congress, slavers could legally expand human bondage across the West, and might even transform the entire nation into a "slavocracy." Indeed, Senator Robert Toombs, of Georgia, vowed that the day would come when he would call the roll of his slaves on Bunker Hill in Boston. The future of the nation, the future of freedom was at stake, Republicans declared.

Once articulated, the Republican ideal spread like wildfire across a dry prairie already inflamed by anti-slavery fervor. Local party organizations sprang up all over the North. On July 6, 1854, the first Republican mass meeting drew hundreds to Jackson, Michigan. The swelling crowd overflowed the town's largest building and was forced to reassemble under a nearby canopy of towering oak trees, which later became sacred to the party. The Michigan Republicans adopted a platform to give identity to their organizing efforts. Cheers erupted when it was resolved that "in view of the necessity of battling for the first principles of Republican government, and against the schemes of an aristocracy, the most revolting and oppressive with which the earth was ever cursed, or man debased, we will cooperate and be known as Republicans until the contest be terminated."

Seven days later, on the sixty-seventh anniversary of the Northwest Ordinance, a document that had explicitly forbidden slavery in the Northwest Territory, Republicans held state conventions in Ohio, Indiana, and Wisconsin to nominate candidates for the 1854 mid-term congressional and state elections. In the fall, the results of their efforts shocked the nation. Throughout the North, Democrats who had won handily two years earlier, were defeated in droves. The fledgling Republican party had a role in the upset, but so too did the Native

American party also known as the Know-Nothings, suddenly energized by Whig converts who joined its ranks and brought it to the polls. Secretly, the Know-Nothings, who were rapidly growing in numbers, voted in concert against all Democrat office-holders.

Additionally, temperance crusaders, out to ban the demon saloon, joined the effort to vote out "Rum Democrats" in states like Pennsylvania. Six months after Douglas' notorious Kansas-Nebraska bill was passed, the immediate result was a net loss of 31 Democratic seats in the House and a stunning defeat in all but two Northern states. To the United States Senate, the Illinois legislature sent Lyman Trumbull, a friend of Abraham Lincoln and the man who would become author of the Thirteenth Amendment in years to come. There, he joined anti-slavery activist, former Whig, and new Republican, William Henry Seward, of New York, who predicted an "irrepressible" conflict over slavery. Seward would become Lincoln's Secretary of State.

The nation was in political turmoil. President Pierce was under attack. Congress was rudderless. No single rebellious party could take total credit for the victory. The political landscape was buckling beneath them all. Republicans won in some states. Know-Nothings, who were incensed that Pierce had appointed a Catholic to his cabinet, won in others. And the Temperance party, Fusion party, and People's party candidates had scored victories in still other states. Republicans were hopeful that with the right candidate they could challenge, even win, the Presidency in 1856.

On June 19, 1855, the Republican Association of Washington, D.C., was formed, charging that the Kansas-Nebraska Act had inflicted "deep dishonor... upon the age in which we live." The association's platform asserted "that Congress possesses no power over the institution of slavery in the several states; but that, outside of state jurisdiction, the constitutional power of the federal government should be exerted to secure life, liberty, and happiness to all men, and therefore; Second. There should be neither slavery nor involuntary servitude, except for the punishment of crime, in any of the territories of the United States."

The Republican Association also called for the popular election of all officers (implying U.S. Senators). It sought to make Francis Preston Blair, Sr., the Democratic publisher of the *Congressional Globe*, its candidate for President, but he declined. The group then formed a committee to work with like-minded "friends of freedom" and clubs "in every city, town, and village in the Union... to expose and fairly meet the sophistry of pro-slavery demagogues." And it hired a hall to house a national committee for the Republican Party in "Washington City ... a city dedicated to slavery." They began collecting funds for pamphlets and also hired German translators to spread the Republican message to the immigrant population across the nation.

By 1856, hundreds of men, women, and children had been shot, burned, or stabbed to death in the Kansas war. With the help of 5,000 "ruffians" crossing over from Missouri to pose as voters and armed with Bowie knives, revolvers, and Sharpe's rifles, the slave faction won the state's first election and established its slave government and constitution at Lecompton. The free-staters counter-organized their own government and passed the "Topeka Constitution," which while banning slavery also outlawed blacks from state residency. Kansas had two competing governors, two legislatures, and two military forces facing off against each other. Blood freely flowed and the economic and moral question of slavery that blighted the soul of the young nation begged to be settled.

Still, Democrats dominated Congress. On January 24, 1856, the U.S. House of Representatives, voting on the Kansas issue, recognized the Lecompton slave constitution and branded the Topeka government guilty of "treason" and "revolution" for resisting the results of the violent election. Guerrilla warfare escalated. President Pierce, the young patriot from New Hampshire who had won election by representing the spirit of "young America" and "Manifest Destiny," regarded it as his constitutional duty to enforce the federal law and uphold the Union at all costs. He removed territorial governor Andrew H. Reeder, originally from Pennsylvania, who opposed slavery and refused to certify the fraudulent election results, and used the U.S. Army to enforce the oppressive state laws of the Lecompton slave legislature. For that decision, President Pierce further fell from grace. Swept into office in a landslide, Pierce was now denounced throughout the North as a "criminal." His political career was finished. He would retire to isolation and bitterness for the rest of his life.

Meanwhile an epic struggle was taking place on the floor of the House of Representatives. For two months, beginning on December 3, 1855, and ending on February 2, 1856, the House fought to pick its next Speaker, but was deadlocked between Democrats, Whigs, Know-Nothings, and Republicans. Finally, after 133 ballots, a coalition including Know-Nothings, elected Nathaniel Prentiss Banks, an antislavery leader from Massachusetts, over William Aiken, of South Carolina. Banks, in only his second term, was the first Speaker to win votes from only one section of the nation.

The new Republicans were not the only political hopefuls with their eyes on the Presidency. On Washington's birthday, February 22, 1856, the national Know-Nothing lodge kicked-off the 1856 Presidential election season by coming above ground to meet in convention in Philadelphia. The secretive Know-Nothings, who got their name because members professed to "Know-Nothing" about their party when asked, kept internal cohesion with clandestine oaths, handshakes, and signs. The nationalist movement had grown throughout the 1840s in response to a massive influx of Irish and German immigrants. Anti-Catholic riots had broken out in several cities and Catholic churches were torched. For the most part, Know-Nothings were not engaged in political activity until 1852, when members of the Order of the Star-Spangled Banner in New York pledged to vote against all Catholics or foreigners running for office, regardless of party affiliation. The movement quickly spread as the Order of United Americans.

The Know-Nothings, or Native American party, sent 227 delegates from 27 states to Philadelphia. Only Maine, Vermont, Georgia, and South Carolina fielded no delegates. In assembly, the powerful party reaffirmed its dedication to "Union" above all else. Americanism remained its gospel. But despite efforts to hold the chaotic assembly together, the slavery issue quickly drove a wedge through its ranks. Delegates from New England, Pennsylvania, Ohio, Illinois, and Iowa jointly bolted the convention, leaving a Southern-dominated party.

The remaining group renamed itself the American party and promptly nominated the thirteenth President of the United States, Millard Fillmore, as its Presidential candidate for 1856. The Philadelphia convention elevated Andrew J. Donelson, of Tennessee, as Fillmore's running mate. Former President Fillmore had represented the "Silver Grey" or "National" wing of the old Whig party, a faction committed first and foremost to Union and its preservation. Fillmore who had been Zachary Taylor's Vice President, succeeded to the Presidency on Taylor's death in 1850. But Fillmore failed to gain the 1852 Whig nomination. Instead, the nomination went to General Winfield Scott, who in declaring his abolitionist sympathies during the general election, had carried only four states in the entire Union. Franklin Pierce was elected President in a landslide so great that it all but destroyed the old Whig party of Henry Clay and Daniel Webster. And Democrats swept the 1852 election to a dominant two-to-one majority in both the House of Representatives and the United States Senate.

When the Whigs disintegrated, Fillmore and his associates surreptitiously moved to take over the Know-Nothings and remake it to their own political purposes by working their way into the hierarchy of the secret lodges. Since the party made decisions from the top down, Fillmore's faction was able to influence events. The core membership remained loyal to its founding principles of "100 percent American." The former Whigs added another unifying theme to the Know-Nothings of preserving the Union by standing against "sectional" parties such as the Republicans.

With a former President as its candidate, the American party looked to be a force in the 1856 election. The Know-Nothing platform on which Fillmore ran was popular with many voters. It called for "the perpetuation of the federal Union, as the palladium of our civil and religious liberties." In xenophobic simplicity it declared, "Americans must rule America." The American party further proclaimed, "Native-born citizens should be selected for all state, federal, or municipal offices of government employment...." And it sanctioned the preservation of slavery when it called for "the unequaled recognition and maintenance of the reserved rights of the several states, and the cultivation of harmony and fraternal good will between the citizens of the several states, and to this end, the non-interference by Congress with questions pertaining solely to the individual states...."

The American party also sought to tighten citizenship laws "making a continued residence of 21 years... an indispensable requisite for citizenship... and excluding all paupers or persons convicted of crime from landing upon our shores, but no interference with the vested rights of foreigners." Politically, the American party also declared "opposition to the reckless and unwise policy of the present administration in general management of our national affairs... as shown in an insolent and cowardly bravado toward the weaker powers, as shown in reopening sectional agitation by the repeal of the Missouri Compromise... as shown by the corruptions which pervade some of the departments of the government...." Therefore, it announced that "to remedy existing evils, and prevent the disastrous consequences otherwise resulting therefrom, we would build up the American party upon the principles herein before stated eschewing all sectional questions, and uniting upon those purely national...." Since the Republican party would not bother to run slates in the slave states, the American party was the only viable political challenge left against the Democrats in the South and most former Southern Whigs joined its ranks in 1856.

On the same day the Know-Nothings emerged from secrecy, on the other side of Pennsylvania, in Pittsburgh, the new Republican party commemorated Washington's birthday with its first national meeting in Lafayette Hall. Hundreds of delegates settled in at the Monongahela Hotel. Among them were anti-slavery leaders including Owen Lovejoy, of Illinois, William Denison, of Ohio, Horace Greeley and businessman Edward Denison Morgan, of New York, Governor George K. S. Bingham, of Michigan, J. W. Stone and Nathaniel Banks, of Massachusetts, C. M. K. Puleston, of New Jersey, Congressman Joshua Reed Giddings, of Ohio, William Boyd Allison, of Iowa, and Lewis Clephane and Francis Preston Blair, Sr., of Washington, D. C. Blair was chosen as the president of the Pittsburgh convention. Hundreds were turned away for lack of room in the meeting hall.

The Republican delegates were enthusiastic and demonstrated a "harmony seldom known to political assemblages of this magnitude," Greeley telegraphed the New York *Tribune*. He predicted that the party's "moral and political effect upon the country will be felt for the next quarter century." But the energetic collection of Republican delegates representing business, labor, and farming, as well as immigrant German and Irish factions, was unwieldy. Their fervor made it difficult to pass any resolutions of principle. Still, the new party laid the infrastructure for a national nominating convention to be held in Philadelphia on June 17 of that year, in order to nominate Presidential and Vice Presidential candidates, and to plan for the subsequent campaign and canvass.

The delegates of the Republican party resolved to challenge the remaining Whigs, the Know-Nothings, and Democrats for the nation's allegiance. And they issued a call to others to begin setting up state and county committees, along with "the formation of clubs in every town and township throughout the land." A large mass meeting followed the convention's adjournment and those in attendance were urged "to resist and overthrow the present national administration, as it is identified with the progress of the slave power to national supremacy."

A month later, on March 27, 1856, the Republican executive committee met in the Willard Hotel in Washington to formally issue the national nominating convention call "To the People of the United States, without regard to past political differences or divisions, who are opposed to the repeal of the Missouri Compromise, to the policy of the present administration, to the extension of slavery into the territories, in favor of admission of Kansas as a free state, and of restoring the action of the federal government to the principles of Washington and Jefferson...."

Thus, to nominate its first Presidential candidate, the new political party dedicated to freedom and the repulsion of slavery from the western territories of the United States convened in Philadelphia on June 17, 1856. Symbolically, the young party that had sprung out of the moral indignation of millions of Americans turned to the nation's sacred birthplace, where first the glorious bell of liberty had rung out to people across the land. Philadelphia was to serve as a powerful reminder to the electorate of the founding fathers' unshakeable creed of liberty, taken up by this new party of freedom. From the city's hallowed ground had sprung the Declaration of Independence, which had so magnificently proclaimed what these men who called themselves Republicans held equally dear, "... that all men are created equal, that they are endowed by their Creator with certain unalienable Rights, that among these are Life, Liberty, and the pursuit of Happiness."

From the meeting halls of Philadelphia had echoed the grand oratory of the First Continental Congress that first put England on notice about the complaints of the colonists, the Second Continental Congress that declared American Independence, and of the Constitutional Convention of 1787 where the Republic's founders had defined the institutions, rights, liberty, and laws through which freedom would find ample exercise in the new states. Philadelphia knew the importance of a convention. And the conveners of the First Republican National Convention knew the importance of Philadelphia to the Union and to the cause of freedom.

A steady stream of Republican delegates and supporters flowed into the venerable city. They ventured from as far away as Wisconsin, and from towns and cities across Pennsylvania, Ohio, and west from Indiana, Illinois, and Iowa, as well as from New York and the New England states. Traveling by steam train, by wagon, by canal, and on foot, imbued with dedication to their cause, they arrived in the "City of Brotherly Love" several thousand strong in mid-June 1856. Many of the delegates were housed at Girard House at Chestnut and Ninth Streets, which had opened in 1852. Others took up temporary residence in Franklin House on Chestnut Street, between Third and Fourth Streets. The delegates represented hundreds of local party organizations that had been established all over the North over the last two years in response to the national emergency that had matured since the Presidential election of 1852.

They were warily welcomed by Philadelphia, once a Whig stronghold, which had grown with a huge influx of Irish fleeing the potato famine and other immigrants who voted Democratic. Whigs had dominated city elections from 1841 through 1854. But after the consolidation of greater Philadelphia into one large city on February 2, 1854, power began to shift to the Democrats. As the Whigs disintegrated as a national party, many Philadelphia Whigs joined the Democrats rather than the Republicans, who struck them as dangerous and radical on the slavery issue.

It was a Democratic mayor, 40-year-old Richard Vaux, who presided over Philadelphia as the new Republicans stormed in for their first Presidential nominating convention. Vaux was the popular son of a philanthropist from an old Quaker family who championed the working classes of the city. He replaced Whig Robert T. Conrad, the first mayor after consolidation, a conservative businessman who had won as an "American" candidate with the help of the Know-Nothings. One of the purposes of consolidation was to build unified police and fire departments that could combat the lawless and violent gangs and volunteer fire companies who battled each other for control of city streets. Conrad recruited 900 new police of American birth who cracked down hard with violence of their own. They harassed those who sold liquor or drank on Sundays in violation of the city's "Blue Laws," setting off a number of confrontations and fights with workingmen.

Since no Philadelphia mayor could succeed himself for another two-year term, Vaux easily won the May 1856 election with the backing of angry Democratic voters. His slogan was "No increases in taxes! No excursions of (city) Councils! No Free rum at the expense of Councils!

No Free cigars! No Free Hack Hire! But a frugal and economical administration of municipal affairs!" William B. Thomas, Philadelphia's first Republican candidate for mayor in 1856, received less than 1 percent of the vote. Vaux would bring about pacification among the notorious gangs such as the Moyamensing Killers, the Bleeders, the Blood Thugs, the Death Fetchers, the Hyenas, the Smashers, and the Tormentors, who had terrorized the city's decent residents for a decade. During his tenure, physical assaults on the streets greatly diminished and there were no large riots. Hence he fulfilled the greater goals of city consolidation. The gifted Vaux was later elected to Congress.

The Quaker city may have been the nation's center of scientific and medical progress, home to cultural institutions and great music, affluent and comfortable homes, often a refined city of post-colonial respectability, and now a Democratic city, but it was still excited by a convention. Philadelphia, the delegates soon discovered was an industrial metropolis true to its English, German, and Welsh ancestry, with many well-educated citizens known for their honest and candid views on all topics, including political affairs. But as a city "with a country heart" and William Penn's tradition of tolerance, it welcomed them. More than a few of the residents were closely following the fortunes of the new political party that was about to launch its national voyage from their civic center and soon would be the rage among all the city's most important elements. However, many Philadelphians, particularly merchants whose textile businesses and trade were closely aligned with the South, were less than sympathetic. And the position of blacks, who had lived in Philadelphia as both freemen and slaves since the city's origins, had badly eroded since they were disenfranchised by the Pennsylvania state constitution in 1838.

The city that housed the Liberty Bell now served as cradle for a restless and burgeoning political party that was firmly set upon purging the moral blight of slavery from the nation's tormented soul. To that end, 558 Republican delegates and thousands of new party members supporters filed into Musical Fund Hall, Philadelphia's largest meeting place, to select a candidate to stand for the Presidency in the upcoming canvass of the states. With that prize, Republicans would gain the power to impose their interpretation of Jefferson's great Declaration on the Republic of their own era. The delegates themselves had been selected by no set rules and most of them were unknown to each other.

The acoustically perfect Musical Fund Hall, located on Locust Street just west of Eighth Street, was an old church bought by the Musical Fund Society in 1824 and converted by architect William Strictland. At 11 A.M., June 17, the delegates were gaveled to order in its ornate concert chamber by Edwin Denison Morgan, of New York, chairman of the Republican National Committee. Among the throng were the new party's national leaders such as Charles Francis Adams, descendent of two Presidents, Judge David Wilmot, of Pennsylvania, whose congressional proviso had set off sectional conflict eight years earlier, Congressman Joshua Reed Giddings, of Ohio, Congressman Gerrit Smith, of New York, Governor Salmon P. Chase and John Sherman, of Ohio, Thaddeus Stevens, Joseph Ritner, and George H. Earle, all of Pennsylvania, Senator Henry Wilson, of Massachusetts, Owen Lovejoy, of Illinois, and young James G. Blaine, of Maine, a future Republican Presidential nominee. All the Northern states, along with border slave states of Delaware, Maryland, Virginia, and Kentucky, sent delegates. So did the territories of Kansas, Nebraska, and Minnesota.

Chairman Morgan's loud voice rang out, "Delegates of the convention, representatives of the heart and hope of the nation: The day and the hour appointed for this gathering have arrived.... You are here today to give direction to a movement which is to decide whether the people of the United States are to be hereafter and forever chained to the present national policy of the extension of human slavery."

He then nominated as temporary chairman the "Honorable Robert Emmet" of New York to tumultuous cheering and a unanimous "Aye." Judge Emmet addressed the noisy assembly, extending his thanks and saying, "Certainly it is owing to no merit of mine that I have been singled out for this compliment. Nothing beyond the zeal which I feel in the common cause that has brought us here together could possibly entitle me to it." The crowd hailed his modesty. "I can say that my antecedents have been all Democrats." Again cheers interrupted him.

"Fellow citizens, the formation of a new party in a Republic like ours, after an existence of 80 years, is a singular event in history... that can only be justified by strong and irresistible causes...." Looking back on the founding of the American Republic, he noted that "all the great men of that day foresaw and predicted that slavery, although it could not be summarily and suddenly abolished, would die out in this country. All acknowledged that it was an evil. All acknowledged that it was the policy of the country gradually to get rid of it. That was the policy of the day.

"That policy led to the adoption of what was called the Missouri Compromise.... I say that the Missouri Compromise was adopted in 1820 as the only measure that could give peace to this country... freedom, fortunately had the larger share here, and freedom would never permit slavery to absorb her, and to engross the whole of this fair territory. What was to be done, then? We could not make all the Southern states free at once. We had then to draw a line; and let it be understood that it was by that line, the Missouri Compromise, slavery was to be limited, and that it should never extend north of it."

Judge Emmet then denounced the warfare in Kansas and the Democrats who had met earlier in Cincinnati to nominate James

Buchanan as their 1856 candidate. "Now, gentlemen, I have known the Honorable James Buchanan for 40 years and upwards, intimately; and I say here that some of the dearest and most cherished recollections of my life are connected with my associations with him. I would defend his personal character if assailed. But his political character, if I were not in deadly hostility to that, I would not be here." He was again interrupted by the crowd's approval; then the judge forged on, "I do not blame him for having been a Federalist once, and for having said in the enthusiasm of the moment, he was a young man at the time, that if he thought he had one drop of Democratic blood in his veins, he would let it out." The crowd erupted in laughter.

"But I do blame him in that, after he had expressed his opinion in regard to the Missouri Compromise, after he had bowed in adhesion to it, as every patriot of the day did, yet when he found certain men of his party breaking down the fabric of liberty, he had not the strength enough to resist it.... And I blame him for his very last act; his adhesion to this spurious platform of Democracy at Cincinnati.... He acknowledges that he is no longer James Buchanan, a free agent, with the right of expressing whatever will or opinion he may have of his own; but that he is bound to that platform and to every plank of it... an admission that he has allowed himself to be chained to the juggernaut of slavery...."

Judge Emmet further castigated the Democrats. "They may call us Black Republicans and Negro worshipers. Why, if they were not traitors and buffoons, they would find something better than that to apply to us. They may say that we mean to concentrate and gather under our wings all the odds and ends of parties, all the 'isms' of the day. Be it so. Let them come to us with all their 'isms.' We will merge them all in that great 'ism,' patriotism." The delegates responded with rapturous and prolonged cheering.

Finally, Emmet took upon himself the label that his opponents had hurled against him; abolitionist. "Now I say boldly... there is not an honest man who does not understand his own rights, and the rights of others, who respects the immortal Declaration of Independence, who does not hope to see the day... when such a thing as human bondage shall not exist in the world.... This is an honest abolitionist." After calling for unity to achieve victory, the judge yielded to the vociferous cheering of his fellow Republicans.

Reverend Albert Branes of Philadelphia gave an invocation before delegates were assigned to committees and other procedural resolutions were introduced, including giving honorary convention membership to members of the radical Free-Soil Democracy of New York, who had seceded from the Democratic party of that state in 1848, and who had refused to be "dragged behind the juggernaut of slavery," and who in the 1848 Presidential election had rolled up 121,000 votes and brought about the defeat of the Democrats.

Then the Honorable John Allison, of Pennsylvania, urged the convention to also seat a large number of delegates who had arrived to represent the Pennsylvania Republican State Convention. A delegate from New Hampshire proclaimed that they should be admitted even if they had to sit on the laps of others, rather than be turned away. The Maine delegation offered to give up its seats for them. Both resolutions were triumphantly adopted and more Republicans crammed into the Musical Fund Hall when it reassembled at 4 P.M. that Tuesday afternoon.

Judge Emmet then introduced the convention's Permanent President, Colonel Henry S. Lane, of Indiana, who had been a Congressman from 1841 through 1843, amid clamorous cheers by attendees from the Hoosier State. When order was restored, President Lane began his declaration, "Friends of Freedom and Freemen." Again a demonstration was touched off. Lane was forceful and held his listeners under his spell, reminding them that they convened on the anniversary of the Battle of Bunker Hill and that they now were gathered within sight of Independence Hall "with all its glorious revolutionary recollections." Now ghosts of those heroes gathered "from a sense of common danger." Lane told the convention that he once had been, "a humble and earnest follower of the gallant and glorious Henry Clay of Kentucky" but that "from the time that I heard the Nebraska-Kansas swindle was consummated, I have let the gallant Clay lay in his tomb, to follow the principles which require active support of all true men." Lane's words were drowned out with cheers.

Then he articulated the principles that drew the delegates together: "No more slave states and admission of Kansas as a free state." He blamed the current predicament on "a set of heartless, brainless demagogues; Douglas and the rest." Lane further denounced the Kansas situation where, "Scenes have been enacted which would have disgraced the revolutionary times of France, which would have disgraced the worst times of the middle ages. These things have been done in the middle of the nineteenth century and done through the connivance of the present weak and wicked administration.... We are told that when we endeavor to prevent these things we are revolutionary. If it is, it is a revolutionary feeling sanctioned by God." His joyous listeners burst into sustained applause.

When President Lane completed his inaugural address, the convention voted to follow the recommendation of the Credentials Committee headed by New York's Elbridge G. Spaulding. The rules of the convention would follow those of the House of Representatives on parliamentary proceedings. The president then called for addresses from the Honorable Caleb Smith, of Indiana, and then Owen Lovejoy, of Illinois.

Lovejoy began in earnest, "Nations, as well as individuals, have their destiny. There often appears on the stage of human action in this world, individuals who seem designed to fulfill a certain purpose. So it is with nations. The question here is, what is our mission... the manifest destiny of the American nation? The mission of our Pilgrim fathers was to exhibit the practicality of a church without a bishop and a state without a king.... I thank God for the principles of the Declaration of Independence... that derives power, not from invading 'Border Ruffians,' but from the will of the governed."

Lovejoy solemnly raised his hand. "What then is the mission of America?" He hesitated before affirming what all in the room knew: "To maintain and illustrate the self-evident truths laid down in that Declaration of Independence.... Now what was the principle it set up? It was simply the truth that 'All men are created equal.' " The delegates demonstrated their agreement. Lovejoy concluded by pointing out, "Henceforth this country has been ruled by 250,000 slave-holders and the North has bowed down like an elephant to receive an ass' load, and stagger under the lash. Will we consent to that?" The delegates shouted back their vehement, "No, no!" Then he chided the timid Northerners who "were afraid that we cannot carry Pennsylvania. But they have no cause for such fear, for Pennsylvania is sure to give us a majority, no matter whether it is the son of New York who is our choice," here there was loud applause for Senator Seward, "or the noble son of Ohio, or the gallant Fremont." Again there was strenuous applause. "We will unite to a man and carry our standard barrier triumphantly into the Presidential seat." The delegates and spectators were on their feet and cheering Lovejoy's oration.

Senator Henry Wilson, of Massachusetts, next took the rostrum and proclaimed, "This, sir, is a convention coming here to place in nomination a ticket around which, we trust, the lovers of human liberty all over the country will gather around without reference to the divisions of the past. Sir, our object is to overthrow the slave power of the country, now organized in the Democratic party of the country." The future Vice President of the United States was interrupted by boisterous cheers. "Mr. Buchanan represents this day the Democracy of Franklin Pierce, for he had ceased to be James Buchanan, and must square himself to the platform of that party. The Democratic party, supporting this administration, an administration that has plunged this nation into a civil war, assembled in convention, adopted a platform dictated by the slave interest of the country, nominated James Buchanan, and he ceased to be a Pennsylvania freeman, and must square his conduct by the terms and conditions of that platform."

Wilson turned to the task of uniting their new party. "The old Whigs of the country can make no successful organization alone to

1856 Republican National Convention. Announcement of the nominations at Musical Fund Hall, 808 Locust Street. The Historical Society of Pennsylvania (HSP).

overthrow the slave power. The American party is powerless as an organization alone, to overthrow that power. Independent Democrats who follow the general doctrines of Thomas Jefferson, who believe in pure, unadulterated progressive Democracy can make no successful effort alone for the overthrow of the Democratic party. But sir, men can unite and they can defeat that party." The delegates shouted back, "They will do it!"

Wilson reinforced his appeal. "I call upon Whigs, men who believe in the words of Daniel Webster, that we must on first, the last, and every occasion oppose the extension of the slave power.... I call upon independent Democrats, on the men who have fought not the battles of slavery, who have stood by the Democratic party, but who can follow its black banner no longer, to come here and unite with us in this glorious effort... that shall represent the genuine Democracy of America." Hoarse cheering rose throughout the hall again. "And, sir, I ask Americans, men who profess to exult patriotism and love of country, and broad and expansive nationality, I ask them to come here, and unite with us to save the first principles of American liberty; free speech, a free press, free soil, free Kansas."

Here Wilson was again stopped by the crowd's vigorous reaction, and a voice rang out, "And Fremont." But Wilson forged on. "Then let us, one and all, of all parties, in the words of Whittier, 'Let us forgive, forgive and unite.' " Again the hall was astir with loud yells. Wilson then recounted the sad story of Kansas and took his aim at Franklin Pierce, Stephen Douglas, and James Buchanan, against the physical attack on Senator Charles Sumner by Preston Brooks on the floor of the Senate, vowing that the North "would take care of ourselves" and not bend to the outrages in Washington. "In God's name, gentlemen of the North, resolve to do your duty and blot out the slave power of the country. I feel that today millions are looking with trembling anxiety upon the deliberations of this convention.

"Disappoint them not, gentlemen," Wilson urged, "by any petty little interest in division. Consult with each other in candor and in frankness and then nominate a man upon whom you can unite with the most votes, and who is true to your principles." With its hurrahs, the convention agreed. "If the bold, gallant Fremont is your candidate," the Fremont crowd burst into enthusiastic cheering, "we will rally behind the young, the gallant spirits of the Republic. If McLean, the learned McLean," loud and prolonged cheering met the name of the Supreme Court Justice from Ohio and a voice shouted, "Three cheers for McLean!" These were followed by even louder cheers, then countered by, "Three cheers for Fremont!" The building shook with affirmative response as the real contest for the nomination began to take shape.

Someone shouted, "Take the vote now," but he was met with a

chorus of "No!" Wilson continued when he could finally find a lull in the demonstration, "Gentlemen, if you nominate the present Speaker of the House of Representatives," cheers went up for Nathaniel Banks, "the first man to lead us to victory, let us, all of us of the North, rally around him and sustain the liberty of our country." Someone shouted, "Three cheers for Banks!" and the hall followed with loud accolades.

"If you nominate Salmon P. Chase," Wilson intoned above the chaos, "one of the foremost men of the Republic, let us, all of us, rally around him and place him in the Presidential chair, that he is so qualified to fill. And gentlemen, if in this convention you should place your suffrages upon the foremost statesman of America, William H. Seward," now three frantic bursts of cheering, waving of hats and handkerchiefs broke loose for several minutes for Seward, and Wilson was forced to rest and simply watch the mad exhibition before he concluded, "Aye, gentlemen, I say this foremost statesman of America, and a man fit to lead the movement in which we are now engaged. All of these men I believe are reliable and true... let us, one and all, unite; for our cause is the cause of liberty, and the cause of patriotism." Amid the jubilation that followed came a motion to adjourn the convention's first day and to reassemble at 10:00 in the morning. No one could hear the vote.

On Wednesday morning, President Henry Lane gaveled the party to order and Reverend Anson Rood, of Philadelphia, gave the invocation. Elbridge G. Spaulding delivered the report from the Committee on Credentials and announced the names of the new Republican National Committee. Edwin D. Morgan was reelected chairman of the committee and Norman B. Judd, of Illinois, was appointed secretary of the national body, a move that would have significant consequences in the surprise nomination of Abraham Lincoln four years hence.

Then the Honorable David Wilmot, judge of the Thirteenth Judicial District of Pennsylvania, introduced the platform which had been crafted the day and night before at the Girard House. It was not an abolitionist document. Wilmot presented the assembly with nine resolutions. The platform railed against slavery in the territories and exhorted "maintenance of the principles promulgated in the Declaration of Independence, and embodied in the federal Constitution which are essential to the preservation of our republican institutions, and that of the federal Constitution," but added "the rights of the states, and the Union of the states, must and shall be preserved."

However, the 558 delegates resolved as well that "with our Republican fathers, we hold it to be a self-evident truth, that all men are endowed with the inalienable right to life, liberty, and the pursuit of happiness, and that the primary object and ulterior design of our federal government were to secure these rights to all persons under its exclusive jurisdiction; that as our Republican fathers, when they had abolished slavery in all our national territory, ordained that no person shall be deprived of life, liberty, or property, without due process of all, it becomes our duty to maintain this provision of the Constitution against all attempts to violate it for the purpose of establishing slavery in the territories of the United States by positive legislation, prohibiting its existence or extension therein...." The new Republicans further resolved that, "It is both the right and the imperative duty of Congress to prohibit in the territories those twin relics of barbarism; polygamy, and slavery."

The future of Kansas was foremost in the minds of the delegates. The new Republican platform denounced the fact that, "The dearest constitutional rights of the people of Kansas have been fraudulently and violently taken from them." It asserted that, "The territory has been invaded by an armed force. Spurious and pretended legislative, judicial, and executive officers have been set over them, by whose usurped authority, sustained by the military power of the government, tyrannical, and unconstitutional laws have been enacted and enforced. The right of the people to keep and bear arms has been infringed... the freedom of speech and of the press has been abridged.... Murders, robberies, and arsons have been instigated and encouraged, and the offenders have been allowed to go unpunished."

The 1856 Republican platform boldly and fiercely declared "that all of these things have been done with the knowledge, sanction, and procurement of the present national administration; and that for this high crime against the Constitution, the Union, and humanity, we arraign that administration, the President, his advisers, agents, supporters, apologists, and accessories, either before or after the fact, before the country and before the world." And the delegates warned "that it is our fixed purpose to bring the actual perpetrators of these atrocious outrages and their accomplices to a sure and condign punishment thereafter." The Republican platform further, "Resolved, That Kansas should be immediately admitted as a state of this Union, with her present free constitution" as the best way of "ending the civil strife now raging in her territory."

The party's first official platform was short and direct. It had indicted slavery and stated its intention to try and punish a sitting President of the United States. It also took a direct jab at the Democrat nominee, James Buchanan, when it condemned "the highwayman's plea, that 'might makes right' embodied in the Ostend Circular" (drawn up by Buchanan as Secretary of State, which declared the U.S. would take Cuba by force). Republicans asserted that kind of diplomacy which threatened weaker nations "was in every respect unworthy of American diplomacy, and would bring shame and dishonor upon any government or people that gave it sanction."

The 1856 Republicans also seized upon a passion of one of its new adherents, explorer John C. Fremont, when it, "Resolved, That a railroad to the Pacific Ocean by the most central and practicable route is imperatively demanded by the interests of the whole country, and that the federal government ought to render immediate and efficient aid in its construction, as an auxiliary thereto, to the immediate construction of an emigrant road on the line of the railroad." Democrats opposed federal aid to build the railroad.

The Republican platform embraced an issue popular with old Whigs, "appropriations by Congress for the improvement of rivers and harbors" to further national commerce. The work to be done outlined by the River and Harbor Convention of 1847 in Chicago to which Lincoln and Greeley had been delegates, had been unfulfilled by a Southern-dominated Congress which opposed Northern economic development. The Republicans pledged to use the central government to create the conditions of national commerce.

The platform's anger and determination to criminalize its opponents was a sure prelude to the Civil War that would tear apart the Union five years later. The planks of the platform, shouted out to the gathering, and repeated by other shouters down the rows of delegates, and out the door to the crowd awaiting word outside, were read in utter silence. But each plank and the entire document was adopted to thundering, unanimous applause. The resolution condemning polygamy and slavery received the loudest and longest affirmation. Delegates were certain that it provided a foundation to "invite the affiliation and cooperation of the men of all parties, however differing from us in other respects, in support of the principles herein declared" to guarantee "liberty of conscience and equality of rights among citizens...."

No sooner had the platform been endorsed by acclamation, than John Seeley, of New York, rose to propose that the convention take an informal poll of candidates it sought to elevate to the Presidency. But his recommendation was opposed by General James Watson Webb, of New York, who argued that, "We are here because the country is in danger." They must be deliberate, he said, and "if it will not keep until tomorrow or the next day, it had better not be done."

Governor Kent, of Maine, suggested formation of a committee of three from each state to discuss the matter. But Anthony J. Bleecker, of New York, warned that to wait would mean that they would lose delegates who had to return home. Mr. Elder, of Pennsylvania, agreed. But Charles F. Adams, of Massachusetts, feared that any such conference, by dividing the body, would disrupt the harmony already established. Pennsylvania Governor Joseph Ritner sided with those in favor of a conference.

New York Governor Patterson rose to say that he and his state preferred one name above all others, alluding to its former governor and current Senator, William H. Seward, who was the acknowledged leader of the party. His remarks drew great applause. But, he added to the surprise of the convention, "I have been requested to withdraw his name." Objections rose from the floor. "Not by William H. Seward," shouted General Webb.

"Yes," replied Patterson, "by a delegation, not by Seward himself. But the delegation took that course with a view to show that they were willing to sacrifice all for the cause in which they had engaged." Seward knew that he was a lightning rod and was already aiming for a nomination four years hence when the party's chances would be stronger.

The question was called on Seeley's resolution to go immediately to the balloting. Judge Spaulding, of Ohio, then took the floor. "I have been requested to withdraw from the present controversy the name of a man whom I have intimately known for over 40 years, than whom a better and purer man does not live. I have here a letter, I wish to read." It was dated June 14, and was addressed to the Ohio delegation. "...I have repeatedly declared, as some of you know, that I have no desire for the Presidency, and that I prefer my present position on the bench." As soon as Judge Spaulding read the name of Justice John McLean, Thaddeus Stevens, of Pennsylvania, rose to request an hour for consultation in light of the development. His delegation had been leaning toward McLean. Convention President Lane declared that debate was out of order and that the reading of any other letters would be permitted.

T. G. Mitchell, of Ohio, then read another epistle to the convention dated June 12. After acknowledging the honor that such a nomination implied, the author noted "... the labors of my political life have ever been directed to the promotion of the cause of freedom, progress, and reform, of which, I trust, the convention will be a faithful guardian. The success of that cause is infinitely dearer to me than any personal advancement, and I should look upon any nomination for any office, however exalted, if prejudicial to it, as a calamity to be dreaded and avoided, rather than as a distinction to be sought and desired.... I trust therefore that those generous friends who have been thinking of presenting my name to the convention will consider well the effect of such an action upon our common cause. If, after duly weighing all circumstances, they come to the conclusion that, under existing conditions, the cause will receive detriment through my nomination, I desire that my name be withheld altogether from the convention." It was signed "S. P. Chase." Mr. Mitchell, knowing the way in which Chase's name might be used by those who tried to paint the new Republicans as enemies of Union, chose to then withdraw it. The cheers for Governor Chase, who was a favorite of party members, were loud and repeated.

Thaddeus Stevens sought recognition by the chair, and gaining it voiced his grievance. "The name, the only name, that could save Pennsylvania, has been withdrawn." He meant Judge McLean who was favored by the delegation as the only hope against Pennsylvania's native son, Buchanan. "I fear we will lose Pennsylvania by 50,000 votes." From other states came the shouts of "No, no!" "But I will follow our party, though many here are dissatisfied with the drift of this body," Stevens, a former and future congressman, intoned.

Moses H. Grinnell, of New York, then moved a recess until 5 P.M., so all, but especially the Pennsylvanians, could deliberate. The resolution passed and the delegates broke into caucus, many grumbling that the great momentum from the platform's endorsement had been lost. The first signs of trouble were manifest.

President Lane called the delegates back to order promptly at 5 P.M. and immediately recognized Edwin D. Morgan, the new chairman of the National Republican Committee, who rose to read a letter dated June 17, and delivered to him from New York by hand. Morgan's voice carried across the hall. "Sir, the committee appointed by the National American Convention, to confer with the convention that today meets in Philadelphia, upon candidates to be presented for the offices of President and Vice President, takes pleasure in transmitting to you a copy of the proceedings of our national convention...."

The North Americans who had bolted the Philadelphia Know-Nothings convention had reconvened in New York City June 12-15. They seemed to be offering their votes to the Republicans. Whether they could deliver voters was questionable. Nonetheless, the anti-slavery Americans had met immediately before the Republican convention with the intent of forming a coalition to defeat Fillmore and Buchanan. Through Horace Greeley and Thurlow Weed, the Northern Know-Nothings let Republicans know they wanted to nominate the same candidate for President. They sought to keep correspondence up between the bodies "in the same spirit with a perfect unanimity of sentiment... to give joy to the heart of every lover of freedom throughout the land, and strike terror to the hearts of his enemies." The letter was signed by George Law.

In reply, De Witt C. Littlejohn, of New York, jumped up, calling for a union with the remanent of the American party. He knew that the rump party had courted John Charles Fremont and would settle on Speaker of the House Banks as its candidate, who would then lend its secret organization to the election of the Republican standard barrier. But Littlejohn went further. "It is only right that the great party represented by the North American Convention should have one candidate on the ticket nominated by the Republican convention."

But Giddings, of Ohio, responded, "It pains me to be compelled to oppose that motion." He argued that Republicans had opened their convention to all, and that if special communications were to be carried on with the North American party, they ought to be carried on with those representing citizens of foreign birth as well, and he moved to table all correspondence. His resolution passed, and official correspondence with the Know-Nothing faction halted. It was essential to gain the foreign voters who counted for so much and not alienate them with a coalition with the Know-Nothings.

President Lane then called for an informal polling for candidates for the Presidency. Suddenly Judge Spaulding, of Ohio, rose and addressed the president. "I simply wish to withdraw my earlier withdrawal and keep in the minds of all the worthy Judge McLean, of Ohio, for candidate for President of the United States." His act caused surprise among some, hope in others, and concern among the supporters of Fremont.

Then the tabulations began with a roll call of states. Maine cast 13 votes for Fremont and 11 for McLean. New Hampshire followed with 15 for Fremont and 14 for McLean. The race looked tight. But then Vermont threw 15 votes to Fremont. Massachusetts added 39 to the young explorer. Rhode Island cast 12, and Connecticut 18 for the "Pathfinder" Fremont. Then New York added its weighty 93 for Fremont, along with just 3 for McLean, 1 for Banks, 2 for Senator Sumner, and only 1 for its favored native son, Seward. New Jersey braced McLean's fall with 14 for the Supreme Court Justice and just 7 for Fremont. Pennsylvania lifted the old jurist with 71 more and only 10 for Fremont. Delaware threw another 9 into McLean's corner and cast none for Fremont.

Finally, Maryland broke the counter momentum with four for Fremont; three for McLean. Virginia abstained. Kentucky shouted, "five for Fremont." Ohio cast 39 votes for McLean, its native son; but added 30 for Fremont. Indiana lifted its neighbor McLean with 21 votes, while tossing 18 Fremont's way. Illinois gave McLean 19 votes; Fremont 14. But the young and vigorous Fremont caught the imagination of Michigan with 18 votes; Iowa fell in line with 12 for the hero of the West; and Wisconsin jumped on the bandwagon with 15. Fremont's adopted state of California gave him 12 more. Kansas followed with nine for the national hero; none for McLean. That gave Fremont 359 to 190 for McLean. McLean was more than 70 years old, a favorite of the Whigs in the convention, but hardly represented the youth and vitality of most of the delegates. Fremont was 43 years old, one of the youngest candidates for President in the nation's history.

On the instant, General Webb was on his feet. "I move that John C. Fremont, of California, be, and he hereby is, unanimously nominated by this convention by acclamation, as the Republican candidate for the President of the United States." He was loudly cheered.

But Pennsylvania's Wilmot caught the eye of President Lane, who recognized him. "I have not a doubt in my mind that this vote is indicative of the sentiment of this convention and is the honest sentiment of this nation." He was cheered on by the Fremont partisans. "It seems hardly necessary to go to formal ballot."

He was interrupted by shouts of "No, no!" countered by yells of "Yes, yes!" Someone shouted, "Let us stand on our record." But Ohio's Congressman Giddings suddenly rose to discuss again the correspondence with the North American convention. Though he believed the Republican party should be open to all, he did not favor special relationships with any group, he told the confused crowd. But his friends in the convention, he said, disagreed, and so he moved to reconsider his earlier motion.

Mr. Littlejohn jumped up to respond. "I do not propose to receive the communication because of any particular sympathy I have with the Know-Nothings, but I believe if they do not cooperate, James Buchanan will ascend to the Presidency.... This communication does not imply we wish to exclude foreigners. Certainly not."

Thomas D. Elliott objected, declaring, "I have just been given the pleasure of casting all of Massachusetts' votes for the nomination of John C. Fremont. I hope this convention does nothing to lessen the strength of the Republican party in Massachusetts."

But former Governor Cleveland, of Connecticut, reminded the delegates that the North American Convention was composed of those who had bolted from the Know-Nothing convention in February rather than accept a pro-slavery position. The Republican convention had invited them; they had responded; now it was the new party's duty to receive them. He hoped the body would support him on this.

However, Owen Lovejoy did not. "We did not invite them," he angrily countered. "If this convention receives the Know-Nothings as a body, that demagogue, Stephen A. Douglas, will tickle the senses of the foreign born of Illinois, and Illinois will be lost. Let the North Americans come as individuals. Let them answer the call of freedom as individuals and Illinois will be saved." The cheers supported him.

Mr. Gazzam, of Pennsylvania, took the floor to say he wished to do the American party of Pennsylvania the justice to say that they had become an open party that constitutes the bulk of the Republican party in his state. Then Judge Hoar, of Massachusetts, reminded the convention that it had already received the group of 100 from New York, and no harm could be done in admitting another group who were lovers of freedom. Mr. Sherwood, of New York, begged the indulgence of delegates to see how their action would be akin to inviting a man to dinner and then kicking him out into the street. The North Americans wanted to confer about platforms and candidates.

Confusion descended upon the hall and lasted for many minutes before Pennsylvania's old Governor Ritner sought to redirect attention back to Fremont, which brought another burst of applause. Finally, the motion to move directly to formal nomination was taken up by President Lane. And another roll call of states began immediately. This time Fremont attracted 520 votes, to 37 for MeLean, and 1 for Seward.

Again General Webb rose and declaimed, "Resolved. That this convention do unanimously nominate John C. Fremont, of California, to be the Republican candidate for President of the United States."

President Lane interjected, "All in favor give three hearty cheers." His instruction was followed by three upon three rousing cheers, and many more, as the convention became delirious in wild and boundless enthusiasm, baffling all description. Hats flew through the air, following upon shouts of joy. On the platform at the front of the hall, Fremont's name was hoisted on a large, white banner. Other star-spangled banners were waved. Fremont banners were dropped from windows, and the large crowd in the streets awaiting the news of the new nominee burst into celebrations of its own.

When at last the jubilation subsided, Judge Emmet moved that the convention be adjourned until the next morning. The delegates and spectators poured into the streets where they took up their festivity with the crowds outside. The new Republican party had its platform and its candidate for President, John Charles Fremont, the Pathfinder and Liberator of California.

The relative ease with which John C. Fremont won the first Republican Presidential nomination was the result of the work of behind-the-scenes power brokers. They had been pondering the problem of a first nominee since their first national meeting in Pittsburgh in February. Meeting at the estate of anti-slavery Democrat Francis Preston Blair, a confidant of former Senator Benton, several of them had decided upon Fremont as a man of youthful vigor and adventurous spirit to serve as their first standard-bearer. Fremont was a national hero of youth, romance, vision, and vitality, who had led the nation west to its manifest destiny.

Fremont had been born in Georgia in 1813, son of a French emigre and a Southern woman. He learned surveying while working for a projected railroad through Carolina and Tennessee. In 1838, he began his army career in the U.S. Topographical Corps as a lieutenant. Fremont was popularly known throughout the land as the "Pathfinder" because, while still in his twenties and early thirties, he led several expeditions across the western plains into the Oregon Territory, mapping the Oregon Trail, opening the land to settlement. His father-in-law, Missouri Democratic Senator Thomas Hart Benton, had exercised his considerable influence to secure Fremont's first reconnaissance into the Missouri Territory in 1842.

The colorful frontiersman Kit Carson served as his guide through the South Pass crossing of the Continental Divide. Newspaper readers across the land followed their exploits through the rugged and dangerous wilderness. Fremont's wife, the beautiful, bright, and witty Jessie Benton Fremont, daughter of the Senator, co-wrote most of the accounts and made sure that her husband's grueling adventures were widely distributed so that the foundation for his political career was firmly established. She was his political advisor and staunchest supporter, and used her many Washington social connections to promote his projects, including the Presidency.

In 1843, Fremont led his second expedition into the Rocky Mountains, through the Cascade Range and the Sierra Nevada, which he traversed in the depths of winter to survey the Oregon Territory. The trip was outrageously bold and dangerous and his expedition was feared lost for several months. His unexpected return to St. Louis in August, 1844, caused a national sensation that brought him lasting fame as an American hero. Fremont then published maps, scientific reports, and colorful accounts of his trip, further engaging the nation's imagination.

Fremont was also a political "Pathfinder." On his third exploration in 1845, he led 60 men up the Colorado and Grand rivers and across the Sierra Nevada to California, and in June of 1846, helped civilians seize the town of Sonoma, north of San Francisco, from a Mexican military force. There, Fremont proclaimed a new California Republic, raising the new state's Bear Flag. In the Mexican-American War, Fremont's "California Battalion" forcefully put down Mexican revolts near Monterey. Fremont became the personification of "Manifest Destiny" and helped to unite the continental United States from sea to shining sea.

But late in 1847, Fremont's career took an unexpected detour when he became involved in what came to be known as the "Stockton-Keary Dispute." Some of Fremont's California exploits had been under the command of Commodore Robert F. Stockton. When Stockton resisted being relieved of his duties by General Stephen W. Keary, Fremont sided with Stockton, who had named Fremont Governor of California. Keary won the dispute and young Fremont was arrested and sent back to Washington, D.C., where he was court-martialed, convicted, and dismissed from the army in early 1848.

Amidst a public outcry, he was reinstated on the orders of President Polk himself, who reputedly had given him secret orders that explained his behavior. Instead of time in the stockade, Fremont voluntarily retired and led private explorations through the rugged terrain of the West. Two years later he was elected one of the first two U.S. Senators by the new California state legislature and he served until 1851, when he was beaten in the state legislature in his reelection bid for the U.S. Senate because of his strong position against the spread of slavery.

In May of 1853, Fremont led another expedition in search of a southern transcontinental railroad route. In 1854, the still youthful but hardened explorer arrived back in Washington to make his congressional report on his latest findings. His beautiful wife had been residing in the house of her father, former Senator Benton (who had also been turned out of his Senate seat from Missouri for opposition to slavery). Fremont joined her there, and also spent time in New York cultivating business ties. In the spring of 1855, a terrible fire destroyed their Washington residence, consuming a lifetime of priceless mementos, including the Senator's second-volume manuscript of "Thirty Years' View."

President Pierce, a family friend who had known Jessie since she was a child, offered them all refuge in the White House. But Fremont permanently retreated to New York and Jessie spent the summer on Nantucket island trying to recover from shock. Afterwards, the entire family reunited in New York City to entertain and practice informal politicking from their residence at 56 West Ninth Street where many influential visitors were pleased to meet Fremont.

By the spring of 1856, Fremont's name was being circulated among leaders of the Democratic, Know-Nothing, and Republican parties as a possible Presidential candidate. But candidate or not, Fremont remained busy every day in the studio of Matthew Brady, working to make photographs from plates taken along the rugged route he had only recently trod. Jessie entertained and was very much in society.

Fremont did not make speeches, but still managed to make clear his views on the burning question of the day, the repeal of the Missouri Compromise and the westward spread of slavery. Writing to a convention of anti-slavery men that had gathered in New York City, the Pathfinder proclaimed, "I heartily concur in all movements which have for their object 'to repair the mischief arising from the violations of good faith in the repeal of the Missouri Compromise.' I am opposed to slavery in the abstract and upon principle, sustained and made habitual by long settled convictions. While I feel inflexible in the belief that it ought not to be interfered with where it exists, under the shield of state sovereignty, I am as inflexibly opposed to its extension on this continent beyond its present limits."

Fremont had long been a loyal Democrat, tutored by his father-in-law, who had objected when he eloped to marry his daughter. Because Fremont was free of the bloody politics of Kansas, and was a hero whose courage and integrity were unquestioned, many Democrats had been intensely interested in making him their Presidential nominee, to replace Pierce. Former Virginia Governor John B. Floyd even invited Fremont to join in negotiations about the position at the St. Nicholas Hotel in New York, on behalf of a powerful Southern Democrat and Know-Nothing alliance. The Know-Nothings approved of Fremont because he was an exclusionist, not on grounds of racial superiority, but on the pragmatic position that the country would be more tranquil without an influx of foreigners from east or west.

Floyd actually offered Fremont the Democratic Presidential nomination. Fremont knew Floyd was offering the Presidency itself and that he expected Fremont would naturally accept. Negotiations lasted several days. At Fremont's side was Nathaniel Banks, the Massachusetts Democrat and Free Soiler who became Speaker of the House earlier that year with Know-Nothing support. But the covert alliance wanted the Southern-born Fremont to pledge allegiance to both the Kansas-Nebraska Act and the Fugitive Slave Act, something he refused to do. Fremont and Banks protested vigorously that no such agreement could be accepted. The argument became so heated that negotiations broke off and the offer was left dangling before him.

Fremont traveled to Nantucket to consult with Jessie. They walked along the beach to Lighthouse Hill near Siasconset as he described his options, telling her that one Democrat had said to him, "No woman can refuse the White House," a low comment directly aimed at her vanity. "There was no shadow of doubt in our minds," Jessie wrote in her diary. "At the foot of the bluff on which the lighthouse stood, were the remains embedded in the sands of a ship, the seas washing into her ribs. Above, steady and brilliant, flashed the recurring light." She said to Charles, as she called him, "It is the choice between a wreck of dishonor, or a kindly light that will go on its mission of doing good." They both knew he would never stoop to the enforcement of the Fugitive Slave Law.

Fremont returned to New York where he tendered his final "No" to the Democrats and, he thought, the Presidency. He would not run in a party that stood for repeal of the Missouri Compromise and the spread of slavery to the lands he had opened up through his explorations, even if it meant he would not become President of the United States. But with such principle manifest, he instantly became the leading contender for the nomination of the new Republican party.

Then, prior to the Philadelphia convention, Republican powerhouse leaders had met in Silver Spring, Maryland, at Blair House, and had chosen Fremont as their candidate, picking him over Seward and Chase, whose high profiles as anti-slavery advocates made them less likely to pull moderate voters who feared the break-up of the Union if a Republican were elected President.

Before the convention, Banks had made a trip to New York City to try to persuade William Cullen Bryant, editor of the New York *Evening Post* to beat the drum for Fremont. Bryant sent his assistant editor, John Bigelow, to make an assessment of the potential candidate. Bigelow caught the Fremont bug and convinced Francis P. Blair, Edwin P. Morgan, a future New York governor and U.S. Senator, and Edward

Miller to back the Pathfinder. Meanwhile, the *Evening Post* took up the Fremont cause, as did the Cleveland *Herald* and *The Herald of Freedom* published by the Emigrant Aid Society that was rushing free-state settlers into Kansas. Fremont fever had swept the West, "like a prairie fire."

But many eastern Republicans remained committed to either Chase or Seward. Chase, seen as an abolitionist by Democrats, could hurt the party in southern Indiana and Illinois, two essential states for the hopeful Republicans. And the Know-Nothings despised Seward. Pennsylvania, New Jersey, and Illinois, including Lincoln, favored Supreme Court Justice John McLean, but his age, in comparison with Fremont's vigor, ruled him out in the eyes of many younger party members. The American party had remained interested in Fremont as well.

By Republican convention time, Fremont had a full head of steam and his name was cheered every time it was mentioned by delegates and party members in Musical Fund Hall. An aura of moral righteousness and evangelical mission pervaded the enthusiastic body. A New York *Tribune* correspondent, J. S. Pike, one of 80 newsmen in attendance, reported, "The fact is not disguised, that as a general thing the outright, progressive movement men are in favor of Fremont, while McLean is the candidate for the slow and hunkerish part of the convention. The general sentiment of all is conciliatory." "Hunkers" were conservative New York pro-slavery Democrats who had opposed Martin Van Buren.

When the Republican convention reconvened the next morning, the 19th of June, 1856, the tired but exuberant Republicans prayed with the Reverend Levy, of Philadelphia. Then a call went out for a national convention of young men in favor of "free speech, free soil, free men, and Fremont" to meet in the city of New York in September. Mr. Edward W. Whelpley, of New Jersey, stood to move that the convention take up the question of a Vice President, and proposed the name of Judge William Lewis Dayton, a former U.S. Senator from the same state and a Princeton graduate. Dayton's name was greeted with cheering, this time a bit hoarser than the day previous. Whelpley then read Dayton's address to the state Republican convention that had been held earlier, calling for a return to the Missouri Compromise. Dayton had insisted that, "freedom is national, slavery is sectional." The audience took up this affirmation in thunderous rolls of cheers and whoops.

Then the Honorable John Allison, of Pennsylvania, took the floor to nominate a man from Illinois who was less well known. Allison recommended the former Whig congressman, Abraham Lincoln, as, "a prince of good fellows, and an old line Whig." Cheers lifted Lincoln's name for consideration. Colonel William B. Archer told the gatherers, "I have lived in Illinois for 40 years and during 30 of that period have known well Abraham Lincoln... he was born in gallant Kentucky and is in the prime of life, about 55 years of age, and enjoying remarkably good health. He is as pure a patriot as has ever lived. Illinois is safe with Lincoln on our ticket." Then he hesitated, "Well, Illinois is safe whoever we chose to stand with Fremont, but with Lincoln, Illinois is doubly safe." The crowd joined in his laughter. "Can he fight?" Judge Spaulding shouted. "Yes, I told you he was born in Kentucky. He's strong mentally, strong physically. He's strong every way."

An old-line Democrat, Mr. Jay, of New Jersey, spoke on behalf of Dayton. Mr. Fisher, of Pennsylvania, then "took the liberty of naming a man... who is a tower of strength in Pennsylvania; I mean David L. Wilmot. If you nominate him, I have no doubt Pennsylvania will ratify your decision in November." John Allison then asked to suspend business to read proceedings from the Pennsylvania Republican State Convention, held the previous evening, June 18, 1856, in the same Musical Fund Hall. It endorsed the national party's platform and Colonel John C. Fremont.

Judge John Palmer, of Illinois, followed, by seconding Lincoln's name. He said he admired Dayton and was going to name his next son after Judge Wilmot, but that, "I think we can do it a little easier if we have Lincoln on the ticket with John C. Fremont." From Massachusetts, Mr. Elliot read a dispatch. "Great rejoicing. Give us a good Vice President. Clear the track!" The convention applauded its own work and the reception it had provoked. Mr. Bleecker, of New York, answered the call with his nomination of John A. King, of the Empire State.

Just then Judge Wilmot rose to read another communication from the North American convention in New York, asking for a committee to be formed with which it could communicate. The Republicans responded by appointing such a committee headed by Francis P. Blair, of Maryland. The North Americans had wanted to nominate Fremont as well. But Greeley and Weed persuaded them to hold off, since it might cause a voter backlash for the Pathfinder if Know-Nothings were too closely associated with the new party. Instead, the North Americans nominated Speaker of the House Nathaniel Banks for President and William F. Johnston, of Pennsylvania, for Vice President, with the understanding that Banks would step aside for the eventual Republican nominee after their convention was over.

President Lane brought the Republican convention back to its main business by calling for an informal vote for Vice President. The result saw 253 votes cast for William L. Dayton; 110 votes for Abraham Lincoln; 46 for Nathaniel P. Banks; 43 for David Wilmot; 35 for Senator Charles Sumner; 9 for John King; 7 for lieutenant Governor Thomas H. Ford, of Ohio; 3 for Cassius M. Clay, who was an anti-slavery former Whig from Kentucky; 15 for Jacob Collamer, of Vermont, who had been Postmaster-General under President Taylor; 2 for Joshua R. Giddings, of Ohio; 2 for Whitefield S. Johnson, of New Jersey; 3 for Henry C. Carey, of Pennsylvania; 1 for Aaron S. Pennington, of New Jersey; 2 for Henry Wilson, of Massachusetts; 8 for General Samuel C. Pomeroy, of Kansas.

The informal vote was quickly followed by withdrawals of the names of Sumner, Banks, and Wilson, all of Massachusetts, at their requests and because of their current importance in Washington. Their names were cheered as they showed dignity and commitment to the new party. Then the names of Wilmot and Ford were withdrawn by their loyalists, before the convention went to a formal vote. Dayton took the prize with 511 votes, to 20 for Lincoln, 6 for Banks, and 1 each for King, Ford, and Sumner.

Judge Palmer took the floor. "Illinois has asked nothing for itself. We knew that in Abraham Lincoln we had a soldier tried and true... but we prefer harmony and union to the success even of our cherished favorite." Then he swung the Illinois votes to Dayton. Finally, the nomination was made unanimous and the convention rose in nine hearty cheers for their new Vice Presidential nominee. Amid much laughing, a notification committee was formed to formally contact Fremont and Dayton. After the convention, Abraham Lincoln, who was back in Illinois, commented that the Vice Presidential votes at the convention must have been for "the distinguished Mr. Lincoln of Massachusetts," referring to Ezra Lincoln, of Boston. And he wrote John Van Dyke, one of the delegates, "When you meet Judge Dayton present my respects and tell him I think him a far better man than I for the position he is in, and I shall support both him and Colonel Fremont most cordially."

Mr. Fisher, of Pennsylvania, reported to the convention that the 31 hands in his Philadelphia manufacturing plant, all Democrats, had declared for Fremont. Governor Cleveland proposed three cheers for the 31 Democrats, and the convention, in good humor, obliged. Mr. Schneider, of Illinois, a German-language newspaper editor, announced that the German population of Illinois was with Fremont. "A majority of the German newspapers across the country have already come out for Fremont.... We look upon the struggle as one between slave labor and free labor."

Then Senator Wills, of California, was called upon to acknowledge the nomination of his state's favorite son. He aroused the delegates, saying, "...in this revolution, for we live in revolutionary times... John C. Fremont is a man of military education, of personal courage, of daring adventure, of unblemished character, a man who, with the field before him, and with the example of Washington in his eye, will become a second Washington by the redemption of his county.... California knows John C. Fremont. He is, as it were, her foster-father, her discoverer, her conqueror as against her foe, the assertor of her freedom, and her first representative in the Senate... and I assert, in no spirit of exaggeration, that if the State of California can be carried by any human being on our platform, John C. Fremont can, and will do it." His remarks provoked vehement applause.

Representatives of other states heaped on their praise for the convention, its platform, and ticket. Mr. Zachariah Chandler, of Michigan, read a dispatch describing 100 guns that had been fired by the soldiers of Detroit in support of Fremont. Then he noted that it was appropriate that this reaction come from the state first "to inaugurate the Republican party of the United States." But from the crowd came dissension. "No, Maine was first," "Ohio was first," "Pennsylvania was first."

Mr. Van Dyke, of New Jersey, reported that although his state had favored McLean, it would win with Fremont, "the man who has traced the paths of the buffalo through the windings and gorges of the Rocky Mountains, who has planted the standard of the United States in the golden regions of California, the man who grappled with the grizzly bear upon the snow-capped summits, the man who through toil, suffering, trial, danger, hunger, and snow has done all these things, and with the capacity of Caesar himself, has gained such magnificent results... a gentleman, whose fame is already too large for this continent...." As for its native son, Senator Dayton, Van Dyke asserted, "He is a scholar, a gentleman, a learned lawyer, a distinguished judge upon the bench... who had with all his energy opposed the Fugitive Slave Law."

A resolution was passed encouraging conventions of young Republicans in the separate states. Henry Wilson rose to congratulate everyone on the results of their proceedings. "You have a ticket standing on your platform worthy of the suffrages of the Christian freemen of the United States... a glorious ticket." Then, after thanking the residents of Philadelphia for their "hospitality and kindness," President Lane gaveled the First Republican National Convention to a close.

In his Ninth Street home in New York City, Fremont calmly received word of his nomination. His nerves "preserved their usual tranquility." On June 25, the New York ratifying rally broke up with a torchlight march down Broadway to the Fremont residence, where he and Jessie appeared before the crowd to thank them. Fremont's July 9, 1856, acceptance letter again made clear his position on the great issue of his day. "Nothing is clearer in the history of our institutions than the design of the nation, in asserting its own independence and freedom, to avoid giving countenance to the extension of slavery. The influence of a small but compact and powerful class of men interested in slavery, who command one section of the country and wield a vast political control as a consequence in the other, is now directed to turn back the impulse of the revolution and reverse its principles. The extension of slavery across the continent is the object of the power which now rules the government; and from this spirit have sprung those kindred wrongs of Kansas so truly portrayed in one of your resolutions, which prove that the elements of the most arbitrary governments have not been vanquished by the just theory of our own.

"It would be out of place here to pledge myself to any particular policy that has been suggested to determine the sectional controversy engendered by political animosities, opening on a powerful class banded together by common interest. A practical remedy is the admission of Kansas into the Union as a free state. The South should, in my judgment, earnestly desire such a consummation. It would vindicate its good faith. It would correct the mistake of the repeal; and the North, having practically the benefit of the agreement between the two sections, would be satisfied and good feeling be restored."

Throughout the canvass that followed, Fremont remained dignified and above the fray. He spent time fencing each morning and walked throughout New York City for exercise. His campaign was managed by Francis P. Blair, John Bigelow, Isaac Sherman, Thurlow Weed, and Fremont's friend, Colonel James. They often consulted with Mrs. Fremont on questions of strategy. Although he met privately with visitors, and greeted well-wishers who gathered in front of his Ninth Street home during the next few months, Fremont made no further comment on policy or the campaign until the people themselves spoke in November. The conqueror of the West, remained humble, silent, and dignified despite the personal attacks that showered him. The man who had turned aside a certain Democratic Presidency for principle, now confronted a damaged party whose primary purpose was victory and retention of power at all costs.

As the Republican's first nominee, John C. Fremont stood against established political giants of the sturdy Democratic party that had elected its nominees almost in grand succession since the time of Jackson. The Democrats had already rallied in Cincinnati on June 2 to nominate James Polk's Secretary of State, James Buchanan, as their Presidential candidate. The party of Jackson was entrenched and powerful, with thousands of patronage jobs to dispense across the nation in exchange for support. That was the skeleton and flesh of its campaign apparatus.

At that convention, anti-slavery Democrats who supported Buchanan, turned back the renomination run of Franklin Pierce and the hopeful challenger, Senator Stephen A. Douglas, of Illinois, whose legislation had set off the epic national crisis. He would become a divided party's candidate four years later, to stand against Lincoln, and for a fractured Union. In Cincinnati, Pierce and Douglas tried to stave off Buchanan through a coalition of delegates. Buchanan was utterly unorganized, having returned from England only a month earlier, where he had been serving as U.S. Minister to Great Britain.

But the country was in a state of hysteria caused by the May 22 attack on abolitionist Senator Charles Sumner, of Massachusetts, in the chambers of the United States Senate, by South Carolina Congressman Preston Brooks. Sumner had crudely attacked Brook's uncle, South Carolina Senator Andrew Pickens Butler, in his "The Crime Against Kansas" speech. Brooks evened the score by beating Sumner into unconsciousness with repeated blows to the head with his cane. Violence had invaded the sacred chambers of government. Violence also came to Kansas the next day when slave state forces raided and looted the free state stronghold of Lawrence. In retaliation, John Brown led a force of free state raiders who murdered five slave state settlers. Panic and fear shook the nation.

In the Democratic convention held a few days later in early June, a standoff developed. With two-thirds of delegates needed for the Democratic nomination, Buchanan charged to an early lead. Pierce had solid support from his patronage base. Douglas followed in third. After 14 ballots, the Pierce forces conceded and changed to Douglas, but Douglas already had his eye on 1860 and had thrown his support to Buchanan. Buchanan's calm and reasoned approach to all problems promised much needed stability to national affairs, and on the seventeenth ballot, he was nominated by the Democracy. Kentucky Congressman John C. Breckinridge was given the Vice Presidential nomination after a contest with Commodore Robert F. Stockton, Fremont's former California guardian. The South's candidate, John A. Quitman, of Mississippi, was neglected as well, much to the displeasure of Southern Democrats who had little use for Buchanan, an avowed opponent of slavery.

Buchanan had a long political career behind him. Born in 1791 in Mercersburg, Pennsylvania, he graduated from Dickinson College in 1809 before being admitted to the bar three years later. After serving in the War of 1812, and resuming his legal career, Buchanan was elected to the U.S. House of Representatives for five terms between 1821 and 1831, rising to chair of the Judiciary Committee. In 1834, he was appointed to the post of U.S. Minister to Russia for two years, before his election by the Pennsylvania legislature to the United States Senate, where he served from 1834 to 1845. President Polk then appointed him Secretary of State. In that capacity Buchanan negotiated the treaty at the end of the Mexican War and futilely sought to buy Cuba from Spain.

In 1853 Buchanan became U.S. Minister to Great Britain where he joined American Ministers to France and Spain in drawing up the Ostend (Belgium) Manifesto of 1854, which declared that possession of Cuba was essential to peace for the United States and warned Spain that if it did not sell the island, the United States was "justified by every law, human and divine" in taking it by force. President Pierce's Secretary of State, William L. Marcy, promptly repudiated the manifesto. Buchanan returned home in 1856 in time to fulfill his life-long aspiration to run for

President. Compared to Buchanan, Fremont had no international experience. But Fremont represented the fervent desires of most Northerners, and everyone knew the real issue of the election was not international, but the domestic division of slavery.

The "National Democracy" as the Democrats called themselves in 1856 to point out the contrast with the sectional Republicans, defiantly defended the Kansas-Nebraska Act that they had crafted in Congress to keep the Union together. To solve the problems it presented, the delegates placed "their trust in the intelligence, the patriotism, and the discriminating justice of the American people." The National Democracy regarded that principle as "a distinctive feature of our political creed... as the great moral element in a form of government springing from and upheld by the popular will: and we contrast it with the creed and practice of Federalism, under whatever name or form, which seeks to palsy the will of the constituent, and which conceives no imposture too monstrous for the popular credulity."

The Democratic platform insisted, "1. That the federal government is one of limited power, derived solely from the Constitution .... 2. That the Constitution does not confer upon the general government the power to commence and carry on a general system of internal improvements. 3. That justice and sound policy forbid the federal government to foster one branch of industry to the detriment of any other... that every citizen and every section of the country has right to demand and insist upon an equality of rights and privileges...."

Democrats touted as democratic the Kansas-Nebraska Act's method of popular vote in each state to solve the slavery question locally. The Democrat party, with its heavy Southern base, also declared that it would resist any and all efforts to reopen the slavery debate in Congress. At the same time, the party of Jackson denounced its rival "Know-Nothing" movement for its violation of "the spirit of tolerance and enlightened freedom."

To fill out the Presidential field of 1856, the disintegrating Whig Party held its convention in Baltimore and also nominated former President Fillmore as its standard bearer.

During the campaign, Fremont was surrounded by a band of hangers-on from his various expeditions and business deals. Republican founders like Gideon Welles, John Bigelow, Francis Blair, Horace Greeley, and others found these hangers-on unsavory in various degrees, but Fremont trusted them. (Throughout his career his trust was often betrayed, particularly in business).

Horace Greeley outlined the Republican strategy. The South and border states provided the Democracy with 108 electoral votes. The Republicans could count on 114 electoral votes from the northeast joined by New York, Ohio, Michigan, Iowa, and Wisconsin. In dispute were

Pennsylvania's 27 critical electoral votes, along with 13 from Indiana, and 11 from Illinois, 8 from Maryland, 7 from New Jersey, and 4 from Fremont's California. The disputed states accounted for a total of 70 electoral votes. The winner needed 149. That meant good news for the Republicans. Victory was within their grasp if Pennsylvania, and Indiana or Illinois, followed the example of their neighbors. John Charles Fremont could become President of the United States, if only Republicans could organize a victory in Pennsylvania, and Indiana, or Illinois.

The Republicans saw clearly what must be done. But the Democrats took the offensive everywhere. Democrat stump speakers denigrated their white Republicans opponents as "Black Republicans" and warned that their "sectional" fanaticism would tear apart the Union, that peace would be drowned out by their abolitionist passions. Republican victory meant a Southern revolution, Northern voters were warned and Southern voters were promised by their angry saloon and soap box orators.

Despite rumors to the contrary, loyal Democrats like Fremont's father-in-law, Thomas H. Benton, no longer a Senator, but a congressman from St. Louis running for Governor of Missouri, stood up for Buchanan and his party against the anti-Nebraska Act defectors. In one oration at the Buchanan ratification meeting in St. Louis on June 21, 1856, Benton exclaimed, "I will assist the new President, for I look upon Mr. Buchanan's election as certain, in doing what I am sure he will do, that is to say, all in his power to preserve the peace of the country at home and abroad, and to restore the fraternal feelings between the different sections of the Union now so lamentably impaired...." The former Senator added, "It is unnecessary for me to speak of these [other] parties: I adhere to my own, and support it, and that to the exclusion of all the rest. One only I allude to, one with which the name of a member of my family is connected, and in reference to which some persons who judge me by themselves... attribute to me a sinister connection...." Then he pounded his fist, "I am above family and above self, when the name of the Union is concerned."

Ratification rallies for Fremont were held in every state that sent delegates to the Republican convention. In Newark, on a hot Monday evening in July, 1856, New Jersey Republicans were asked to ratify Fremont's nomination. The large crowd "was the most enthusiastic political gathering which has been called together since the days of 'Tippicanoe and Tyler too,' " wrote the New York *Herald* the next day. " 'Fremont and Victory was the cry.' " Other political rallies were staged throughout the summer in the free states and the enthusiasm for Fremont rose with the August thermometer. Speaker Banks, Bryant, Chase, and Charles A. Dana, Greeley, Hannibal Hamlin, Judge Hoar, and Senator Sumner spoke on behalf of the grand cause and their heroic nominee. So did the esteemed Ralph Waldo Emerson, William M. Evarts, and Roscoe Conkling, of New York, Schuyler Colfax, of Indiana, and Carl Schurz, of Missouri.

A rally of 25,000 was staged in Massillon, Ohio. In Kalamazoo, 30,000 Republicans listened to orations and marched in support of Fremont. Beloit, Wisconsin, was site to a rally of equal size. In Alton, Illinois, 35,000 supporters were mesmerized by Lincoln's piercing, high-pitched appeal for Fremont. "Let us in building our party," he said, "plant ourselves on the rock of the Declaration of Independence and the gates of hell shall not prevail against us." During the campaign, Lincoln delivered 50 addresses on behalf of the new party. Lyman Trumbull sat on a reviewing stand in Jacksonville, just west of Springfield, as a mile-and-a-half long Republican procession paraded past. A rally of equal size was reported from Indianapolis where as night fell upon the city, the streets flowed with the flames of torchlights as far as the eye could see and the night air was filled with the orators' flamboyance for "Fremont and Victory." Everywhere the Wide Awakes, bands of dedicated and well-drilled young Republican men and Fremont glee clubs appeared at party events and filled concert halls. The celebrants saluted, "Jessie Bent On Being Free," and "Fremont and Jessie." In the streets, Democrats were denounced as "Buchaneers."

In New York, the *Tribune*, the *Evening Post*, and the *Times* all clamored for the election of the Republican candidate, as did *The Philadelphia North American*, edited by Morton McMichael and *The Chicago Tribune* published by Joseph Medill and Horace White. Old Whig and Democratic papers, like the New York *Herald*, converted to the new party and repeatedly ran headlines celebrating the crusade and Fremont. Many papers offered special campaign subscriber rates to readers. John Greenleaf Whittier composed a campaign poem, "The Pass of the Pierras," extolling Fremont's legendary exploits. John Bigelow worked with Jessie to write her husband's biography, and hundreds of thousands of copies were shipped across the North and sold for $1 each. Republican women added a new character to politics as they spread the word for Fremont and carried out party tasks as they never had before. Old timers agreed that the political excitement rivaled William Henry Harrison's "log cabin and hard cider campaign" of 1840. Republican strategists were optimistic.

Buchanan carried on a front-porch campaign, greeting visiting guests to his estate of Wheatland outside Lancaster, Pennsylvania, but following tradition, did not comment on the issues raging about him. He was a statesman and heir apparent. But his supporters were less than statesman-like, spewing rumors of all sorts against their Republican opponent, including accusations of drunkenness, although Fremont rarely drank. Some charges were absurd, such as the one accusing him of owning slaves. Fremont and Jessie had refused the slaves offered them as a wedding gift by their Southern relatives. Fremont's financial difficulties associated with his California gold mine were also magnified. Some Democratic stump speakers claimed he was actually a Canadian, since his father was from the land north of the border, and hence not qualified for the Presidency. Others slandered his "illegitimate" birth, calling him "a Frenchman's bastard." The Democratic campaign charge that he exaggerated his role in the conquest of California was nullified by Buchanan's own assertion while in England that "in my opinion [Fremont] is better entitled to be called the conqueror of California than any other man." However, his business dealings in the California mines and a record of debt led to considerable resentment in the new state. But his supporters formed "Bear Clubs" across California and campaigned hard to reverse the damage.

Fremont's nomination infuriated the Southern politicians. Preston Brooks, who had beaten Massachusetts Senator Sumner into unconsciousness on the floor of the Senate, jeered that "Union or Disunion" was the sole issue of the contest. He urged the South to prepare to take Washington by force if Fremont won. Others bitterly charged Fremont with being an "abolitionist." Support began to evaporate for Millard Fillmore when Southern Whigs saw he had little Northern backing. With the Whigs no longer a real electoral threat, the Southern Democrat bloc hardened to defeat at all costs the new Republican champion who cut such a dashing figure with his cropped beard and Christ-like hair. The political atmosphere through the nation became ugly as slurs were hurled back and forth.

Meanwhile the war in Kansas raged on, heightening the fears of many that the Union was tottering on the precipice of disaster. Fillmore warned on more than one occasion that "in the event of the election of Colonel Fremont to the Presidency, the Southern states in a body, ought to, and will, withdraw from the Union." Fremont was labeled a "traitor" for trying to break up the Union with his anti-slavery stance. Though the candidates, in public at least, remained above the fray, the mudslinging and slandering of candidates escalated. One popular cartoon depicted Fremont riding a broken-down "abolition nag" led by New York Senator William H. Seward. Democratic posters called Fremont a "Woolly Horse," who had "the full size of a horse, a Negro head, abolitionist body, tail of a snake, and the feet of an elephant... with black curled wool covering his head." The "Black Republicans" were called America's first "sectional party." This frightened many who opposed slavery but also feared dissolution of the Union.

The new minister to Mexico, John Forsyth, insisted that were Fremont elevated to the Presidency "the South ought not submit to it, and will not submit. The government of the United States will be at an end."

Southerners who dissented were threatened with lynching. Northern Whigs fearfully turned to Buchanan to preserve the Union. Sectionalism was judged more dangerous than slavery. Meanwhile, radical abolitionists, unsatisfied with the Republicans' timid stance in limiting their fight against slavery to the territories, but in not calling for its total abolition, attacked the Republicans as well.

More scurrilous were the Southern Know-Nothing charges that Fremont was secretly a practicing Catholic who would bring the Pope to power. His father was a French Catholic, opponents charged. Others claimed that when young John and Jessie eloped to escape Senator Benton's disapproval, they were married by a priest. And as if that weren't bad enough, doubters were informed that during one of his expeditions Fremont had placed a cross at Independence Rock. The charges roused enough suspicion that a delegation of Republican clergy visited Fremont to confirm that he was actually an Episcopalian. But publicly, Fremont refused to make religion a political issue and would not answer the slanderous charges that circulated in political quarters, even when Thurlow Weed and 40 other Republican leaders urged him to do so, thus adding to the malicious rumors' credence.

Fremont responded that the issue of the campaign was freedom, including religious freedom. He would not do anything to perpetuate the religious bigotry that had brought so many wars to Europe. The widespread prejudice across the country against Catholics and fear that they "take orders from the Pope," was skillfully played upon by Fremont's Democrat opponents. But Catholics did not rally to Fremont's side either, thinking he was really a stand-in for the Know-Nothings. Other critics challenged his discoveries as an explorer and tried to chip away at his heroic status in the popular imagination. Every detail of his career was misrepresented by his frenzied opponents.

But in every Northern city and town, Republican meetings were large and spirited and the crowds sang campaign songs celebrating their new hero, their "Columbus of the golden West." The Republicans intoned together, "All hail to Fremont! Swell the lofty acclaim; Like winds from the mountains, like prairies aflame! Once more the Pathfinder is forth on his hunt; Clear the way for free soil, for free men, and Fremont!" Republicans promised in their lyric, "Oh! The land that we love shall be sacred from slaves; from the tyrant's misrule, and the plunder of knaves; We'll baptize the Union in liberty's font; And the faith of our fathers shall live with Fremont!"

Various Republican delegations visited the young political leader at his home. One visitor described the scene inside. "In the midst of the group sat a small, intense, earnest, determined looking man, who bore the traces of hardship and toil, yet his countenance beamed with such an expression of good nature that it seemed to preserve a magnetic attraction for his guests.... Intelligence was breathed in every utterance; resolution was portrayed upon every feature; modesty, ability, integrity were written as plainly as the alphabet upon the whole man."

Fremont counted among his admirers the literary elite of the nation; Bryant, Emerson, Longfellow, and Whittier, and religious leaders such as Henry Ward Beecher. The entire campaign carried an aura of a religious revival. Fremont was a general directing a political battle as great as the forging of a new state like California; winning back the soul of a nation that had been burned in hell by slavery.

Fremont was a handsome figure. Another Fremont visitor wrote, "The prints fall exceedingly short of doing justice to his appearance." Visitors perceived a "rare union of gentleness, refinement, and delicacy, with resolute energy and firmness, which are so remarkable in his features and in the expression of his countenance." Republican partisans across the country were inspired by their candidate and the platform the party had crafted.

Carl Schurz, the German revolutionary of 1848 who had been banished from his fatherland, and co-founder of the Republican party, asserted, "The Republican platform sounded to me like a bugle call of liberty, and the name of Fremont, the Pathfinder, surrounded by a halo of adventurous heroism, mightily stirred the imagination. Thus the old cause of human freedom was to be fought for on the soil of the new world. The great final decision seemed to be impending."

But rumors persisted about Fremont and the hidden power of his wife and thus of her Democratic father, the former Missouri Senator. Others doubted that Fremont was prepared for the Presidency. *New York Evening Post* reporter John Bigelow visited Fremont at the Metropolitan Hotel as the campaign escalated, and noted that the candidate was in "no proper sense a statesman. He owes such success... to his wife, a remarkably capable and accomplished woman; to her father, through whose influence with the Democratic portion of the coalition, he was naturally expected to profit and his utterly neutral gender in politics. But he rendered his country as a candidate all the service he was capable of rendering it, by incarnating in that character the principles of the Free Soil party, and thus combining in the free states the force upon which the perpetuity of our Union was to be dependent, and the doctrine of popular sovereignty vindicated as it had never been before."

The national election was preceded by several staggered state elections which portended the ultimate results. On October 14, 1856, Pennsylvania voters turned out. Democrats stood against the Union party, a coalition of Republicans, Whigs, and assorted Native Americans. Democrats were already organized and waged a battle well-funded to the tune of $500,000, raised from New York and Pennsylvania merchants who relied upon Southern products. August Belmont, of New York, contributed $50,000 and other Wall Street brokers and bankers added $100,000 to the cause. The Union forces counted on 200 stump speakers, including Wilmot and Hannibal Hamlin, who would become Lincoln's first Vice President. The Pennsylvania press, beyond the confines of Philadelphia, spoke up for its favorite son, Buchanan.

Despite a cold, steady drizzle, voters turned out heavily for each side. Two days passed before the outcome was clear. In the end, Buchanan's Pennsylvania state party took the prize by fewer than 3,000 votes. Fremont believed his party had committed a strategic error in picking New Jersey's Dayton over Pennsylvania's Simon Cameron for Vice President. The choice proved fatal in Pennsylvania, although it may have made little difference in Indiana or Illinois. And, in the national election three weeks later, Pennsylvania Whigs who outnumbered Republicans three to one in Philadelphia alone, turned out for Millard Fillmore instead of Fremont. State elections held on the same October day in Indiana brought a similar victory to the Democrats. Only Ohio, which voted alongside its neighbors, turned out for Fremont. Republicans were crestfallen. The ultimate outcome in November was clear, a narrow but decisive defeat for the new party.

On November 4, 31 states cast ballots. The Pathfinder polled 500,000 fewer votes than Buchanan. The Democrat won 19 states. Fremont took 11. The new Republican party carried all but five free states. New York, Ohio, Michigan, Wisconsin, and Iowa all stood with the Pathfinder. Fourteen slave states and the five free states, including Pennsylvania, Indiana, and Illinois went for Buchanan. Fillmore, the former President, carried only one slave state, Maryland, but made the difference for Buchanan in New Jersey, California, and Indiana. Democrats lost ten states that they had carried four years earlier.

In the Electoral College, the vote was 174 for Buchanan, 114 for Fremont, and 8 for Fillmore. The popular vote stood at 1,836,072, or 45.3 percent for Buchanan; 1,342,345 or 33.1 percent for Fremont; 873,053 or 21.5 percent for Fillmore, about 300,000 of those coming from the North. The Know-Nothing votes represented the difference between defeat and victory. In Philadelphia, Buchanan won 56 percent of the vote, while Fillmore drew 36 percent from the city's strong Native American contingent, and Fremont received just 11 percent in the city of his nomination. Philadelphia did not relish the idea of war with the South. Buchanan was a minority President left simply to carry on the failed policies of Pierce.

As feared, Fillmore was the spoiler for the new Republicans. But it was both the Whigs' and Know-Nothings' last hurrah. As for the Republicans, their future, dimmed by momentary defeat, was as bright as an approaching comet that would soon illuminate the darkness that slavery had cast across the history of the nation, but not first without the cataclysmic explosion of civil war.

Had Fremont won, and somehow prevented secession, perhaps his family connections with Benton might have led to a slow abolition of slavery. Fremont wanted to compensate slave owners from the federal treasury for giving up their slaves. Fremont worked on such a plan during the election with Judge Jeremiah S. Black, of Pennsylvania, who subsequently became Buchanan's Attorney General and Secretary of State. But had the South reacted in the manner urged by its most reckless politicians, Fremont, a military man might have carried the war to a quicker conclusion than Lincoln, although Fremont's contemporaries feared his impetuous, erratic, and rash judgments might have led the North to defeat. The speculative "ifs" of history, of course, remain forever unresolved.

Fremont was only 43 at the time of his defeat. In the spring of 1857, he took his family to Paris for the season. Then they traveled back to California through the Panama Canal to settle on his ranch, "Bear Valley" in Mariposa. Large gold strikes had been recorded that could make him a multi-millionaire, but his claims were disputed in court. Still he amassed a small fortune, that within a year would vanish with railroad ventures that failed to link the continent. A few years later, the family retired to a "cottage" on a bluff overlooking the Golden Gate in San Francisco.

Then came the war of secession. Lincoln appointed Fremont commander of the Department of the West. He organized an excellent army, but when he declared Martial Law in Missouri and ordered the freeing of slaves before the Emancipation Proclamation, Lincoln was politically embarrassed and removed him from command. His political supporters got him reassigned to the "Mountain Division," but he soon stepped down from this post. After the war, he retained the faith of the "Radical Republicans" who sought to punish and transform the South. But his political career never again neared the heights of 1856. However, he did not fade away, serving as Governor of the Arizona Territory from 1878 to 1883. He finally retired, moving as he always had, between Washington, New York, and Los Angeles. In 1890, shortly before his death in New York City on July 13, Congress elevated John Charles Fremont to his final army rank of major general.

**James Buchanan
1856 Democratic Presidential
Nominee**

The 1872 National Union Republican Convention: Renominating A Hero

Convention-at-a-Glance

Event: Fifth National Union Republican Convention
Date: June 5-6, 1872
Location: Academy of Music, Broad and Locust Streets
Philadelphia Mayor: William S. Stokley, Republican
Philadelphia's Population: 674,022 (1870)
Convention's Permanent President: Judge Thomas Settle, North Carolina
Number of Delegates: 752
Number Needed to Nominate: A majority
Candidates for Nomination: President Ulysses Simpson Grant, Illinois
Presidential Nominee: President Ulysses Simpson Grant
Age at Renomination: 50
Number of Ballots: One; nominated unanimously
Vice Presidential Nominee: Senator Henry Wilson, Massachusetts
Largest Audience: About 3,000
Platform Positions: Payment of the national debt; enforcement of the Thirteenth, Fourteenth, and Fifteenth Amendments; suppression of the Ku Klux Klan; Civil Service reform
Campaign Slogan: "Grant Us Another Term"
Campaign Song: "Rally Round Our Leaders"

President Ulysses Simpson Grant
1872 National Union Republican
Presidential Nominee

Senator Henry Wilson
1872 National Union Republican
Vice Presidential Nominee

1872

The 1872 National Union Republican Convention:
Renominating A Hero

Not until 1872 did the Republican party return to Philadelphia, site of its first national Presidential nominating convention. The new party that had met in Philadelphia in 1856, won the Presidency four years later with the man that the first convention had turned aside as its first Vice Presidential nominee. Abraham Lincoln, who originally had been a Whig, was elected as the first Republican President with a 39.9 percent plurality of the popular total and without a single Southern electoral vote. Almost immediately, the South seceded and the nation plunged into four bloody years of civil war. Philadelphia sent over 90,000 men into the field, including 11 regiments of black soldiers. Among its war heroes was Major General George Gordon Meade, whose victory at Gettysburg saved the Union.

In 1864, while the conflict still raged, Lincoln broadened his adopted party and created the National Union Party. It convened in Baltimore as a fusion of Republicans and "War Democrats," such as Andrew Johnson, of Tennessee, Lincoln's Vice Presidential choice. As late as mid-summer 1864, Lincoln and his advisors had all but given up hope of holding on to the White House. The nation was tired of the costly conflict and mired in a military stalemate. The "Peace Democracy" and its candidate, General George Brinton McClellan, whom Lincoln had dismissed as Commander of the Army of the Potomac, held the initiative. But Old Abe's second term was secured, in part, by the late summer and fall military victories by an unknown Union officer from Illinois, whose eventual elevation to the rank of Commander of the Armies of the United States led to a Northern victory, restoration of the Union, and the emancipation of a long-enslaved race. Philadelphia gave the war President its vote.

After his assassination on April 14, 1865, Lincoln's funeral train passed through Philadelphia and he lay in state in Independence Hall while 85,000 people passed by his black-draped bier to pay their deepest respects. On August 14, 1866, President Andrew Johnson, Lincoln's successor, seeking to build support for his reconstruction programs and Presidential renomination in 1868, held a mid-term convention for the National Union Party in the "Philadelphia Wigwam," a temporary building erected on Girard Avenue between Twentieth and Twenty-first Streets. (Political meeting halls were often called Wigwams, an Algonquin word for temporary building. The term was associated with the political tradition of Tammany Hall which celebrated Tammanend, chief of the Lenni Lenapes or Delaware Indians, later dubbed St. Tammany, who had reputedly signed the Great Treaty of Friendship with William Penn in 1682.)

But after the 1868 failed congressional impeachment of Johnson, the war hero, General Ulysses Simpson Grant, was instead nominated in Chicago and elected as the nation's second Republican President over New York Governor Horatio Seymour by a 52.7 to 47.3 percent margin on his slogan of "Let Us Have Peace." As with the war he had waged, Grant had a strategic plan to rule. He promised to offer no policy "to enforce against the will of the people," but ceded power to Congress and only proposed programs from time to time. The void created an opportunity for power and money grabbers, and for scandal. Grant's appointment of close friends to high posts, such as General John Aaron Rawlins to the office of Secretary of War, and to big campaign contributors, such as Adolph Edward Borie who became Secretary of the Navy, created a post-war atmosphere of spoils for the taking. The humble Grant, who had failed in business before the war, surrounded himself with wealthy advisors and slipped into comfortable luxury.

Domestically, Grant did press Congress to pass the Enforcement Acts in order to quell the Ku Kluxers who terrorized new black citizens. Despite arrests, federal raids, and suspension of habeas corpus in some Southern counties, his success in repressing Klan behavior was sporadic. Grant's Republican critics feared that his tough reconstructionist attitude would politically backfire. They believed Republican control of the South would slip away to the Democrats, and with it the rights of the newly enfranchised blacks.

The Civil War had created a generation of millionaires, accelerated the industrialization of the land, and ushered in the Gilded Age of American capitalism. Grant's laissez-faire policy seemed to fuel its excesses, even as it stabilized the national economy. In 1869, Grant's own wife was caught up in a sinister plan by financier Jay Gould and "Jubilee" Jim Fisk to corner the gold market and make a financial killing. When Grant got wind of the scheme, he reversed his policy at the last moment to foil the gold diggers by dumping government metal reserves on the market. "Black Friday" resulted in a Wall Street crash, but the national economy survived.

However, Grant seemed oblivious to the cries of Western farmers to put more money in circulation so they were not captive to the Eastern banks. Grant held to his "hard money" policy that encouraged deflation as he paid off the war debt. He signed the Specie Resumption Bill; this put the nation to the rigid task of recalibrating paper money to the actual amount of gold and silver held in government reserve.

Meanwhile, Grant's foreign policy yielded mixed results. In 1871, his Secretary of State, Hamilton Fish, managed to resolve the "Alabama Affair" with the Treaty of Washington. The United States received $15,500,000 in claims against Great Britain for damage done by a British vessel sold to the Confederates. But Grant's ambition to annex Cuba and to make Santo Domingo a black state in the Union was blocked by his nemesis, Massachusetts' radical Republican Senator Charles Sumner. All the while complaints against Grant grew ever louder. The carping of Liberal Republicans especially struck President Grant as disloyal and vindictive. Whatever his shortcomings as a statesman, no matter how vicious the attacks against him in the press, the people still loved their hero. He had saved the Union. He had forced the South to live up to the ideals of freedom and citizenship for all. Grant was, after all, one of the humble people like the masses for whom the star-spangled banner of freedom flew.

In June 1872, regular Republicans gathered in Philadelphia to renominate President Grant to continue his work as the chief magistrate of the land. His main opponent had already been chosen in convention a month earlier in Cincinnati. He was an unlikely opponent; a founder of the Republican party and a Grant partisan four years before. In fact, he had named the Republican party. Indeed, many founding members of the Republican party who were prominent at its first Philadelphia convention were not in Philadelphia in 1872 to participate in Grant's renomination. They had bolted from the regular party to form the Liberal Republican party. They threatened to take with them the party's moral high ground. Not only that, the Democrats who were scheduled to meet a month later, might offer no candidate of their own but endorse the Liberal Republican standard-bearer in an unholy alliance to elect "anyone but Grant."

Grant's behavior in office and his ill-formed policies, his profligate patronage that filled federal jobs with individuals who the Liberal Republicans found unqualified and unfit, had driven them from the party. From the time the general failed to consult Republican congressional leaders on the appointment of his new cabinet, Republican loyalists had begun their retreat from the party they had created in 1856. Many in the Washington establishment found Grant vulgar and uncouth in his habits, inept in his execution of political duties, and careless in his appointments. As had been the case in the military, he was rumored to be drunk much of the time.

Liberal Republicans also objected to his policies. In late 1871, Grant persuaded Congress to pass the Ku Klux Klan Act, which they feared gave the federal government too much power to suspend individual rights. Liberal Republicans felt that their party's only hope in the South was to show greater leniency toward former rebels and to restore home rule. They complained that Grant's policies solidified Democratic support. And the farmers of the West who wanted inflationary money policies and free trade to reduce their costs and open the world to their produce, saw the old Galena tanner spending more and more time with rich Wall Street speculators who controlled their fate. They no longer trusted him.

Liberal Republicans, in coalition with Democrats, first swept into office in Missouri, electing B. Gratz Brown governor and a Republican founder, General Carl Schurz, as their new Senator. In opposition to regular Missouri Republicans, they demanded universal amnesty for former rebels and a policy of free trade. At their state convention in January 1872, the Missourians put out a call for a national Liberal Republican Convention to be held in Cincinnati on May 1, at the Music Hall to nominate someone to run against Grant.

Throughout the spring the insurgents gained momentum. Old Republican stalwarts joined them, including Lincoln's Secretary of Treasury, Salmon P. Chase, now Chief Justice of the U.S. Supreme Court; economist David A. Wells; Francis P. Blair, Jr., of Missouri, who had run as the 1868 Democratic Vice Presidential nominee; Grant's former Secretary of the Interior, Jacob B. Cox, a former Ohio governor was active as well. In New York, former Governor Reuben E. Fenton and his wing of the party joined the rebellion. They had been ousted and cut off from patronage positions, with Grant's approval, by the dashing, golden-haired, orator Senator Roscoe Conkling, whom Mrs. Grant wanted her husband to appoint to the Supreme Court. Conkling, the "King of Patronage," declined the offer which had little patronage reach.

Powerful newspaper editors such as Samuel Bowles of the *Springfield Republican*, Murat Halstead of the *Cincinnati Commercial*, Colonel Henry Watterson of the *Louisville Courier-Journal*, and Horace White of the *Chicago Tribune* also turned on Grant and fueled the party realignment. For a time, the Republican reformers hoped they could stop Grant's renomination in the Republican party itself and replace him with a reform candidate such as Senator Lyman Trumbull or Governor John M. Palmer, both of Illinois. When that hope faded, these luminaries became contenders for the Liberal Republican Presidential nomination.

As May neared, the leading candidate for the Liberal nomination, and the favorite of many professional politicians, was Supreme Court Justice David Davis, of Illinois, the man who had been Lincoln's campaign manager in 1860. But many liberals distrusted Davis, especially since he had actively sought the Democratic nomination just four years earlier. They doubted his reform credentials. Chief Justice Chase, who had been a contender for the Republican nomination in 1860, also made himself available to the Liberal Republicans and had a goodly number of supporters at the Cincinnati convention. Massachusetts Senator Charles Sumner, attracted strong antislavery veterans and radical Republicans, but did not himself seek the nomination.

Others, including Carl Schurz and B. Gratz Brown, favored the aristocratic son and grandson of two former Presidents, Charles Francis Adams, of Massachusetts, who had been spurned by Grant for the Secretary of State post. In comparison to Grant, his moral character and manners were sterling. By most accounts, the nomination could have been his had he worked for it. But Adams was too cold and remote to stoop to such trivialities, though he desired the designation and believed he could beat Grant. Instead of coming to Cincinnati as his supporters urged, he sailed for England.

To further Adam's chances on the eve of the Cincinnati convention, Murat Halstead, Horace White, Samuel Bowles, and Colonel Watterson mounted a last-minute editorial attack on Davis that crippled his campaign for the nomination. The delegates, who numbered twice each state's electoral number and were often self-appointed devotees to the liberal cause, still were split on candidates and issues as they gathered for the first session.

The Liberal Republican platform was frank: "We demand the immediate and absolute removal of all disabilities imposed on account of the rebellion, which was finally subdued seven years ago, believing that universal amnesty will result in complete pacification in all sections of the country. Local self-government, with impartial suffrage, will guard the rights of all citizens more securely than any centralized power. The public welfare requires the supremacy of the civil over the military authority, and freedom of person under the protection of the habeas corpus." That did not mean the Liberal Republicans were abandoning newly-freed slaves. Rather, their platform declared, "We recognize the equality of all men before the law, and hold that it is the duty of government in its dealings with the people to mete out equal and exact justice to all of whatever nativity, race, color, or persuasion religious or political."

Going to the heart of some complaints against Grant, the Liberal Republicans asserted, "The Civil Service of the government has become a mere instrument of partisan tyranny and personal ambition and an object of selfish greed. It is a scandal and reproach upon free institutions and breeds a demoralization dangerous to the perpetuity of republican government. We therefore regard such thorough reforms of the Civil

Service as one of the most pressing necessities of the hour; that honesty, capacity, and fidelity constitute the only valid claim to public employment; cease to be a matter of arbitrary favoritism and patronage, and that public station become again a post of honor. To this end it is imperatively required that no President shall become a candidate for re-election."

Ending the tariff and promoting a policy of free trade had been the motivating force for many Liberal Republicans. But when they arrived in Cincinnati, they were disappointed. In part, to satisfy the powerful newspaper publisher Horace Greeley, whose New York *Tribune* would be an essential ally in their fight, the new party wrote a compromise plank that recognized "... there are in our midst honest but irreconcilable differences of opinion with regard to the respective systems of protection and free trade." Greeley had sent his second in command, Whitelaw Reid, to the Cincinnati convention to work on his behalf and to make sure the Liberal platform did not include a call for free trade. So the party decided to "remit the discussion on the subject to the people in the Congress districts, and to the decision of Congress thereon, wholly free of executive interference or dictation." Finally, the Liberal Republicans, asserted, "We are opposed to all further grants of lands to the railroads or other corporations. The public domain should be held sacred to actual settlers."

With a clear and decisive platform hammered out, the Liberal Republicans, got down to the business of nominating a candidate to take on Grant. After the first ballot, Adams had the lead with 203 votes. Surprisingly, Horace Greeley tallied 147. Illinois Senator Lyman Trumbull, author of the Thirteenth Amendment to the U.S. Constitution, was third with 110; Governor B. Gratz Brown drew 95 votes, while Justice Davis corralled 92 ½.

But after the first round, Brown suddenly broke with Schurz and withdrew, throwing his support behind Greeley and working for him in "secret maneuvers." During the second ballot the legendary New York editor took a two vote lead. Adams surged back into the front on the next two tests, but could not secure a majority. On the fifth ballot, Greeley regained the lead as Davis and Trumbull supporters shifted allegiance.

On the sixth ballot the New Yorker gained a few more votes, tallying 332 to 324 for Adams. Then suddenly delegates began to switch their votes in rapid succession and wild Greeley demonstrations broke out throughout the hall. Upon the final tabulation, Horace Greeley was given the majority on the sixth ballot. An attempt to make the nomination unanimous was defeated and many Liberal Republicans, especially the free traders, charged "fraud" and felt betrayed. Horace Greeley, who had the longest record as a reformer of almost any living American and had often envisioned himself as President even though he had been but a one-term congressman, now had his opportunity, to the utter surprise and bewilderment of voters throughout the land. In exchange for his support, B. Gratz Brown was nominated to the second spot on the Liberal ticket. (Justice David Davis was subsequently nominated by the National Labor convention.)

Stunned and incredulous that a political maverick like Greeley had absconded with the nomination, several prominent Liberal Republicans abandoned their own rump party. They charged that they had been "swindled by political idiots and political buccaneers." The convention broke up with the new party in turmoil. Greeley, who had long desired to become President, received word of his success in his *Tribune* office where he was swamped with congratulations. Elsewhere he was showered with ridicule. His detractors called him "scatter-brained" and a moral zealot. But in New York City, tens of thousands of Greeley supporters turned out for a "monster meeting" around Cooper Institute, jamming all the streets to ratify Greeley and Brown, "The People's Choice." Greeley clubs spontaneously formed throughout the states and his supporters donned white hats like the famous one worn by their political hero. Support was so strong that a few weeks after the convention, Greeley declared, "The people have already ratified Cincinnati."

A month after the Cincinnati affair, regular Republicans trooped to Philadelphia to endorse their leader. The convention site had been chosen at the Chicago gathering of 1868 where Grant was first nominated. Each state sent delegates equal to twice the number of Senators and Representatives they had in Congress, while each territory dispatched two delegates. The event was staged in the magnificent, four-story Academy of Music at Broad and Locust Streets, which had opened in 1857 and replaced Musical Fund Hall as Philadelphia's premiere concert hall. The acoustically perfect conservatory was designed by Napoleon Le Brun and its grand interior mirrored his design of the great opera house, La Scala, in Milan. The convention assembled just south of where construction was to begin on Philadelphia's new city hall in Penn Square.

The once simple "Quaker City" of red brick homes was now an industrial marvel prosperous beyond its early dreams. Its postbellum wealth was added to by new industries such as petroleum and publishing. It was home to over 40 banks, including the house of Jay Cooke who had helped finance the Civil War. Its Board of Trade, insurance firms, and sugar trade were bustling. Convention delegates arrived from all directions on the powerful Pennsylvania Railroad. Over the city's administration presided Republican Mayor "Sweet William" Stokley, who got his name from the confectionery business he owned. Stokley didn't fit the gentlemanly ideal that the city aspired to in earlier times, but he was likeable. His policies, however, were far from candied. To combat the new wave of riotousness and civic disorder that involved both outright criminality of gangs and outlaws, and violent clashes between the city's volunteer fire companies, Stokley clamped down with a beefed up police force that used violence of its own. As a result, there were no bank robberies at all during his term. But his political machine was heavy with patronage. Nonetheless, the Republican mayor served as a generous host to the Republicans who arrived to renominate their President.

At exactly noon on Wednesday, June 5, 1872, Governor William Claflin, of Massachusetts, chairman of the Republican National Committee, gaveled the fifth quadrennial National Union Republican Convention to order. "Gentleman of the convention," he boomed to the unruly assemblage, "elected according to the usages of the Republican party, in conventions of the people held in every state, you have assembled for the purpose of placing in nomination candidates for the two highest offices in the gift of the American people. You represent a party founded on the broadest principles of freedom, justice, and humanity; and whose achievements have been the wonder and admiration of the civilized world. The promises of reform and progress made four years ago have been faithfully fulfilled."

Now the governor had their attention and applause swept through the Academy of Music. "In the guarantee by the nation of equal rights for all; in the reduction of the public expenditures and the public debt; in the decrease of the public burdens; in the improvement of the public credit; in the establishment of the public faith that no act of repudiation shall ever stain the statute book, and in securing peace and order throughout the entire Republic," the party staked its claim.

Claflin continued in clarion voice, "You are summoned to declare anew your fidelity to those principles and purposes which have brought such benefits to the nation. We will not fear that the people will desert those who have been faithful to their high trust, for other men and other organizations, although they may adopt our principles and promise to adhere to our policy. Let us go forward with confident faith that our cause will triumph, not withstanding the unexpected defections, over all combinations, however skillfully planned, because in its continued success are centered the best interests and the highest hopes of the country."

As Claflin concluded his remarks the convention rose in rousing cheers. Then the governor invited Reverend Dr. Alexander Reed, of Philadelphia's Central Presbyterian Church, to bless the proceedings, which he did, with a prayer twice the length of the governor's opening remarks, recalling the "dark and dangerous days of division and strife," that the nation had endured during the Civil War, and thanking God for "our new birth of freedom."

Governor Claflin, then introduced the convention's temporary

The chairman announces the nomination of Grant inside the Academy of Music. Sketch by James E. Taylor in *Frank Leslie's Illustrated Newspaper, June 1872.* The Library Company of Philadelphia.

chairman, Morton McMichael, former Republican mayor of Philadelphia, to great applause. He thanked the crowd. "I am the more gratified because as a delegate from Pennsylvania and a resident of Philadelphia, it gives me the occasion to welcome you to our state and city, and to say how glad we are to have you among us." The crowd expressed its pleasure to be there. "Under any circumstances, it would be a source of satisfaction to have the presence of so many distinguished men, gathered from all parts of this mighty land, which grows and stretches so rapidly that in these recurring quadrennial convocations new states, new territories, and in this case, happily for the cause of humanity and progress, a new race," here McMichael was interrupted with thunderous applause, "new at least in the possession of political rights and functions, and soon to be endowed with all the attributes of equality, are represented: under any circumstances your presence would be a source of satisfaction."

Then he took the convention's first shot at their opponents, the Liberal Republicans and the Democracy. "The malcontents who recently met at Cincinnati were without a constituency; and the Democrats who are soon to meet at Baltimore will be without a principle." His phraseology elicited great laughter. "The former, having no motive in common but personal disappointment, attempted a fusion of repelling elements, which has resulted in an explosion; the latter, degraded from the high estate they once occupied, propose an abandonment of their identity, which means death. Unlike the first, you are authentic exponents of a great national organization, based upon principles... unlike the last, your object is to preserve, not to destroy."

Then the Philadelphian launched into a defense of his party's leader. "On the subject which has most perplexed, and must continue to perplex their councils... there will be absolute harmony. With us the selection of a Presidential candidate is a foregone conclusion. In that regard the people have decided for us in advance, and we have only to put their will into proper shape by formally nominating Ulysses S. Grant." At the first mention of the President's name, the Republican convention burst into enthusiastic and sustained cheering, with the entire assemblage jumping to its feet; "... not withstanding all the malignant venom that has been spit at him; all the odious calumnies that have been heaped upon him; all the disgraceful slanders that have been circulated in regard to him, General Grant at this moment enjoys more of the confidence of his countrymen, is believed by them to be an honester, truer, and better man than any of his detractors."

McMichael's listeners cheered their assent. "No one in our day has been more causelessly, more shamelessly vilified: no one will be more thoroughly vindicated. The great heart of the American people beats responsively to truth and justice, and as they have tried and tested and trusted him; as they know that his administration has been wise and faithful; as they have seen the nation prosper under his rule as it has never before prospered; they will stand by and defend, and when the ballot box gives them a chance to do so, avenge him." The crowd shouted "They will, they will!"

McMichael continued, "Remembering the sore trials which, along with his fellow soldiers, he underwent during the war, his sacrifices of ease and comfort, his perils by day and night, the exposure of means of which those who now revile him were able to secure luxurious repose at a safe distance from danger, they are quite willing that he should indulge in 'palace cars and cigars and seaside loiterings.' " The laughter arose again as McMichael mocked Grant's critics. "And they mean to furnish him with the opportunity of enjoying these for at least four years to come."

McMichael's entertaining remarks concluded, the band broke into a musical interlude and the convention fell to the mundane work of appointing committees on credentials; on permanent organization; on resolutions; and on rules and order of business. But the body of distant travelers was not ready to disband and wanted more speeches from its luminaries, shouting out the names of Senator Logan, of Illinois, Senator Morton, of Indiana, Representative Banks, of Massachusetts, and finally one of the party's venerable founders, Gerrit Smith, of New York, "the oldest pioneer in the cause of emancipation."

All over the hall, delegates waved handkerchiefs, tossed hats and yelled out Smith's name, while the band played "Hail to the Chief." Smith was hoarse from informal speeches the night before, but gamely accommodated the convocation. "Gentlemen, the time has nearly come round again when the American people are to choose their chief magistrate. Who shall it be?"

The delegates shouted back "Grant, Grant!" "Why do we all say Grant?" he answered them. "Because he was the savior of the country. Because he has blessed his country in time of peace." Smith recounted Grant's victories in war, then turned to his record as President. "I say that he has helped us in peace also. He has preserved us on terms of amity with all the nations of the earth. He has preserved the policy of kindness towards the poor, erring, deluded Indians. And he is doing what he can, and if you give him time he will fully accomplish it, to crush out Ku Kluxism and save the Negro and the few white men who defend the Negro from the bloody, fearful, and terrible vengeance threatened against them."

Smith then answered the Liberals call for one-term Presidents by defending Grant's right to a second term. "My friends, my doctrine is that his having proved a good President once, proves him fitted for it in a second term. That was the doctrine of the American people when they reelected Washington, the first savior of the country. It was their doctrine when they re-elected Lincoln, the second savior of his country. It is their doctrine in regard to the third savior of the country, and they will re-elect General Grant accordingly." Smith's declaration was met with wild applause.

Then the delegates called upon the great war governor of Indiana, now Senator Oliver Perry Morton, whose infirmity required him to speak from a chair. "In the enthusiasm which prevails here today, I see the unmistakable evidence of victory in November. This enthusiasm is not manufactured; it is spontaneous; it comes from the hearts of this audience here today representing the great mass of the people of the United States. You represent the Republican party, and that party has a great mission to perform, a mission that is no less than taking care of this country."

The crowd was with the old Senator as he recounted how Grant had taken care of the country by reduction of public debt and keeping of contracts made during the war. "It is for the Republican party to establish the Fourteenth and Fifteenth Amendments, to plant them in the Constitution, beyond peradventure, so that they shall be recognized by all parties, so that there shall no longer be any considerable party in this country which shall dare to question the legality or the validity of these amendments." Delegates shouted in agreement.

"It is for the Republican party to establish fully the rights of the colored men of this country." Again applause shook the hall. "Our work will not be done until they shall be conceded by all parties, and they shall have the full and free enjoyment of their rights in every portion of this country." Again applause answered Senator Morton. "Until they shall be in the full and free enjoyment not just of their political rights, but all their civil rights, our work will not be done until there shall be equal protection under the law extended to the men of every race and color, and to all men of all political views in every part of the United States.

"The mission of the Republican party will not be performed as long as there shall remain a Ku Klux organization in any state of this union." Again the delegates interrupted Morton. "For that organization but sleeps in some states, and it will awake to active, terrible life, shortly before the Presidential election if there shall not be proper legislation, if there shall not be a firm, bold administration of government which shall afford protection for all." Now the delegates were on their feet shouting their agreement.

"In passing what is called the Ku Klux law, we did not intend to place an arbitrary power in the hands of the President of the United States, to be exercised with caprice or for selfish or partisan purposes. That power was placed there for the purpose of protecting, or enabling him to protect, the lives, liberty, and property of hundreds and thousands and even millions of people in some of the Southern States, where the

"Monster Meeting" around Cooper Institute, New York City, to ratify the nominations for Horace Greeley and Gratz Brown. *Frank Leslie's Illustrated Newspaper*, June 1872. The Library Company of Philadelphia.

state governments have been unable or had failed to grant such protection.

"We knew, when placing that power in the hands of the President, he would not abuse it. He has not abused it. And allow me to say that the Ku Klux law has done more good in a shorter time than any law ever enacted by the Congress of the United States. It has protected thousands and thousands of people from murder, from outrage, and from exile. And those in the South who denounce that law, and who oppose the re-enactment for another year of the power of the President to suspend the writ of habeas corpus in the case of revolution or rebellion, do not oppose it because any wrong has been done, because any rights have been violated, but they oppose it because they are unwilling that such an instrumentality shall be crushed out, which being left uncontrolled, may control, may absolutely sway, the political action of certain states of the Union. We desire only fair elections. We want men of all parties and of all colors, without regard to previous condition, to have perfect liberty in the exercise of their political rights. And it is because they have not been accorded hitherto that we enacted it."

When Senator Morton concluded his stirring oration and the vast assemblage returned to some semblance of order, more orators went to the podium, including Governor John L. Orr, of Ohio, and Governor Richard J. Oglesby, of Illinois, Grant's home state, who spoke warmly about its native son. "The little man, who but a few years ago was an unknown to fame and to this country as that poor colored man now redeemed and sitting in your midst; the young man who passed through West Point unnoticed, who passed through the Mexican War in the same way, unnoticed to retire to private life; you and I know that among all the great names but a few years ago, this little man's name, Ulysses S. Grant, was unknown.

"How came the American people to select him for their general? Can you tell? Can history tell? No; no man can tell, unless it is written upon the necessities of the times by the invisible finger of almighty God. Who brought him from obscurity? It was a mere circumstance in his life that he lived in our proud state. He came trudging along from obscurity step by step. He marched to the front. When the dark clouds of war were rolling and reverberating around the angry horizon; when none of us, not even our gallant generals, our other magnificent soldiers in the East and West, worthy of all praise, worthy of our gratitude, when none of us knew where to look or what to do, this little shadow of Ulysses S. Grant fell upon us." Oglesby was interrupted by applause. "To give us relief; and although that mighty voice assailed him but yesterday in the Senate [he referred to Senator Sumner]; today the feeble voice of an obscure man who fought under his orders and by his side must now defend and uphold him." Immense applause swept the hall.

"He was an enigma from the hour of birth to this moment; his character has not yet been fathomed by this American people. He is purer and greater and nobler than we have ever thought him to be.... I stand before you today, uttering in my feeble way the voice of the great Prairie State, the state that gave to the country the immortal Lincoln..., to say that our confidence is unshaken in the deep and pure patriotism of General Grant, as has been shown in his magnanimity, and in his bright and shining intellect. He is not a man of words. He cannot utter a speech to defend himself at any time; upon no occasion can we hope for that, and therefore those of us who are gifted with speech, I am not sure but that some of us have a little too much of that element [the delegates laughed], are quite free in our comments and strictures.... I come here today to say that we have perfect confidence in General Grant and are willing to trust him four years longer, without so much as a shadow or suspicion of a doubt."

When Governor Oglesby stepped down from the stand, the audience's appetite for oratory was not yet quenched and a cry for William H. Grey, of Arkansas, filled the hall. As the statuesque African-American made his way to the rostrum, a hush fell upon the animated assembly. "Gentlemen of the convention, for the first time, perhaps, in the history of the American people, there stands before you in a national convention assembled, a representative of that oppressed race that has lived among you for 250 years, lifted by the magnanimity of this great nation, by the power of God, and the laws of war, from the degradation of slavery to the proud position of American citizenship." Grey's pronouncement was met with thunderous cheers.

"Words fail me, upon this occasion, to thank you for this evidence of the grandest progress in civilization, when a people of such magnitude, the grandest and greatest nation on the face of the earth, not only in the recognition of the merits and the glory of the war which her noble sons waged so successfully, have, in convention assembled, been willing to listen not only to the greatest of her orators, but to the humblest citizens of this great Republic.

"I scarcely know where to begin upon an occasion like the present. If I raise the curtain of the past, then I open the doors of the sarcophagus from which we have but just emerged. If I should go back to the primary history of my race in this country, I would open up, perhaps, to discussion things and circumstances that would make us blush, and the blood in our cheeks to tingle in view of the evidences of the shameful and horrible condition such in its degradation as the American people have thought of, from which we have just escaped.

"But that is hardly necessary. We are ready to say in the words of the Good Book, 'let the dead past bury its dead.' While we remember those errors, while we remember all these degradations, there is no vengeance, thank God, found in our hearts; no revengeful feelings, no desire for retaliation. But God has given us a heart to thank the American people for the position in which we stand today.... It is the wonder of the world, the miracle of the nineteenth century, that this tremendous struggle which rocked this great country from center to circumference, that amid the debris of 250 years, a living people were found by this great nation and lifted from degradation by the strong arm of power, and at once, without preparation and without forethought, placed upon the broad plane of American citizenship....

"I happened to be present on that occasion, in Chicago in 1868, when General Grant was nominated, and I know very well, and there are men here who can attest it, that through that political contest it cost the lives of over 300 black men in Arkansas to carry the state for Ulysses S. Grant. Today, the Ku Klux problem is being worked out.... But had it not been for the passage of the Ku Klux law and the man at the helm who had the nerve to execute it, that organization would be today in full venom in that section of the country. Therefore we urge upon the American people to give us Ulysses S. Grant for our candidate, for his name is a tower of strength that the South, and the only name that the unrepentant rebels respect." Loud cheers resounded at Grey's appeal.

"... We stand, many of us, in a prominent position in the Southern states... but the law is weak and the public sentiment so perverse that the common civilities of a citizen are withheld from us. We want the Civil Rights bill." His appeal met with more applause.

"We ask of the American people as the natural result of their own actions, that we shall be respected as men among men, and as free American citizens." Here Grey was cheered again. "We do not ask that for any small reason. There are always two classes of people we have to be afraid of: those who love us too well and that class who hates us too bad. All we ask is a fair chance in the race of life. Give us the same privileges and opportunities that are given to other men.... So far as the colored people of the South are concerned, they are a unit for Ulysses S. Grant."

When he stepped away from the stand, Grey received a prolonged ovation that lasted several minutes. But the convention was treated to more insight into the oratorical skills of the new members of its party as Robert Brown Elliott, an African-American congressman from South Carolina and James H. Harris of North Carolina were successively urged to the rostrum.

They were followed by the first committee report, presented by General Albright, of Pennsylvania, who informed the body that the Committee on Permanent Organization had nominated Judge Thomas Settle, of North Carolina, as the convention's president. The nomination and committee report were unanimously adopted and Judge Settle came

FRANK LESLIE'S
ILLUSTRATED
NEWSPAPER

Entered according to the Act of Congress, in the year 1875, by Frank Leslie, in the Office of the Librarian of Congress, at Washington.

No. 1,013—Vol. XXXIX.] NEW YORK, FEBRUARY 27, 1875. [Price 10 Cents. $4 00 Yearly. 15 Weeks, $1.00.

Grant's administration began to crumble after his 1872 victory. *Frank Leslie's Illustrated Newspaper,* February 27, 1875.

to the stand. He accepted the honor, "... not so much as a personal tribute to myself, but as the right hand of fellowship extended from our magnanimous sisters of the North to the erring, wayward, punished, regenerated, patriotic sisters of the South." His comments sparked immense applause and cheering on the floor of the convention. He added, "We of the South recognize and demand Ulysses S. Grant as necessary for law and order in that portion of the country, and for the freedom of all men." Then Judge Settle entertained a motion from Charles S. Spencer, of New York, to adjourn until the next morning, which was done.

The second day of the convention, June 6, 1872, was packed with real business. Most of the committees had met late into the evening to prepare for the session. When Judge Settle gaveled the proceedings back to order, Oliver Ames, of Massachusetts, chairman of the Committee on Rules, reported and urged passage of a package which closely followed procedures used in the House of Representatives, and which set the standard of a majority vote for nomination of candidates for President and Vice President.

Isaac Pendleton, of Iowa, chairman of the Committee on Credentials, reported that "no seats are contested except those of Utah and Dakota." A delegate from California objected that he understood that the delegates had been excluded from Utah "because of their being Mormons." That was denied by Mr. Pendleton and a motion to overturn the committee's ruling was defeated. Appointments to the National Executive Committee were announced and included William H. Kemble, of Pennsylvania.

Then, as the delegates awaited the report of the Committee on Resolutions, delegates heard a report from the National Council of the Union League of America that had been meeting in Philadelphia. The city's Union League Club, which had raised tens of thousands of dollars for the Union war effort and whose members now included the city's richest businessmen, was located a few doors north at Broad and Sansom Streets in an imposing red brick French Renaissance edifice. "We reject, as utterly unfounded," its resolution read, "the idea that the mission of the Republican party has been accomplished...." The Union Leaguers also declared, "Whatever may be its pretenses, the Democratic party remains unchanged in character and ultimate purposes. What it was from April 1861 to April 1865, it still is, and will continue to be. Incapable of reform or improvement, it will always be unfit to direct or govern the nation." The Union League also denounced the Liberal Republicans who had met in Cincinnati. And it urged the House of Representatives "to pass the civil rights and enforcement bills pending in it...." The Republican delegates cheered and endorsed their resolutions.

Cries from the floor arose for Colonel George W. Carter, of

Texas, who spoke briefly. "I appreciate your desire to hear something... from a Confederate, who believed he was right.... I am an ex-Confederate soldier who needed reconstruction, and if I am any judge of the matter, I believe that I have been reconstructed." He conceded that he thought "our people down there are learning." As for the contest between Grant and Greeley, Carter asserted, "They prefer a man who does not cry over them as they weep over their distresses, but tells them they must work if they would be happy.... I believe today if the Democrats endorse Mr. Greeley, General Grant will get more straight Democratic votes than Greeley will in Louisiana."

Mr. Paul Strobach, of Alabama, a naturalized German, walked to the stand and told delegates his former countrymen were with Grant. Then he horrified listeners with a story of the Ku Kluxers in his territory, including an attack on a racially-mixed husband and wife. "This band of assassins went at the hour of midnight and destroyed their little cabin," he indignantly shouted, "and after killing the husband, burned the wife alive. This is one of the many instances to show you that the Ku Klux are not as the Democratic papers present them, a myth, for there are facts and accusations so plain that we must have the strong arm of government to protect us in the South."

A succession of speakers was called to the podium by delegates on the floor. Emery A. Storrs, of Illinois, mocked the verbal jibes against Southern carpetbaggers, noting, "In 25 years the carpetbaggers of Illinois have built a magnificent empire, and on the shores of that great lake, one of the most magnificent cities that the world has ever seen. I say, then, that if the carpetbag tree produces this kind of fruit, for God's sake, plant it all over the nation." He was cheered heartily. "As proud as I was of my great city a year or two ago, I was prouder still of it after the flames had swept over it, when out of the still unextinguished fires, I saw the spirit of the carpetbagger rising unconquered and unconquerable."

Storrs was followed by former Senator John B. Henderson, of Missouri, where the dissident Liberal Republican movement first took hold. He bellowed, "Whatever you may think of Missouri, I am here to say that now the Republican party of that state is united. There will come from the prairies and the valleys of that state one universal shout for the nominations of this convention. It has been most unfortunate the quarrel in our state, but it is healed now. There have been Liberals and regulars, but now they are upon the same platform.

"Some of us in the state favored repeal of constitutional restrictions against those who have been engaged in the rebellion. I, for one, after the war was over, and we had secured everything we could, was in favor of the constitutional amendments adopted by the Republican party to enfranchise the rebels; not that they deserved it, but simply because it was dangerous in a republican government to keep a part of her citizens excluded, and I therefore went for repealing the constitutional restrictions."

Then he explained how Governor Gratz Brown had associated himself with the Democrats and Liberal Republicans, and how Carl Schurz had crossed over from the Republican party without winning support for his free trade position from the Cincinnati convention. "I understand that in a short time, he is to visit Europe, and I suppose, for the purpose of getting a large supply of 'pretzel seed' for his candidate." That elicited much laughter from his audience.

When Henderson stepped down, W. D. Bickham, of Ohio, rose and shouted, "I move a suspension of the rules, and that we proceed to ballot for President of the United States." But the motion was voted down.

Then Mr. Hill, of Mississippi, addressed the body from the floor. "Mr. President, I desire to suggest that while the various delegations are presenting to this convention from different sections, eloquent orators, we propose to this convention that it listen to the eloquent colored Secretary of State from Mississippi, the Honorable James R. Lynch."

Loud cheers resounded from the floor in agreement and Lynch made his way to the podium. James Roy Lynch, who would be elected to Congress in the subsequent contest, began, "I should be constrained to silence on this occasion, knowing that 400,000 colored people of the state of Mississippi, and the Republicans of other color, are waiting with anxious hopes to hear the announcement by telegraph that General Grant has been renominated for President of the United States." Lynch was interrupted with great applause.

"I will not trespass on your valuable time by entering into any argument in favor of the Republican party. It needs no more argument to convince patriotism, justice, reason, and intelligence that it is the only party that can bless and save the country, and realize the hopes of its founders, than does the glorious sun, scattering his rays everywhere, bathing the world in glory, to make men believe it is necessary to warm our air to make it capable of supporting human life." Lynch's rhetorical flamboyance elicited more applause.

"I heard gentlemen say here that we would kill the Democratic party. With all due deference to those who have superior political sagacity and knowledge to that which I possess, I beg leave to suggest that the Democratic party is dead." His audience laughed. "Some may ask, then, why invoke the Divine Master to retard its progress? Because a dead body lying on the ground in the summer time may do more harm than a living one." The delegates roared with laughter.

"I behold this Democratic party dead: its hydra head in the waters of the lakes, its cloven feet stuck out in the waters of the Gulf, one of its cold, clammy, bony fingers grasps the Pacific, and the other the Atlantic, and the stinking carcass emits an odor that breeds disease, and that disease threatens the Union soldier, one-armed and one-legged, and the widows and orphans, clothed in the habiliments of mourning with national disgrace. That contagion threatens the nation with repudiation; threatens men who, in the field, in the cabinet, and in the national councils, saved to the world the glorious heritage and the hope that made the victims of European despotism and tyranny smile amid their tears as in chains they were confined within the walls of the bastilles and dungeons all over Europe. It threatens them with disgrace, and we propose to turn out next November in the State of Mississippi, with the colored citizens all over our broad land, under the leadership of General Ulysses S. Grant, now President of the United States, and dig a grave for this corpse so deep and so wide, and bury it so that it will never more be resuscitated." The crowd applauded thunderously.

Next, Governor E. F. Noyes, of Ohio, sought to move the convention to action. "Now, we want to get to work.... Mr. President, I renew the motion to suspend the rules, and proceed first and only to the selection of our candidate for President." The building resounded with cheers as the motion carried.

Mr. Shelby M. Cullom, of Illinois, ascended to the platform, and said, "On behalf of the great Republican party of Illinois and that of the Union, in the name of liberty, of loyalty, of justice, and of law, and in the interest of economy, of good government, of peace, and of equal rights of all, remembering with profound gratitude his glorious achievements in the field and his noble statesmanship as chief magistrate of this great nation, I nominate as President of the United States, for a second term, Ulysses S. Grant."

His words were greeted by wild excitement among the delegates and the thousands of spectators who were crowded into every corner of the spacious Academy, and rose tier upon tier into the galleries, in deafening, prolonged, tumultuous cheers, swelling from the pit to ceiling dome, while a perfect wilderness of hats, caps, handkerchiefs waved in a surging mass reverberating in thousands of voices as the band played almost inaudibly "Hail to the Chief." At that moment, a life-size equestrian portrait of General Grant unfurled, as if by magic, and filled the entire backdrop space of the stage.

When order had at last been approached, Governor Stewart L. Woodford, of New York, addressed the throng. "Mr. President and gentlemen of the convention, New York, the home of the distinguished editor who has been placed in nomination for the Presidency in Cincinnati, asks you to pause one moment before you record the formal nomination that is the prophecy of election, that she may reach across the continent, strike hands with Illinois, and second the nomination of Ulysses S. Grant."

After praising Grant, Woodford recalled a recent attack upon the President by Senator Sumner, of Massachusetts, "as I read it according to the gospel of the *Tribune*, the text is probably correct. He said that Stanton, just before he passed from earth, spoke thus: 'I know General Grant better than any other person in the country can know him. It was my duty to study him, and I did it, day and night, when I saw him and when I did not see him, and now I can tell you what I know; he cannot govern this country.'"

A rumbling passed among the delegates before Woodford continued, "Let the history of those perilous days reply that the great War Secretary indeed knew Grant through and through; that until the hour when Grant assumed personal command in Virginia, Stanton had been compelled to discharge not only his ministerial duties as Secretary, but to watch and guide the actions of the commanders in the field; that from that hour he and Lincoln alike trusted, leaned upon, and confided in Grant; and left him free, according to his own judgement to fight the rebellion in his own resolute and sure way."

Then Woodford recounted the most prominent deeds of Grant's career in battle. "Aye! Stanton knew Grant well, so well, that Mr. Stanton pleaded for his election, endorsed his fitness, and labored for his success. These very walls still ring with the echo of that great speech, one of the last utterances of that great statesman in his own Pennsylvania, from the grave where he was killed from overwork in the cabinet, as much a martyr to the war as though he had wasted in a hospital or died on the field. His cold lips speak this day as in life they spoke from this very platform. From the grave the dead Stanton rebukes the living Senator, and I hear his earnest and solemn approval of Ulysses S. Grant as soldier, man, and patriot. In the name of millions of our loyal people, in the name of an enfranchised race, in the name of his old comrades, the living and the dead Secretary of War, New York endorses the nomination, and asks God's blessing on the cause." As Woodford fell silent, the auditorium's inhabitants filled the stillness with tremendous applause.

Grant was then seconded as well by M. D. Boruck, of California, before the call for the roll of the states, which proceeded quickly without interruption. When all had cast their ballots, President Settle announced, "It is the pleasure of the chair to announce that Ulysses S. Grant has received 752 votes, the entire vote of every state and territory in the Union." Again the delegates and spectators expressed their unrestrained approval and the band played a new Grant campaign song, while a large choir of gentlemen on stage sang it.

> "Rally round our leaders, men,
> We're arming for the fight,
> We'll raise our glorious standard,

And battle for the right.
To swell our gallant army,
Come from hill and plain,
Grant shall win the victory
For President again."

When all the verses were sung, a cry went up from the multitude for, "John Brown!" and the band struck up the familiar, electrifying strains which Union soldiers had sung when marching to the front and the entire concourse stood and rolled out the grand old hymn of freedom.

There then were calls from the floor for Lucius B. Church, of Montana, who came to the podium and spoke. "Twelve years ago, in the Wigwam at Chicago, preparatory to the nomination of Mr. Lincoln, I was called upon for a patriotic song. My selection at that time was our army and navy song, 'The Red, White, and Blue.'" Church sang it again, with great effect. Then the crowd demanded a chorus of "Marching Through Georgia," and standing sang along with Church, who concluded, "Now I ask for three cheers for those loyal black men who stood by us during that march through Georgia to the Sea." And those three cheers echoed through the hall. When the festivities subsided, President Settle, determined to finish the day's business, promptly called for nominations for Vice President.

Normally, there would be little fight against an incumbent Vice President. But Grant's current partner, Schuyler Colfax, of Indiana, had been tainted in what became known as the Credit Mobilier scandal which would break into full public view in the spring of 1873. Credit Mobilier of America was a construction company organized by the Union Pacific Railroad immediately after the Civil War. To win public land grants for its right of way, its lobbyists had bribed congressmen by selling them stocks at half the market value in return for favorable legislation. Colfax had been exposed for taking a small quantity of stock from Oakes Ames as the first unraveling of the Credit Mobilier scandal began. Not only that, some said Grant was displeased by the former Speaker of the House's own Presidential aspirations. So to minimize the damage, many in the party wanted to select Henry Wilson, who had served as chairman of the Senate Committee on Military Affairs during the war. Little did they reckon that he too would be touched by the scandal in coming months, as would be James A. Garfield, a future Republican President and James G. Blaine, a future Republican nominee.

Morton McMichael, of Pennsylvania, rose and spoke. "Sir, the Republican party had both its birth and its baptism on Pennsylvania soil. At Pittsburgh it was called into existence by voluntary gathering, and in Philadelphia it received the solemn sanction of the people, and from the hour of its organization to this, Pennsylvania has always steadfastly upheld the principles upon which it was founded. You sir, and all who hear me, remember it, and when because of the successes of those principles, the South plunged madly into revolt, and with formidable martial preparations challenged the North to mortal combat, Pennsylvania was the first in the field and foremost in the fight."

He continued with the history of his state's contributions to the war and party, and catalogued a few patronage complaints as well, then declared, "I am here, under the unanimous instructions of the Pennsylvania delegation, to present the name of a statesman known to the country as an honest, upright, able man, who has labored, and is laboring still, earnestly in behalf of the laboring masses of the country, and for the good of the whole country; I mean Henry Wilson of Massachusetts." His nomination set off a wild demonstration in support of Wilson.

Then Dr. Loring, of Massachusetts, seconded Senator Wilson, (who had been born Jeremiah Jones Colbath but had changed his name in 1833) saying, "Henry Wilson represents, in all his attributes, more than any man I know of, the power of high principles, of thorough devotion, to overcome all the obstacles which fall in the path of childhood, and youth, and mature years. For more than a quarter of a century, he has adhered to the great principles of this party. He was devoted to them long before it was a party, and when Massachusetts stood almost alone in the great cause, it was Henry Wilson whose voice was early heard in the cause of freedom. I ask you to name to me the commonwealth in the Union where that voice has not been heard in the cause. I ask you to point to me the down-trodden and oppressed citizens of the United States who have not been encouraged by Henry Wilson, and aiding in lifting themselves above the oppressor." Although there was another candidate whose name would be offered, the entire convention cheered Dr. Loring's description of Wilson.

Loring was followed by Ossian Ray, of New Hampshire, who noted, "Coming as I do from the state in which Henry Wilson was born, it gives me unbounded pleasure to announce that we are united on Massachusetts' favorite and great Senator, Henry Wilson. We ought to nominate him as Vice President because he is a good man and true, because he has always been the friend of the people, whose instincts and impulses are always right.... Like General Grant, he has been the architect of his own fortunes. He commenced life poor, by graduating from the shoemaker's shop. It is the pride and glory of American civilization that by industry, honesty, and perseverance the highest offices within the nation's gift are within the possible reach of the humblest youth in the land.... I pray you, gentlemen, to nominate the honest and noble Henry Wilson."

When the cheering for Wilson subsided, Richard W. Thompson, of Indiana, addressed the convention. "In behalf of the united Republican party of Indiana... I am instructed to nominate the Honorable Schuyler Colfax." At the mention of the name of the sitting Vice President, and a man that in 1868 Grant had called "the most popular man in the land," the convention burst into prolonged applause. "I do this because it is the just reward of eminent ability and devoted public service, of devotion to country and the integrity and honor of the Union; but that satisfaction is somewhat alloyed by the fact that we find our older and better sister Massachusetts presenting one of her eminent and honored sons, for whom we have the highest possible respect."

Thompson then lavishly praised Wilson, before returning to his task. "Feeling, therefore, as we do, that by joining the name of Colfax with that of Grant, we utter the same old battle cry which has been repeated by every child in the land, 'Grant and Colfax,' and that it will be the signal of victory, we present his name."

William A. Howard, of Michigan, followed the call in support of the former Speaker of the House. "I represent that state which first perfected a Republican state organization, that state which first applied the name to a state organization, with all due deference to my friend from Pennsylvania. The oak tree still stands where that organization still stands.... In the border of that state, before the state had a name, there came a stripling youth from the great Empire State of New York. He located within five miles of our border. In a little room he opened a printing office. He was compositor, pressman, and editor before he was of age, and in that way supported a mother and built up his business, developed his intellect, cultivated statesmanship, and is now the second officer in the great United States.

"Ten years ago, when the war was raging, he was made the presiding officer of the popular branch of this great government. So steadily did he hold the reins, with such exact justice did he administer parliamentary law, so firmly did he support the Union, that his present associate, General Grant, in the field of war proved a success. Four years ago his name was associated with that of General Grant on the Presidential ticket. 'Grant and Colfax' became the rallying cry throughout the land. Both have proved eminently faithful and successful. In God's name, we ask why should those names today be separated?"

Then Mr. Lynch, of Mississippi, made his second appearance at the rostrum, to urge support for Colfax. Gerrit Smith, of New York, did the same, as did Cortlandt Parker, of New Jersey. J. F. Quarles, of Georgia, stood up for Wilson. But as James B. Sener, of Virginia, attempted to address the convention to place in nomination the name of John F. Lewis, of his state, vast confusion and argument on the floor prevented his comments from being heard as the delegates fiercely debated among themselves the virtues and dangers of replacing Colfax. The same problem confronted Mr. Flannagan, of Texas, as he tried to nominate E. J. Davis, of Texas, for the second spot. And so was the voice of David A. Nunn, of Tennessee, swallowed as he presented for consideration Horace Maynard, of Tennessee, whom he said "was at the head of the party in Tennessee that crushed out Andrew Johnson when he proved false to the party, that crushed out the Democracy and struck the death blow to Ku Kluxism."

Before any vote for the second spot could be taken, President Settle announced that the Committee on Resolutions was finally prepared to present the platform, and delegates divided their attention between that and the thorny problem of deciding who would run with Grant.

Mr. Scofield, of Pennsylvania, chairman of the Resolutions Committee, presented Governor Hawley, of Connecticut, to read the document. The Republican's first resolution declared, "During the 11 years of supremacy it has accepted with great courage the solemn duties of the time, it suppressed a gigantic rebellion, emancipated four millions of slaves, decreed the equal citizenship of all, and established universal suffrage. Exhibiting unparalleled magnanimity, it criminally punished no man for political offenses, and warmly welcomed all who proved loyalty by obeying the laws and dealing justly with their neighbors. It has steadily decreased with a firm hand the resultant disorders of a great war, and initiated a wise and humane policy toward the Indians. The Pacific railroad and similar vast enterprises have been generously aided and successfully conducted, the public lands freely given to actual settlers, immigration protected and encouraged, and a full acknowledgment of the naturalized citizen's rights secured from European powers.

"A uniform national currency has been provided, repudiation frowned down, the national credit sustained under the most extraordinary burdens, and new bonds negotiated at lower rates. The revenues have been carefully collected and honestly applied. Despite large annual reductions of the rate of taxation, the public debt has been reduced during President Grant's Presidency at the rate of a $100 million a year, great financial crises have been avoided, and peace and plenty prevail throughout the land. Menacing foreign difficulties have been peacefully and honorably composed, and the honor and power of the nation kept in high respect throughout the world. This glorious record of the past is the party's best pledge for the future. We believe the people will not entrust the government to any party or combination of men composed chiefly of those who have resisted every step of this beneficent progress."

The accomplishments of the party elicited sustained support from the delegates. Then Governor Hawley read the second plank. "The recent amendments of the national Constitution should be cordially sustained because they are right, not merely tolerated because they are laws, and should be carried out according to the spirit by appropriate legislation, the enforcement of which can safely be entrusted only to the party that secured those amendments.

"Third," Hawley intoned. "Complete liberty and exact equality in the enjoyment of all civil, political, and public rights should be established and effectually maintained throughout the Union by efficient and appropriate state and federal legislation. Neither the law nor its administration should admit any discrimination in respect of citizens by reason of race, creed, color, or previous condition of servitude. Fourth. The national government should seek to maintain honorable peace with all nations, protecting its citizens everywhere, and sympathizing with all peoples who strive for greater liberty.

"Fifth. Any system of Civil Service under which the subordinate positions of the government are considered rewards for mere party zeal is fatally demoralizing, and we therefore favor a reform of the system by laws which shall abolish the evils of patronage, and make honesty, efficiency, and fidelity the essential qualifications for public positions, without practically creating a life tenure of office." The plank was aimed at undercutting Liberal Republican criticism. The sixth resolution took on the railroads. "We oppose the further grants of the public lands to corporations and monopolies, and demand that the national domain be set apart for free homes for the people."

The seventh resolution would become one of the hottest issues during the remainder of the century: the tariff. "The annual revenue, after paying current expenditures, pensions, and interest on the public debt, should furnish a moderate balance for the reduction of the principal, and that revenue, except so much as may be derived from a tax upon tobacco and liquors, should be raised by duties upon importations, the details of which should be adjusted as to aid in securing remunerative wages to labor, and to promote the industries, prosperity, and growth of the whole country." (Philadelphia's tariff interests were well represented in Congress for over a quarter of a century by a former judge, William B. Kelley, who carried the nickname "Pig Iron" for his successful defense of one of the city's great industries.)

The eighth Republican resolution insured a pension for soldiers and survivors of the war between the states, while the ninth protected the rights of immigrants and naturalized citizens from claims of European powers, who asserted "once a subject, always a subject." The tenth resolution called for abolition of franking privileges, or free mail for Congress and others, and called for a reduction in postal rates. The eleventh resolution sought to balance the growing tensions between labor and capital. "The Republican party recognizes the duty of so shaping legislation as to secure full protection and the amplest field for capital, and for labor, the creator of capital, and the largest opportunities and a just share of mutual profits of these two great servants of civilization."

The twelfth Republican resolution of 1872 thanked Congress and the President for "suppression of violent and treasonable organizations in certain lately rebellious regions," notably the Ku Kluxers, "and for the protection of the ballot box." The thirteenth resolution denounced repudiation of public debt "in any form or disguises, as a national crime... and expect that our excellent national currency will be perfected by a speedy resumption of specie payment," by which Republicans meant basing it dollar for dollar upon gold or silver reserves held by the government.

The fourteenth resolution acknowledged the growing political influence of women and declared, "The Republican party is mindful of its obligations to the loyal women of America for the noble devotion to the cause of freedom. Their admission to wider fields of usefulness is viewed with satisfaction, and the honest demand of any class of citizens for additional rights should be treated with respectful consideration." The fifteenth resolution approved of the acts of Congress in extending amnesty to "those lately in rebellion."

The sixteenth resolution of the Republican platform urged limited government and "respect (for) the rights reserved by the people to themselves as the powers delegated by them to the state and federal government," and disapproved "of the resort to unconstitutional laws for the purpose of removing evils, by interference with rights not surrendered by the people to either state or national government," while the seventeenth resolution called on the national government to "encourage and restore American commerce and shipbuilding." Finally, the eighteenth and nineteenth resolutions called for support for the party's Presidential and Vice Presidential candidates.

General Burnside, of Rhode Island, rose and "moved the adoption of the platform as a whole," and his resolution unanimously carried. With this important interlude completed and a platform adopted that in many regards was identical to that of their Liberal Republican opponents, delegates returned to the disturbing question of picking a Vice President from among equally beloved party leaders. Governor Noyes, of Ohio, spoke briefly for Henry Wilson, but no sooner had he stepped aside than Mr. Bickham, also of Ohio, raised his voice for Colfax. He was followed by Governor Clayton, of Arkansas, who put in a brief word for Wilson, as cries of "Vote, vote," resounded through the hall.

At last, President Settle called for a roll call of the states to settle the matter. But after the first round of balloting the convention stood equally split. Then Virginia, West Virginia, and Georgia abandoned their votes for Southern candidates to support Wilson and put him over the top. With 377 votes needed to nominate, the totals stood at 399 ½ for Senator Henry Wilson; 308 ½ for Vice President Schuyler Colfax; 26 for Horace Maynard; 16 for Edmund J. Davis; 1 for Joseph R. Hawley; and 1 for Edward F. Noyes. With the announcement of Wilson's success, the convention broke into wild cheering. Finally, former-Senator Henry S. Lane, of Indiana, who had been president of the first Republican convention, reached the podium to move that the nomination of Wilson be made unanimous, which was done with one swelling shout of "Aye."

President Settle then formally announced the Grant and Wilson ticket. Within minutes a telegram arrived from Washington and was read to the body by the convention president. It was addressed to John W. Foster, of the Indiana delegation. "Accept for yourself and delegates my sincere gratitude for your gallant contest. I support the ticket cheerfully. Men are nothing, principle everything. Nothing must arrest the Republican triumph until law, like liberty, from which it springs, is universally acknowledged, and the citizenship of the humblest becomes a sure protection against outrage and wrong, as was Roman citizenship of old." The communique was signed "Schuyler Colfax" and was received with warm appreciation.

Finally, Charles S. Spencer, of New York, resolved, "That thanks of this convention are hereby heartily given to the generous citizens of Philadelphia, from whom its delegates have received the kindest treatment and greatest courtesy." The resolution was adopted. Spencer also offered thanks to President Settle, who in turn said, "There remains for me but one more official act to perform, which is to declare, as I now do, this convention adjourned sine die." And amidst cheers the delegates filed out into the streets of Philadelphia ready for the electoral canvass.

On June 10, 1872, at half-past one in the afternoon, Judge Settle and other officers of the convention entered the office of the President of the United States in Washington, D.C., to formally notify him of the convention's recommendations. President Grant replied, "It is sincerely gratifying to me to know that after holding for three years the exalted office I now occupy, and without any political training whatever, I am again endorsed by kind friends and former supporters. I am, of course, deeply gratified."

General Solomon D. Meredith, of Indiana, a vice president of the convention, said, "Now let me say for Indiana that she will give you 15 electoral votes. I'll say nothing now as to the precise majority, but of the state you may be sure."

President Grant replied, "At any rate, General, don't let your people vote but once each," and laughed. Later that day, the President drafted a formal reply, which noted, among other points, "If elected in November and protected by a kind Providence in health and strength to perform the duties of the high trust conferred, I promise the same zeal and devotion to the good of the whole people for the future of my official life as shown in the past.

"Past experience may guide me in avoiding mistakes inevitable with novices in all professions and in all occupations. When relieved from the responsibilities of my present trust, by the election of a successor, whether it be at the end of this term or the next, I hope to leave to him, as executive, a country at peace within its own borders, at peace with outside nations, with a credit at home and abroad, and without embarrassing questions to threaten its future prosperity. With the expression of a desire to see a speedy healing of all bitterness of feeling between sections, parties, or races of citizens, and the time when the title of citizen carries with it all the protections and privileges to the humblest that it does to the most exalted, I subscribe myself, very respectfully, your obedient servant." His epistle was signed "U. S. Grant."

Senator Wilson's formal reply to the convention was equally revealing about his reaction and intentions. Referring to Philadelphia, he noted, "Sixteen years ago, in the same city, was held the first meeting of men who, amid the darkness and doubts of that hour of slave-holding ascendancy and aggression, had assembled in national convention to confer with each other on the exigencies to which that fearful domination had brought their country. After a full conference, the highest point of resolve they could reach, the most they dared to recommend, was the avowed purpose to prohibit the existence of slavery in the territories.

"Last week the same party met by its representatives from 37 states and 10 territories, at the same center of wealth, intelligence, and power, to review the past, take note of the present, and indicate its line of action for the future. As typical facts of the headlands of the nation's recent history, there sat on its platform, taking a prominent and honorable part in its proceedings, admitted on terms of perfect equality to the leading hotels of the city, not only colored representatives of the race which was ten years before in abject slavery, but one of the oldest and most prominent of the once despised abolitionists, to whom was accorded, as to no other, the warmest demonstration of popular regard and esteem, an ovation not to him alone, but to the cause he had for so many years represented, and to the men and women, living and dead, who had toiled through long years of obliquity and self-sacrifice for the glorious fruition of that hour. [He referred to abolitionist Gerrit Smith.] It hardly needed a brilliant summary of its platform to set forth its illustrious achievements. The very presence of those men was alone significant of victories already achieved, the progress already made, and the great distance which the nation had traveled between the years 1856 and 1872.

"But grand as has been its record, the Republican party rests not on its past alone: it looks to the future and grapples with its problems and duties." Wilson, the former Natick shoemaker, then outlined the difficulties of enforcement of equality and suppression of violence in the South, the problem of obtaining fair wages for labor, the adjustment of duties on imports, Civil Service reform, a new role for women, and the other issues raised in the Republican platform.

A month after the Republicans adjourned, the Democrats convened in Baltimore on July 9, 1872, for perhaps the strangest of all their conventions. The party which first held a Presidential nominating convention in that city in 1832, deliberated for but six hours before adjourning. Coming in, the party was split down the middle on strategy. Many members of the Democracy favored an unorthodox coalition with the Liberal Republicans to throw out Grant and the Radical Republicans who still made their lives miserable with federal troops and oppressive statutes. They had formed "Reunion and Reform Associations" to further that goal. But many of the "Bourbon Democrats" of the South were loyal to their party and balked at any such coalition. However, Democrats agreed with Liberal Republican Greeley's opposition to free trade.

Support for a ticket headed by their long-time nemesis, Horace Greeley, had been building all spring. By the time they reached Baltimore, the choice seemed clear; Greeley or Grant. The Democracy couldn't stomach Grant. With Greeley as a fusion candidate with the Liberal Republicans, they calculated that they had a chance to defeat the hated general. No nominating speeches were entertained, and 686 of the 732 delegates endorsed Greeley. To solidify the shotgun marriage, Democrats adopted the Cincinnati platform by a 671 to 62 vote.

The election that followed the three national conventions was one of the most contentious ever, one in which the future of the Union was not as vigorously debated as the characters of the Presidential candidates were defiled. It was tainted by personal tragedy as well.

"The Galena Tanner and the Natick Cobbler" stood for peace at home and abroad. Grant remained detached from the corruption that bubbled up in his administration and disdainful of the high-minded reformers who nipped at his heels. While Greeley was an experienced orator, Grant could not "deliver himself of even the simplest sentence," said a British observer. Still, the silent general loomed loud over the loquacious editor, even as the President stayed close to the White House. The campaign raged beyond its walls in states across the land.

The reformer Horace Greeley, who had a half-century history of championing reasonable and quirky new movements, was known throughout the nation as a political and literary oracle whose pronouncements were often as compellingly correct as they were often foolishly wrong. In 1834, the 23-year-old farm boy and apprentice printer who had arrived impoverished in New York City three years before launched his long career as a literary and political critic by founding the *New Yorker*, a weekly magazine of poetry, short stories, and political commentary. Seven years later, in 1841, the tall and thin editor began publishing the New York *Tribune*, initially a Whig, then a major Republican daily paper, that was "anti-slavery, anti-war, anti-rum, antitobacco, anti-seduction, anti-grogshop, anti-brothel, and anti-gambling house."

Easily caricatured for his balding crown, long blond strands of disheveled hair tumbling down the side of his head, clean-shaven but ashen-white face with chin whiskers, and keen pale eyes peering out from his elliptical, wire-rimmed spectacles, Greeley wore a long white coat called a duster and a broad white hat. The brilliant editor was as generous as he was eccentric, as persuasive as he was moralistic. In his long career, he had stood against efforts to exploit the Indians of New York and the West. He favored essential public works for the nation's development, but promoted fiscal responsibility and opposed fraud. He swooned over the European idea of associations of like-minded people working together as economic units. He yearned for a utopian and moral paradise in the land of the free and a utopian community in Colorado had been named after him. Greeley was a crusading reformer through and through.

The "Farmer of Chappaqua," as Greeley was sometimes called, having been born on a farm in New Hampshire and owning one in New York once he could afford it, touted his theories on agricultural reform and envisioned the day when mechanical tractors would transform farm drudgery. He preached the need for education reform in a democracy. He rallied the civic reform forces of New York. To the editor, government was a necessary evil. Above all, "Honest Horace" believed in America's progress, in its future blossoming upon the post-war horizon. He was an odd yet passionate spirit of American enlightenment.

Under his editorial tutelage, the *Tribune* sought to lift the intelligence of democracy and make more moral its instruments of power. Yet the high-minded *Tribune* was also a sensational and partisan paper that covered all of the urban vices in vivid detail. Its avid readers devoured its pages and its arguments as gospel. Democrats of all kinds had been its favorite political target. Greeley had called Jackson "violent and lawless." He labeled the Democratic party of Buchanan and Douglas a "Sham Democracy." He had been a founder of the Republican party in 1854 and in Chicago, during the 1860 Republican convention, Greeley had stood against his old Whig allies Thurlow Weed and Senator William Henry Seward, of New York, inadvertently making way for Lincoln as nominee, a man he underestimated.

Under a kind of war psychosis brought on by massive war costs in lives and material, Greeley had called for premature peace without victory and a restoration of the antebellum Union. Reaction against him was bitterly critical. His later support for Civil War conscription and the $300 exemption which allowed rich youth to escape the draft led anti-draft rioters marauding through New York's City Hall Park in March 1863 to sing, "We'll hang Horace Greeley from a sour apple tree."

But Greeley had worked hard for and celebrated Lincoln's reelection in 1864. After the war he had urged reconciliation, and in response to an appeal by Varina Davis had posted part of the $100,000 bail to free the Confederate President, Jefferson Davis, in 1867, an act he never lived down. Greeley argued for Andrew Johnson's impeachment in 1868. And though he had favored the Presidential nomination of Supreme Court Justice Salmon P. Chase, he had worked for Grant once he was the Republican nominee later that year.

Under Grant's administration, the old editor had fought for the Ku Klux enforcement acts and implementation of the new national voting and civil rights amendments. During his southern trip before receiving the Liberal Republican nomination, he attacked Ku Kluxers, argued for universal amnesty, lambasted carpetbaggers and scalawags, and chastised Southern conservatives for not standing up for voting rights needed for reconciliation. It was his erratic and contradictory record that made voters incredulous at his Liberal Republican nomination.

And of Grant, who was now his political antagonist, Greeley had written in 1862, "Our soldiers are being driven into Tennessee today. Our Generals are drunk. Buell ought to be shot, and Grant ought to be hung." But President Grant had tried to appoint Greeley to diplomatic posts, including Minister to England. Greeley resisted and resented Grant's intrusion into New York politics in favor of Roscoe Conkling's faction. Greeley continually turned down White House dinner invitations. When Grant appointed Conkling underling Chester A. Arthur to the patronage-rich post of collector of the port of New York, Greeley took aim at Grant.

Despite being elevated to nominee of the Liberal Republican movement, Greeley cared little about the Civil Service reform trumpeted by his new party and was a life-long enemy of free trade. However, he despised the corruption that was beginning to mount in the Grant administration and favored greater leniency toward reconstructed rebels. Now the lifelong conservative, who distrusted the masses as much as he understood their poverty and hopes, needed their support. So Greeley called the nation to a "New Departure" that put all of the wounds of the war behind them, that allowed the regions to join hands "in joyful consciousness that they are and must henceforth remain brethren."

Amidst the early onslaught of interviews and visitors, speeches and pronouncements, Greeley fell ill with a bout of "brain fever" and as the summer progressed his invalid wife, Mary, took for the worse. She was crippled by rheumatism, unable to walk, and relied upon her daughter and her husband who spent hours by her side. Greeley persevered through personal hardship and continued some of his editorial duties, answered hundreds of letters, and made more speeches than any Presidential candidate before him. In July, he traveled to Boston and to Newport to give talks.

Endorsement by his perennial enemy, the Democrats, including their acknowledgment of the Thirteenth, Fourteenth, and Fifteenth Amendments as stipulated by the Liberal Republican platform, gave Greeley hope that his New Departure message was viable, that principled Republicans and Democrats could find common ground. By mid-July Greeley's supporters were convinced that he could win. His message of reconciliation was reaching the heart of many voters. During the summer, he made many appearances, but tried to restrain his sporadic cantankerous outbursts.

As fall approached, Greeley's campaign hit high gear. Greeley and an array of stump speakers denounced Grant and his spoilsmanship, patronage, and corruption. They looked to a better future through regional reconciliation and denounced Grant as a dullard and drunk who was lost in his cigar smoke. Greeley would bring back good government and Civil Service reform, they insisted. "Honest Horace" wore the "White Hat of Peace." Friendly magazines such as *Leslie's* depicted him beating swords into ploughshares. Greeley's unofficial campaign song was "The Old White Hat."

"There's a good old man who lives on a farm,
And he's not afraid to labor;
His heart is pure and he does no harm,
But works for the good of his neighbor.
He always wears an old white hat,
And he doesn't go much on style;
He's kind to the poor that come to his door,
And his heart is free from guile."

Despite the corruption becoming evident in his administration, Grant too was cheered for his personal integrity. His supporters, angry at the slings and arrows aimed at the good old general, were not hesitant to fire back at "Old Chappaquack." They called Greeley a "Know-Nothing," a slave trader, and a secessionist. His long record of support of diverse reforms from temperance to cooperativism were recounted far and wide. He was called a supporter of women's rights and a follower of Victoria Woodhull's doctrine of free love. (The new Equal Rights Party nominated Victoria Clafin Woodhull as the first woman Presidential candidate. Frederick Douglass, the first national African-American candidate, was her running mate for Vice President.)

Greeley was depicted as being in cahoots with the Ku Kluxers. His greatest tormentor in the campaign was cartoonist Thomas Nast who on the pages of *Harper's Weekly* characterized him shaking hands with John Wilkes Booth over Lincoln's grave, and showed him making secret agreements with boss Tweed of Tammany Hall in the name of reform.

That charge stuck despite the fact Greeley had once said Tammany men drank at a Hickory pole representing Jacksonian democracy "from the ground, like hogs." His quotes made the rounds in anti-Greeley campaign flyers. Another Nast drawing caricatured the lifelong enemy of the Democratic party seated on a high stool eating a big bowl containing "red hot" porridge of "My Own Words and Deeds."

Greeley had pontificated on every major issue on the political landscape since 1834 and made a fool and champion of himself more times than Don Quixote. His enemies remembered the bitter sting of his high-principled tongue and these opponents reminded voters of his blunders and his wild idealism. One pundit argued, "I have always regarded Greeley as an awkward, ill-bred boor, and though a sort of inspired idiot, neither a scholar, statesman, or gentleman, I wouldn't give Grant's little finger for a congressional district full of him. Yet, I want him elected."

The fall canvass was foreshadowed by elections for state offices. On August 1, 1872, regular Republicans beat back the Liberal Republicans in North Carolina. In September, the regulars kept control in Maine and Vermont. While the elections in October states loomed with disastrous implications, Greeley took to the stump, traveling by rail and carriage through New Jersey, Pennsylvania, Ohio, Kentucky, and the bellwether Indiana, making more than 200 speeches.

Greeley promised a new dawn and national rebirth through thrifty and honest government, productive labor working in cooperative movements, universal amnesty for the South, and equal rights for all where black and white stood "on a common platform of American nationality." In Ohio, "Old White Hat" exhorted, "Let us forget that we have fought. Let us remember that we have made peace.... Our triumph is not the triumph of a section; it is not the triumph of a race; it is not the triumph of class. It is the triumph of the American people; making us all in life, in heart, and purpose, the people, the one people of the great American Republic. Fellow citizens, to the work of reconciliation I dedicate myself."

Swelling crowds greeted Greeley everywhere. But Grant parades, bands, and hecklers disrupted his meetings. "I hardly know if I am running for President or the penitentiary," he told a friend. Still, large audiences hung on his words and he could be permitted the vanity of believing his hopes were not delusional. But Grant told Congressman James A. Garfield that the Liberal Republicans reminded him of "the deceptive noise made in the West by prairie wolves." Slowly a gloom took hold of the Liberal Republican cause and Greeley's personal fate.

Beleaguered by the barrage of political assaults that accompanied his epic effort, an aging Greeley returned to New York exhausted. Then the Republican states voted Republican in state contests and Greeley felt his political ship begin to sink. As much as he wished the campaign to finish, it dragged on toward November. Meanwhile, Greeley's wife had gamely resisted death with Greeley at her side, until she gave way a week before the election on October 30. "I am not dead," the melancholy old editor wrote a friend, "but I wish I were. My house is desolate, my future dark, my heart a stone."

Greeley told friends he wanted to follow Mary to the grave. Grant gave him his wish. He was buried in a landslide re-election in which Democrats boycotted their own party's suicide wish and free traders abandoned the Liberal Republicans. The vast public, almost oblivious to the concerns of disgruntled politicians, extended their military and political hero an overwhelming vote of confidence. Greeley attracted 43.8 percent of the popular vote, but took only six border and Southern states. Grant received a popular majority three times greater than in his first election. Even Greeley's native New Hampshire and New York jilted him. Grant cornered 286 of 349 Electoral Votes. In the wake of his landslide, Grant felt his personal character had been vindicated by the confidence of the people.

Greeley, humiliated and broken, returned briefly to the *Tribune*, but another visitor was awaiting him. Frenzied he wrote, "I stand naked before God, the most utterly, hopelessly wretched, and undone of all who ever lived." Incoherent, he was committed to a sanitarium and died on November 29, 1872, the election month not yet over. On December 4, President Grant's carriage led a funeral procession that included governors and senators along with the Lincoln Club of New York, the Typographical Society and the Union League Club, in a solemn march down Fifth Avenue in Greeley's honor.

In the election's wake, Mark Twain credited cartoonist Thomas Nast with contributing heavily to Grant's "prodigious victory, for civilization and progress." In his inaugural address on March 4, 1873, Grant confided, "I have been the subject of abuse and slander scarcely ever equaled in political history, which today I feel that I can afford to disregard in view of your verdict." Yet, rather than reform and glory, the public was given a hemorrhaging of corruption and scandal during Grant's second term. In early 1873, more Republican members of Congress were implicated in Credit Mobilier, the "railroad grab" in which they received stock and bribes for votes. William Worth Belknap, Grant's second Secretary of War, who had replaced Grant's closest friend and aide General Rawlins on his death, was forced to resign over fraud in Indian affairs. And despite Grant's long defense of his personal secretary, Orville E. Babock was indicted for his role in The Whiskey Ring. Even worse, in 1873 the nation plunged into a deep economic depression that lasted for the rest of the decade.

The 1900 Republican National Convention: Prosperity and Power

Convention-at-a-Glance

Event: Twelfth Republican National Convention
Date: June 19-21, 1900
Location: Exposition Auditorium, Thirty-fourth Street below Spruce Street, West Philadelphia
Philadelphia Mayor: Samuel H. Ashbridge, Republican
Philadelphia's Population: 1,293,697
Convention Permanent Chairman: Senator Henry Cabot Lodge, Massachusetts
Number of Delegates: 926
Number Needed to Nominate: A majority
Candidates for Renomination: President William McKinley, Jr., Ohio
Presidential Nominee: President William McKinley
Age at Nomination: 57
Number of Ballots: One; by unanimous vote
Vice Presidential Nominee: Governor Theodore Roosevelt, New York
Largest Audience: 20,000 (building capacity 16,000)
Platform Positions: Acceptance of international responsibilities befitting a new world power; construction and ownership of a canal through the Central American isthmus; enforcement of anti-trust laws against "all conspiracies and combinations intended to restrict business, to create monopolies, to limit production, or to control prices;" maintenance of the gold standard and currency stability; renewed faith in the policy of protection and a fair tariff to protect business and labor; a new Department of Commerce
Campaign Slogan: "Four More Years Of The Full Lunch Pail"
Popular Convention Song: "There'll Be a Hot Time in the Old Town Tonight."

**President William McKinley
1900 Republican Presidential
Nominee**

**Governor Theodore Roosevelt
1900 Republican Vice Presidential
Nominee**

1900

The 1900 Republican National Convention:
Prosperity and Power

The Republican party of 1900 gathered triumphantly in the Exposition Auditorium in West Philadelphia on June 19, to renominate William McKinley, Jr., the last nineteenth-century President of the United States, in hopes that he would continue as the nation's first chief magistrate of the twentieth century. The 926 delegates and over 16,000 spectators confidently assembled to pick one President who would reach across the two great eras divided by this momentous year: 1900. Instead, they picked two.

During his first four years in office, William McKinley—Civil War major, congressional author of the McKinley Tariff that imposed a 50 percent tax on foreign goods and protected American industry, former governor of a great Middlewestern state (Ohio), and Republican national party leader—had become the "most popular President since Lincoln." McKinley was the first President since war ripped asunder the states to be embraced again by all sections of the nation. That's because McKinley was the first President of American nationalism and expansionism on the world scene, which meant new wealth at home.

McKinley's popularity with the people was not surprising since the United States was enjoying the greatest prosperity in its 124-year history. The long and deadly depression of the 1890s, which had been the central issue of the bitter 1896 election fight with William Jennings Bryan, was now almost a distant memory. Business was booming. Profits were steady and abundant. Twenty-five percent of the labor force had been unemployed when he entered office; now there was work aplenty for all.

America also had defeated Spain in a war to liberate Cuba and seized distant Pacific territories in the process to assume its place among the great imperial powers of the world. As the delegates gathered, U.S.

troops were in the final stages of suppressing an indigenous rebellion in the Philippine Islands that was the residue "responsibility" of victory over Spain and trusteeship of her Atlantic and Pacific territories. Big business was expanding in every direction in search of new markets.

This Republican convention meant to nominate a leader worthy of the destiny manifest in the mission of the United States of America: to bring freedom and profits to the peoples of the world. The steady and able McKinley had proved to be that man. He was a master politician and a proven statesman. He liked the American people and they liked him.

Throughout the week before the convention, delegates from across the nation arrived by train at the new Pennsylvania Railroad's Broad Street Station, a massive building which already had the nickname, the "Chinese Wall." Other Republicans came into the ornate Philadelphia and Reading Railroad Terminal at Market and Twelfth Streets. On the Saturday afternoon before the convention, a huge Republican parade marched down Broad Street from York Street on the far north to Ritner Street on the far south, passing Philadelphia's recently completed City Hall, the largest building in the United States, topped by a 547-foot tower upon which stood the 37-foot tall, 26-ton bronze statue of William Penn in Quaker garb and hat. Inside the 700 rooms of City Hall were the offices of the Republican Mayor Samuel H. "Stars and Stripes Sam" Ashbridge, so nicknamed because of his rousing patriotic speeches.

But his powerful Republican machine was among the most corrupt in the land, with City Hall grafters taking lucrative cuts from city franchises on electricity, subways, and street cars. The parade then passed Republican party headquarters at 221 South Broad Street. Along the route cheered thousands of Philadelphians, including many of the tens of thousands of new Italian and East European immigrants who now made the Quaker City their home. Philadelphia had grown by 25 percent over the past decade. After the parade, some of the city visitors took a look in at John Wanamaker's department store, the largest in the world, or got a bite to eat at the nation's first Horn and Hardart's automat. On the Sunday night before the convention opened, a mass meeting drawing thousands of local supporters and national guests was held at the Academy of Music, where President Grant had been renominated in 1872.

Philadelphia was ready for another Presidential nominating convention. The first day of the affair was cool for mid-June. Delegates and spectators fought a stiff wind as they rode new electric trolleys out to the large, white marble Exposition Auditorium at Thirty-fourth Street below Spruce Street near the west bank of the Schuylkill River. The neo-classical, Corinthian-columned edifice had been built to house the National Export Exposition of 1899 and was dedicated by President McKinley in 1897. After raising $100,000 to secure the convention, the city made minor changes to prepare the hall for this convention.

Inside, on the giant platform at one end of the hall before the speaker's stand stood Republican national committee chairman, Senator Marcus (Mark) Alonzo Hanna, of Ohio, who gaveled open the convention a few minutes after noon. Befitting his position as the second most powerful man in the country next to the President, the band played "Hail to the Chief" when Hanna had walked to the podium. Senator Mark Hanna was a symbol of the prosperous and mighty Republican party that had ruled in eight of the past ten national elections. The party was no longer the motley collection of passionate crusaders fighting for the principles of the Constitution who had first gathered in Philadelphia in 1856, but protectors of the great wealth that had grown out of the institutions of freedom.

The chairman, who usually shielded himself from public exposure, was a bulky, retired millionaire industrialist whose interest and skills in Ohio state politics had elevated him to the United States Senate in 1897 by the margin of a single vote. He was the conduit to the vast money pools contributed by the likes of Standard Oil, J. P. Morgan, and other Republican financial stalwarts. The press caricatured him during the contentious 1896 election as dressed in a suit covered with dollar bills of large denominations that he collected from the industrial, agricultural, financial, and transportation trusts to elect his friend and fellow buckeye McKinley. Sometimes he was depicted as a hurdy-gurdy man, with the President as his monkey. Hanna had guided McKinley's political and financial fortunes since the future President's 1892 congressional defeat. His word was often the President's.

McKinley assigned Hanna to run the 1900 convention and make it an appropriate send-off for his re-election campaign so he would be permitted to further America's emerging mission in the world. But Hanna, who had never even been seen by most of the delegates prior to this convention, was no longer the bulky and brash insider of four years before. He had been worn down by sickness and nearly crippled by rheumatism. His face lacked the fullness and vitality that once animated him. And he was exhausted from the pre-convention maneuvering over the uncertain Vice Presidential spot.

Only a few moments after Hanna imposed order upon the large convention body, the hall burst into spontaneous and wild cheering to greet the perfectly-timed entrance of New York Governor Theodore Roosevelt. Hanna shivered. Only the night before, Roosevelt had released the latest of a long series of statements insisting that he "would under no circumstances" be a candidate for the Vice Presidential nomination. Hanna knew his appearance in Philadelphia as a delegate-at-large said otherwise. As the governor marched down the aisle to join the New York delegation, he wore a black felt hat with wide brim bent back, resembling the one he had donned as he led his Rough Riders up San Juan Hill to victory in Cuba two years earlier, and to the governor's mansion in Albany a few months later. "Teddy," as his admirers called him, and he hated to be called, was a national hero. Wayne MacVeagh, President Garfield's attorney general, said to his friends on the convention floor, "Gentlemen, that's an acceptance hat."

Roosevelt remained stiff as he marched in, not even acknowledging the wild applause that engulfed him. The military stoic within told him his duty was to remain aloof from praise, that good actions are done for their right reason, not for mere adulation. The ovation lasted two minutes. When the band put an exclamation point on the delegate demonstration with a rendition of "The Star-Spangled Banner," Roosevelt jumped up from his seat and covered his heart with his Rough Rider hat. Then delegates surrounded him shaking his hand as Hanna banged for order.

Chairman Hanna was not among the colonel's admirers. Hanna considered him "erratic, unsafe... too ambitious." In fact, he seethed at the reception the brash governor received, because it clearly marked, in the very first moments of the national gathering, his failure to control this convention whose planning he had for months orchestrated. Hanna pledged to himself to do everything in his power in the days left before the Vice Presidential nomination vote to overturn Roosevelt's band wagon. But New York governors had a traditional link to the Presidency and Theodore Roosevelt had a direct emotional bond to the Republican faithful of the nation who saw him as the personification of American virtue and perfectibility.

Hanna's introductory remarks were brief. "Gentlemen of the convention: In bidding you welcome I also desire to extend congratulations upon this magnificent gathering of the great Republican party. The National Republican Committee made no mistake when they brought the national convention to the city of Philadelphia. This city, the cradle of liberty, the birthplace of the Republican party, this magnificent industrial center, a veritable beehive of industry; what fitter object lesson could be present to those of us who gather here to witness the success of the great principle of our party which has been its foundation—protection to American industry...."

"Delegates, I greet you on the anniversary in Philadelphia of the birthday of our party.... We are called together once more upon the eve of another great struggle. We are now beginning to form our battalions under the leadership of our great statesman-general, William McKinley." He then told the delegates this would be his last function as their party chair. But he wanted to pass on "one suggestion; always trust the people." And he urged them to remember the motto of the national committee in 1896; "There is no such word as 'fail.' "

As worked out in advance, Senator Edward O. Wolcott, of

Colorado, was made temporary chairman of the 1900 convention and Hanna handed him the gavel. He delivered a rhetorical keynote address that praised the policies McKinley had followed to bring the nation back to prosperity. "Since the first party convention in these United States, there was never one gathered under such hopeful and auspicious circumstances as those which surround us today. United, proud of the achievements of the past four years, our country prosperous and happy, with nothing to regret and naught to make us ashamed, with a record spotless and clean, the Republican party stands facing the dawn, confident that the ticket it shall present will command public approval, and that in the declaration of principles and purposes, it will voice the aspirations and hopes of the vast majority of American freemen....

"Yet there is a significance in the fact that the convention is assembled in this historic and beautiful city, where we first assumed territorial responsibilities, when our fathers, a century and a quarter ago, promulgated the immortal Declaration of Independence. The spirit of justice and liberty that animated them found voice three-quarters of a century later in this same City of Brotherly Love, when Fremont led the forlorn hope of united patriots who laid here the foundations of our own party and put human freedom as its cornerstone...." Here Wolcott was amply applauded.

"While we observe the law of nations and maintain that neutrality which we owe to a great and friendly government, the same spirit lives today in the genuine feeling of sympathy we cherish for the brave men now fighting for their homes in the velds of South Africa. It prompts us in our determination to give to the dusky races of the Philippines the blessings of good government and republican institutions, and finds voice in our indignant protest against the violent suppression of the rights of the colored man in the South." Wolcott was again cheered. Despite this declaration of equality, the black men who came to the 1900 Republican convention were denied admission to many of Philadelphia's better hotels.

The Colorado Senator then reviewed McKinley's record. "He has shown unerring mastery of the economic problems which confront us, and has guided us out of the slough of financial disaster, impaired credit, and commercial stagnation, up to the high and safe ground of National prosperity and financial security. Through the delicate and trying events of the late war he stood firm, courageous, and conservative, and under his leadership we have emerged triumphant, our national honor untarnished, our credit unassailed, and the equal devotion of every section of our common country to the welfare of the Republic cemented forever. Never in the memory of this generation has there stood at the head of the government a truer patriot, a wiser or more courageous leader, or a better example of the highest type of American manhood. The victories of peace and the victories of war are alike inscribed upon his banner."

Then Wolcott added praise for McKinley's deceased Vice President. "Had Garret Augustus Hobart been spared to us until today, the work of this convention would have been limited to a cordial and unanimous indorsement of the leaders of '96.... He was always the trusted friend and adviser of our President, sage in counsel and wise in judgement." When the Senator completed his eulogy, committee assignments were made, and on the motion of Joseph G. Cannon, of Illinois, the convention adjourned "until 12 o'clock meridian tomorrow."

On the convention's second day, June 20, 1900, the assembly saluted the National Fremont Association, survivors of the first Republican conventions held in Pittsburgh and Philadelphia 44 years earlier. Senator Wolcott announced, "They bring with them the same old flag that was used in the convention." The white-haired men walked across the auditorium stage bearing a tattered American flag that was barely held together, and the audience spontaneously rose to its feet in an emotional and deafening salutation. Among the party veterans were General Joseph R. Hawley, of Connecticut, and several Pennsylvanians: John Jacobs, Walter Laing, G. W. Holstein, M.D., Edgar M. Levy, D.D., and Jacob Wyand.

When the celebration died down, the convention returned to the mundane task of committee reports. The Committee on Credentials certified 926 delegates. The Committee on Permanent Organization recommended as the convention's permanent chairman, Senator Henry Cabot Lodge, of Massachusetts, and he was unanimously endorsed. Lodge, a Senator since 1893 and long a friend and advisor of the rambunctious Theodore Roosevelt, could use the gavel to aid the governor's cause, if needed. He was escorted to the platform by Governor Shaw, of Iowa, and Governor Roosevelt.

Lodge addressed the convention in crisp language and precise tone. "One of the greatest honors that can fall to any American in public life is to be called to preside over a Republican National Convention.... We meet again to nominate the next President of the United States. Four years have passed since we nominated the soldier and statesman who is now President, and who is soon to enter upon his second term. Since the Civil War, no Presidential term has been so crowded with great events as that which is now drawing to a close. To Republicans they show a record of promises kept, of work done, of unforeseen questions met and answered. To the Democrats they have been generous in the exhibition of unfulfilled predictions, in the ruin of their hopes of calamity, and in futile opposition to the forces of the times and the aspirations of the American people. I wish I could add that they have been equally instructive to our opponents, but while it is true that the Democrats, like the Bourbons, learn nothing, it is too evident that the familiar comparison cannot be completed, for they forget a great deal which it would be well for them to remember." Lodge's audience applauded in cheerful agreement at his witticisms.

"In 1897, we took the government and the country from the hands of President Cleveland. His party had abandoned him and were joined to their idols, of which he was no longer one. During the last years of his term we had presented to us the melancholy spectacle of a President trying to govern without a party. The result was that his policies were in ruin, legislation was at a standstill, and public affairs were in a perilous and incoherent condition. Party responsibility had vanished, and with it all possibility of intelligent action, demanded by the country at home and abroad. It was an interesting but by no means singular display of Democratic unfitness for the practical work of government. To the political student, it was instructive; to the country it was extremely painful; to business disastrous.

"We replaced this political chaos with a President in thorough accord with his party, and the machinery of government began again to move smoothly and effectively.... In four months after the inauguration of President McKinley we had passed a tariff bill.... Would you know the result of our tariff legislation? Look about you!... There is not a state in the Union today which could be carried for free trade against protection. Never was a policy more fully justified by its works, never was a promise made by any party more absolutely fulfilled." The great applause that met Lodge affirmed his statement.

"Dominant among the issues of four years ago was that of our monetary and financial system. The Republican party promised to uphold our credit, to protect our currency from revolution, and to maintain the gold standard. We have done so. We have done more. We have been better than our promise.... But there were still other questions in 1896. We had already thwarted the efforts of the Cleveland administration to throw the Hawaiian Islands back to their dethroned Queen, and to give England a foothold for her cables in the group. We said then we would settle the Hawaiian question. We have done so. The traditional American policy has been carried out. The flag of the Union floats today over the crossroads of the Pacific, and her representatives sit with you in this hall." There was applause for the Hawaiian delegates.

"We promised to deal with the Cuban question. Again comes the reply, we have done so. The long agony of the island is over. Cuba is free. But this great work has brought with it events and issues which no man had foreseen, for which no party creed had provided a policy. The crisis came, bringing war in its train. The Republican President and the Republican Congress met the new trial in the old spirit. We fought the war with Spain. The result is history known of all men." Lodge was interrupted with cheers.

What was the result? "A war of a hundred days with many

victories and no defeats, with no prisoners taken from us and no advance stayed, with triumphant outcome startling in it completeness and in its worldwide meaning. Was ever a war more justly entered upon, more quickly fought, more fully won, more thorough in its results?" The applause gave his response. "Cuba is free. Spain has been driven from the Western Hemisphere. Fresh glory has come to our arms and crowned our flag. It was the work of the American people, but the Republican party was their instrument. Have we not the right to say that, even as in the days of Abraham Lincoln, we have fought a good fight, we have kept the faith, we have finished the work." Lodge was cheered again.

"War, however, is like the sword of Alexander. It cuts the knots. It is a great solvent and brings many results not to be foreseen. The world forces unchained in war perform in hours the work of years of quiet. Spain sued for peace. How was that peace to be made? The answer to this great question was given by the President of the United States. We were victorious in Cuba, in Porto Rico, in the Philippines. Should we give these islands back to Spain? Never! Was the President's reply. Would any American wish that he had answered otherwise? Should we hand them over to some other power? Never! Was again the answer.... Should we turn the islands where we had destroyed all existing sovereignty, loose upon the world to be a prey to domestic anarchy and the helpless spoils of some other nation? Again the inevitable negative. Again the President answered as the nation he represented would have him answer.

"He boldly took the islands, took them knowing well the burden and responsibility; took them from a deep sense of duty to ourselves and others, guided by a just foresight as to our future in the East, and with an entire faith in the ability of the American people to grapple with the new task. When future conventions point to the deeds by which the Republican party has made history, they will proclaim with special pride that under a Republican administration the war of 1898 was fought, and that the peace with Spain was the work of William McKinley." The convention gave their President a long ovation.

"For the islands of Hawaii and Porto Rico, the political problem has been solved, and by Republican legislation they have been given self-government, and are peaceful and prosperous under the rule of the United States. In the Philippines we were met by rebellion, fomented by a self-seeking adventurer and usurper. The duty of the President was to repress that rebellion, to see to it that the authority of the United States, as rightful and righteous in Manila as in Philadelphia, was acknowledged and obeyed. That harsh and painful duty President McKinley has performed firmly and justly.... Unlike the opponents of expansion, we do not regard the soldiers of Otis and Lawton and MacArthur as 'an enemy camp.'... Even now the Democrats are planning, if they get control of the

House, to cut off appropriations for the army and thus compel the withdrawal of our troops from the Philippines.... Their retreat would be the signal for the massacre and plunder of the great body of peaceful inhabitants of the island who have trusted to us to protect and guard them. Such an event would be an infamy." Lodge heard cheers of agreement.

But there was another reason why the Philippines were important in Republican eyes. "We believe in trade expansion. By every legitimate means within the province of government and legislation we mean to stimulate the expansion of our trade and to open new markets. Greatest of all markets is China. Our trade there is growing by leaps and bounds. Manila, the prize of war, gives us inestimable advantages in developing that trade. Today when our legations are in danger, when our missionaries are assailed, and our consuls threatened, it is well indeed that we have ships in the Bay of Manila and troops that we can send to protect our own." The convention concurred. "Manila is the cornerstone of our Eastern policy, and the brilliant diplomacy of John Hay in securing from all nations a guarantee of our treaty rights and of the open door in China rests upon it.

"We ask the American people whether they will throw away these new markets and widening opportunities for trade and commerce by putting in power the Democratic party.... The choice lies between this Democratic policy of retreat and the Republican policy which would hold the islands, give them freedom and prosperity, and enlarge these great opportunities for ourselves and our posterity.... The Democrats assume we will fail. They fall down and worship a Chinese half-breed whose name they have never heard three years ago, and they slander, and cry down, and doubt the honor of American soldiers and sailors, of Admirals and Generals, and public men.... We are true to our own....

Senator Lodge concluded his assault: "There is one question which we will put to the American people in this campaign which includes and outweighs all others. We will say to them, you were in the depths of adversity under the last administration; you are in the heights of prosperity today. Will that prosperity continue if you make a change in your President and the party which administers your government? How long will your good times last if you turn out the Republicans and give political power to those who cry nothing but 'Woe! Woe!' the lovers of calamity and the foes of prosperity, who hold success in business to be a crime and regard thrift as a misdemeanor?...

"Do you know that if Bryan were elected, the day after the news was flashed over the country wages would go down, prices would decline, and that great argosy of American business now forging ahead over calm waters, with fair breezes and with swelling canvas, would begin to take in sail and seek the shelter and anchorage of the nearest harbor?" When Lodge completed his remarks, the convention body stood as one in amazed appreciation, shouting his name.

Then the convention began committee reports, starting with the Committee on Rules and Order of Business. Its chairman, Henry H. Bingham, of Pennsylvania, submitted his findings to the body. But political conventions always offer an opportunity for surprise, and that's what former Senator Matthew Stanley Quay, supreme boss of Pennsylvania politics, had in mind as he rose that second morning to offer an amendment to the carefully crafted document. Quay, whose election certification to return to the U.S. Senate where he had held office since 1887 had been denied on the deciding vote of Mark Hanna, was about to show who had the power in his home state. (Quay's reelection by an evenly divided Pennsylvania legislature on the deciding vote of the governor was rejected by an equally divided U.S. Senate.) Now Quay, who controlled the state patronage machine and was expert in making the money interests "Shake the Plum Tree," received a tumultuous seven-minute welcome from Pennsylvania delegates and the partisan spectators brought to the hall by Mayor Ashbridge to cheer.

Finally, the home state cheers urged Quay to the platform where he walked past Chairman Lodge's "sneering smile" and entered a motion that stunned the gathering and threatened party unity. Quay proposed that the voting power of various states in the Republican convention be based on the tally of votes each state contributed to the Republican nominee in the preceding national election. Since Southern states were solidly Democratic and delivered relatively few Republican votes, the measure would strip them of significant power in the Republican convention.

Quay's proposal was not an abstract one aimed at proportional democratic representation. Instead, he directed his remarks at his arch-enemy, Chairman Hanna, who derived much of his power at the convention through his control of the Southern delegations, whose members were often federal patronage holders. What's more, the amendment was introduced as a covert warning to Hanna that he had better cease his opposition to Roosevelt, whose campaign for the second spot was being orchestrated by Quay and New York Senator Thomas Platt and their political machines. Quay's resolution caused an uproar on the floor, particularly among the Southern delegates, until the former Senator further stated that he wished to table the matter until the following day. "The amendment involves a very radical change in the base of representation, and the convention can scarcely, from the bare reading of the statement by the clerk at the desk, know exactly what it is proposed on, if we take a vote now." Hanna instinctively knew he was beaten. He could not give up the "rotten boroughs" of Southern patronage and power.

Instead of Quay's debate, Senator Charles Warren Fairbanks, of

Indiana, a former railroad attorney and current chairman of the resolutions committee, rose to the rostrum and read the 1900 Republican party platform to the body. The platform showed off the power and prestige of the party. On the tariff, the most hotly debated national issue in the nineteenth century after slavery, the Republicans of 1900 asserted, "We renew our faith in the policy of protection to American labor. In that policy our industries have been established, diversified, and maintained. By protecting the home market, competition has been stimulated and production cheapened." The hot hall began to empty of delegates too bored to endure a reading of the platform. They knew the platform for 1900: McKinley.

Those who remained in the Exposition Auditorium listened intently. On foreign trade, the 1900 Republican platform asserted, in part, "We favor the construction, ownership, and protection of an Isthmian Canal by the government of the United States. New markets are necessary for the increasing surplus of our farm products. Every effort should be made to open and obtain new markets, especially in the Orient, and the administration is warmly to be commended for its successful efforts to commit all trading and colonizing nations to the policy of the open door in China."

On international expansion, Republicans of 1900 declared, "In accepting by the Treaty of Paris the just responsibility of our victories in the Spanish war, the President and Senate won the undoubted approval of the American people. No other course was possible than to destroy Spain's sovereignty throughout the West Indies and in the Philippine Islands.... Our authority could not be less than our responsibility, and where sovereign rights were extended, it became the high duty of the government to maintain its authority, to put down armed insurrection and to confer the blessings of liberty and civilization upon all the rescued peoples." The Republicans also endorsed annexation of the Hawaiian Islands and promised self-rule and independence for Cuba.

On the issue of big business and trusts, the Republican platform of 1900, proclaimed, "We recognize the necessity and the propriety of the honest cooperation of capital to meet new business conditions and especially to extend our rapidly increasing foreign trade, but we condemn all conspiracies and combinations intended to restrict business, to create monopolies, to limit production, or to control prices; and favor such legislation as will effectively restrain and prevent all such abuses, protect and promote competition, and secure the rights of producers, laborers, and all who are engaged in industry and commerce." The plank had been written by Hanna who saw little problem with the trusts, but sensed it would be a Democratic issue to defuse. But the platform declaration also indicated that President McKinley found the trust problem troubling, long before his successor became famous as a "Trust Buster."

On currency, the 1900 platform echoed the 1896 Presidential contest, "We renew our allegiance to the principle of the gold standard and declare our confidence in the wisdom of the legislation of the Fifty-Sixth Congress, by which the parity of all our money and the stability of our currency upon a gold basis has been secured....[And] we declare our steadfast opposition to the free and unlimited coinage of silver." Republicans wanted to remind voters that McKinley had restored prosperity "by means of two legislative measures: a protective tariff and a law making gold the standard of value." The party further called for the creation of a new Department of Commerce.

The platform had been worked out by the President and his cabinet in the White House. It reflected both the achievements of McKinley's active administration and his hopes for his second term. It had been brought to Philadelphia by Postmaster General Charles Emory Smith who handed it to Senator Joseph Benson Foraker, of Ohio, who in cooperation with Senator Fairbanks, made revisions. But much to the chagrin of the White House, the version voted on by the convention had been revised and key passages on the constitutional relationship of the United States to its new territories were cut. Congressman Lem Quigg, of New York, was later blamed. The omission left McKinley more open to charges of "imperialism" by the Democrats in the fall. But whatever its merits or flaws, the 1900 platform was adopted unanimously by Republican delegates who had almost no part in its drafting. With the perfunctory vote taken, the convention was left with little to do but adjourn. Republicans had a three-day contract for the auditorium.

On Thursday, June 21, 1900, the convention finally got down to its real work: the nominations for President and Vice President. Large crowds traveled across the Schuylkill River and descended from streetcars to pack into the Exhibition Auditorium. Spectator tickets were selling at four times their printed price. Although the building was constructed for 16,000, an extra 4,000 managed to squeeze in for the historic day.

Plumes of red, white, and blue pampas grass were handed out as the crowds crushed forward to their seats. The Grand Army Band from McKinley's Canton, Ohio, hometown played the national anthem. Anticipation was in the air, not over the lead spot, but over the choice for McKinley's running mate. Women filed in wearing their summer finery. Everywhere men clutched their summer straw hats. American flags were waving red, white, and blue in every corner of the giant auditorium.

Senator Lodge pounded the gavel to bring the session to order. The proceedings were blessed by Philadelphia Archbishop Patrick J. Ryan. The first order of negotiated business was for Matt Quay to withdraw his resolution, which brought cheers of relief from Southern delegates. Then the roll call of the states began and Alabama yielded to Ohio. Senator Joseph Benson Foraker, a former governor of McKinley's

Exposition Auditorium at 34th Street below Spruce Street, site of the 1900 Republican National Convention. The Library Company of Philadelphia.

home state of Ohio, paraded to the rostrum to make the long-anticipated renomination speech for the President. His words were continuously interrupted by bursts of applause and ovations, as the President's achievements were catalogued.

"From one end of the land to the other," Foraker proclaimed, "in every mind only one and the same man is thought of for the honor which we are now about to confer, and that man is the first choice of every man who wishes Republican success next November.... He has a record replete with brilliant achievements, a record that speaks at once both his promises and his highest eulogy. It comprehends both peace and war and constitutes the most striking illustration possible of triumphant and inspiriting fidelity and successes in the discharge of public duty.... It is no exaggeration to say that in all American history there is no chapter more brilliant than that which chronicles, with him as our commander-in-chief, our victories on land and sea.... In the name of all of these considerations, not alone on behalf of his beloved state of Ohio, but on behalf of every other state and territory here represented, and in the name of all Republicans everywhere throughout our jurisdiction, I nominate to be our next candidate for the Presidency, William McKinley." Foraker's words were resoundingly affirmed by the delegates' loud and prolonged applause and cheers.

President McKinley was an honest and relatively simple man whose greatest skills were the political ones of working every citizen and interest group into the fabric of his political solutions. He could defuse angry opponents with his charm. He was personable and warm, patriotic and religious, and loved meeting the voters whom he greeted on a daily basis as a duty of his office and an opportunity to hear directly the voice of the people whose destiny he sought to further. In all but one election in his long and distinguished career, the voters had trusted him to office. Always they respected him.

Even Hanna, the President's loyal friend who had guided his career from congressional defeat to the White House, was swept away in the hysteria that descended upon the Exposition Auditorium with McKinley's renomination. Despite the crippling effects of rheumatism, he ran from delegation to delegation with a large plume in his grasp, exclaiming, "Isn't this glorious. Take a plume and whoop 'er up." Later he was seen screaming on top of a table on the stage. Whatever the rest of the proceedings promised, Hanna was exuberant for his friend and ally.

After the marching and shouting died down, Lodge again surveyed the 20,000-person throng. The convention had barely caught its breath when Colonel Roosevelt reached the podium to second McKinley's nomination. The house went mad with excited approval. The colonel "stood flushed and almost dazed by the tremendous character of his greeting." Once again the delegates strained their lungs as Roosevelt made his forceful presentation.

"I rise to second the nomination of William McKinley, the President who has had to face more numerous and graver problems than any other President since the days of the mighty Lincoln, and who has faced them.... The Republican nominee, even before a fortnight had passed, had become the candidate not merely of all Republicans but of all Americans far-sighted enough to see where the true interests of the nation lay, and keenly sensitive to the national honor." Now the applause rose to match Roosevelt's oratory. "Four years ago we were confronted with the gravest crisis which this nation has had to face since Appomattox was won and the Civil War came to a close....

"The President faced this duty as he faced all others. He exhausted every expedient to get Spain to withdraw peacefully from the island which she was impotent to do aught than oppress, and when every peaceful means had failed, we drew the sword and waged the most righteous and brilliantly successful foreign war that this generation has seen.... And like every other great feat that has ever been performed in the history of humanity, it left those who performed it not only a heritage of honor, but a heritage of responsibility...."

Roosevelt next turned to the Philippines. "The insurrection still goes on because the allies in this country of the bloody insurrectionary oligarchy in Luzon have taught their foolish dupes to believe that Democratic success at the polls next November means the abandonment of the islands to the savages, who would scramble for the bloody plunder until some other strong civilized nation came in to do the work that we would have shown ourselves unfit to perform. Our success in November means peace in the islands. The success of our opponents means an indefinite prolongation of the present bloody struggle. We nominate President McKinley because he stands indeed for honesty at home and for honor abroad; because he stands for the continuance of the material prosperity which has brought comfort to every home in the Union; and because he stands for the kind of policy which consists in making performance square with promise." When Roosevelt finished, delegates stormed into the aisles, falling in line behind their state banners to display support for their unquestioned leader.

The enthusiastic crowd cheered McKinley and Roosevelt, and then heard seconding speeches from Senator John M. Thurston, of Nebraska, Congressman John W. Yerkes, of Kentucky, John A. Knight, of California, and James A. Mount, of Indiana. The vote was boisterous and delegations shouted their verdict. When the roll call of the states was completed, President William McKinley had been unanimously renominated. The announcement of the results sent the delegates and spectators into another spasm of adulation for their President. The demonstration was feverish and lasted several minutes. Four bands blared out versions of "Rally Round the Flag" and "There'll Be a Hot Time in the Old Town Tonight." Delegates danced down the aisles behind a large paper elephant. McKinley was their man, for no one more typified the age of American confidence and expansion. His re-election would mean more of the same, and better yet to come. In the balconies and on the floor, American flags were unfurled and flapped along with the state banners.

But the great Republican leader needed a worthy running mate. In the weeks before the convention, the President, who represented the culmination of Republican triumph, had magnanimously turned the task of selecting a running mate over to the delegates of the convention itself. Anticipation made the giant convention hall crackle with excitement.

The dynamics that brought Roosevelt's name to the throats of thousands of delegates at that moment was complex and had been laid out over several months leading up to the Philadelphia confab. John Adams had called the Vice Presidency, "the most insignificant office that ever the invention of man contrived or his imagination conceived." Nonetheless, the Vice Presidency had been resurrected by the faithful and useful behavior of McKinley's first Vice President, Garret A. Hobart, of New Jersey, who had died in office in November 21, 1899. McKinley had made Hobart a trusted member of his cabinet.

In his Senate eulogy to Hobart, Henry Cabot Lodge, thinking of Roosevelt, declared, the office should be sought by "our most ambitious men... as a stepping stone to higher honors." Roosevelt's political career to the moment had been meteoric. The cantankerous candidate had been elected to the New York State Assembly as a reformer, run for mayor of New York at age 28, been a U.S. Civil Service Commissioner for President Benjamin Harrison, been elected as an anti-corruption New York City Police Commissioner, and served as McKinley's Assistant Secretary of the Navy for a year between 1897 and 1898, under Secretary Long.

At that time, Hanna called Roosevelt "impulsive, frivolous, unsound." Roosevelt charged, "McKinley has a chocolate eclair backbone," because he wanted a diplomatic solution that averted war. Roosevelt had agitated so loudly for a fight against Spain that many credited the war to him. Long called his assistant "a bull in a china shop." (Years later the hero would become the Bull Moose Presidential candidate.) Roosevelt declared, "We will have this war for freedom of Cuba, Senator Hanna, in spite of the timidity of commercial interests." Then Teddy joined up and became a hero.

McKinley had initially preferred to replace Hobart with William Boyd Allison, of Iowa, the veteran conservative Senate leader. But the "Father of the Senate," who had held his post since 1872 and was chairman of the powerful appropriations committee, declined. Hanna had wanted Elihu Root, Secretary of the War Department, to be elevated to the Vice Presidency, but McKinley preferred to keep him where he was, still active in putting down the Philippine rebels. Root told friends he turned the job down. Hanna and McKinley agreed on McKinley's Secretary of the Interior, Cornelius N. Bliss. Bliss told Hanna he'd agree if Mrs. Bliss agreed as well. Hanna who had battled her in the past gave up hope.

Then, despite disfavoring Roosevelt, President McKinley insisted that the second spot be selected by the convention itself in a free democratic action worthy of the nation's political heritage. McKinley believed in the people; the people as followers, the people as leaders. When Hanna balked at his declaration, President McKinley, who in the early years had been portrayed as the servant of Hanna, showed that he was now his master.

John D. Long, of Massachusetts, the former Secretary of the Navy, and Senator Charles Fairbanks, of Indiana, Representative Johnathan Dolliver, of Iowa, Lieutenant Governor Timothy L. Woodruff, of New York, a Platt machine operative, had all been mentioned for the second spot. Hanna could accept any of them, except Woodruff, who wanted the job so he could use his extensive fortune to entertain Washington. Any of them, were preferable to the one candidate who loomed above them all. Without some kind of unified opposition, Roosevelt could not be stopped.

Working on Roosevelt's behalf was a machine coalition concocted between New York and Pennsylvania. Before making him governor, by only 17,000 votes, Senator Thomas Collier Platt, "The Easy Boss," had told a friend, "I don't particularly like Theodore. He has been a disturbing element to every situation to which he has been a party." Still Roosevelt was a useful vehicle for the machine to retain power. When he came back from the war, Platt put him in office. The new governor worked closely with Platt, meeting with him every Sunday morning at the Fifth Avenue Hotel where the Senator resided. The newspapers called the conferences "Platt's Sunday School Classes."

But Roosevelt fought Platt on key issues such as a new corporate franchise tax the governor imposed and over patronage appointments such as the lucrative Commissioner of Insurance post. Platt reminded Roosevelt of his pledge to work with the boss. "You did a thing which has caused the business community of New York to wonder how far the notions of populism, as laid down in Kansas and Nebraska, have taken hold on the Republican party of the State of New York," Platt reprimanded him. Roosevelt vetoed Platt's commissioner, calling his appointment "a stench in the nostril of the people." The Senator began investigating distant diplomatic appointments for Roosevelt, before thinking of his scheme to "kick him upstairs to the Vice Presidency."

Platt enlisted Quay in his plan. With Roosevelt on the national ticket, Platt could install his own man in Albany. The New York Republican state boss told the Pennsylvania state boss, that Roosevelt was "a bloody anarchist... and an enemy of the people." Listening to the exchange was Quay's lieutenant, Senator Boies Penrose, of Pennsylvania, who had gone to school with the New York governor. "I know Theodore well. If you can get enough people hollering for him to take the job, common people, mind you, not nice people, he'll insist on being Vice President." Penrose, who was an independently wealthy heir of Philadelphia shipbuilders, would eventually succeed Quay as the dominant Republican power in the Keystone State.

Platt and Quay took Penrose's advice and initiated a draft Roosevelt campaign in the Western states and among other Republican delegations. Teddy was tempted. But eventually, Roosevelt discovered Platt's Machiavellian motives. On February 6, 1900, Roosevelt released a statement that "... under no circumstances could I or would I accept the nomination for the Vice Presidency. My duty is here to the state whose people chose me as governor." He kept vacillating all the way up to the convention.

To assess the situation, the governor traveled south to the federal capital. He was taken aback that official Washington regarded him with amusement when he came in early June. Should he take the Vice Presidency? T.R. inquired of the Secretary of War Elihu Root. "Of course not," Root, replied with a tight smile, "you're not fit for it." John Hay reported that "nobody in Washington, except Platt, had ever dreamed of such a thing...." That was an over-estimation. Senator Henry Cabot Lodge, Roosevelt's friend and ally, assured him the Vice Presidency was a stepping-stone to the Presidency in 1904. After two popular terms, McKinley was certain to step aside. Lodge had told Roosevelt, "If you go to the convention, you'll be nominated."

T. R. arrived in Philadelphia for the convention with Senator Platt on Sunday and set up camp at the Walton Hotel. Confronted with the enthusiastic response he received wherever he strolled, Roosevelt seemed swayed to his Washington option. "I think up to this moment, Roosevelt was against it," Charles Dick, of Pennsylvania, who was secretary of the Republican National Committee, told McKinley's secretary George B. Cortelyou over the new long distance telephone, "but they have turned his head."

McKinley still could have intervened and anointed someone else, but he stuck to his commitment of letting the delegates decide democratically. But Hanna was out to stop the Rough Rider, without disobeying his President. The fight went back and forth all convention week. On Monday, the national chairman moved into the Walton where he could operate, twist arms for votes, and keep an eye on Roosevelt.

Hanna told Roosevelt's friend Nicholas Murray Butler, of Columbia University, that T.R. would not be the nominee under any circumstances, because he would not permit it. But his appeals got nowhere against the rising tide of support for the one-time Dakota cowboy.

Roosevelt may have made up his mind to give in to the draft that was building all spring because of Platt's duplicity and the opposition of New York businessmen upset by his franchise tax. Even if he won a second term as governor, he would be out of the two-year term two years before the next Presidential election. In Washington, at least, he would still be a public servant when 1904 rolled around. Roosevelt was, as President Harrison had said years earlier "a young man, impatient for righteousness." Roosevelt also feared that with his children in college he wouldn't be able to afford the lavish entertainment bill of the Vice Presidency.

In the halls of the hotels like the Walton, spontaneous demonstrations for Roosevelt were staged by various delegations every evening. On Monday evening, the night before he graveled the convention to order, Hanna felt he had turned the tide. But on Wednesday morning, Wisconsin and several Western states came out for Roosevelt. "Do what you please," Hanna shouted at a Wisconsin national committeeman supporting the New York governor. "I'm through, I won't have anything more to do with this convention!" Then he threatened, "I won't take charge of the campaign! I won't be chairman of the national committee again!... McKinley won't let me use the power of the administration to defeat Roosevelt. He is blind, or afraid, or something."

All day, delegates debated the issue among themselves. The California caucus decided to back no one, although if there were a candidate, Roosevelt would be their man. The Kansas caucus declared for the Rough Rider. The final night before the nominations, the pressure on Hanna mounted, especially from Southern delegates threatened by Quay's resolution.

Hanna called Roosevelt to his chambers and accused him of a breach of faith in breaking his public statements to run "under no circumstances." Hanna told the New Yorker he would injure the national ticket with rumors of machine politics as practiced by Platt and Quay. Roosevelt had, Hanna told him, already hurt the party and himself. Roosevelt withered under the political browbeating Hanna handed him and consented to make yet another denial speech. He proclaimed he could best help the party by running for governor in New York. His backers were confused. In the interim, the New York delegation voted to support Woodruff. Rumors circulated that "Roosevelt was out of it." Hanna was temporarily heartened.

But as Hanna said, "You can't beat someone with nobody." Fairbanks, of Indiana, withdrew his name to let the draft go forward for

Roosevelt, and was rewarded with the Vice Presidency four years later. Platt played hard ball and told Roosevelt that he would not be renominated in New York, that Benjamin Odell, one of his lieutenants, would get the nod. Roosevelt had no option but to accept the draft. By this time, Lodge believed Roosevelt didn't want the prize and was wearing a button for John D. Long. Meanwhile, Platt and Quay plotted a final stampede. The Pennsylvania delegation voted 53-4 to vote for Roosevelt.

Fairbanks and Allison recommended that the President take Roosevelt. Charles G. Dawes, of Illinois, was a trusted Hanna lieutenant who had worked Illinois for McKinley in 1896, against his former Nebraska acquaintance, William Jennings Bryan. The future Vice President under Coolidge and Nobel Peace Prize winner (for his post-World War I reparations plan) warned Hanna of the rumors that Roosevelt was being manipulated out of the nomination by party bosses. He cautioned that it could hurt McKinley. Dawes also called McKinley, through his secretary, George B. Cortelyou (who later became Roosevelt's secretary and eventually, Secretary of Commerce, before becoming national chairman of the party).

Dawes reported to the White House that, "The Roosevelt boom is let loose and it has swept everything. It starts with the support of Pennsylvania and New York practically solid and with California and Colorado back of it also. The feeling is that the thing is going pell-mell like a tidal wave."

Finally, McKinley himself sent directions to Hanna, through his secretary Cortelyou and Charles Dawes, that, "The President's close friend must not undertake to commit the administration to any candidate. It has no candidate. The convention must make the nomination."

Dawes showed the President's message to Hanna who could read the inevitable. He picked up one of the hotel phones and called Roosevelt in his room. "Teddy, you're it," he announced, then hung up. Then Hanna told his aides, "Don't you realize there is only one life between this madman and the White House?"

Next, a reluctant Hanna, still the President's most important power broker, called Lafayette Young, of Iowa, and told him to "put in San Juan Hill and the proper coloring." Then as midnight neared, Hanna released a press statement, "The administration has had no candidate for Vice President. It has not been for or against any candidate. It has desired that the convention should make the candidate and that has been my position throughout... several eminent Republicans have been proposed, all of them distinguished men with many friends.... In the present situation with the strong and earnest sentiment of the delegates from all parts of the country for Governor Roosevelt, and since President McKinley is to be nominated without a dissenting voice, it is my judgement that Governor Roosevelt should be nominated for Vice President with the same unanimity."

No sooner had the wild whirlwind for McKinley's nomination by acclamation subsided on Thursday afternoon than Lafayette Young was granted the floor. He promptly placed into nomination for Vice President the name of Theodore Roosevelt and the hall burst into even more delirious hysteria for a man whose enthusiasm for American virtue was unsurpassed. The mention of Roosevelt's name, the buoyant hero of America's daring adventure against Spain, in association with their beloved, wise, and cautious McKinley, set the Twelfth Republican National Convention into a convulsion of pandemonium.

Then Senator Chauncey DePew, the former president of the New York Central Railroad, spoke up for his friend Roosevelt. "We stand in the presence of 800 million of people with the Pacific as an American lake, and the American artisan producing better and cheaper goods than any country in the world, and my friends, we go to American labor and to the American farm, and say that, with McKinley for another four years, there is no congestion for America. Let invention proceed, let production go on, let the mountains bring forth their treasures, let the factories do their best, let labor be employed at the highest wages, because the world is ours, and we have conquered it by Republican principles and by Republican persistency in the principles of American industry and America for Americans....

"We have the best ticket ever presented," DePew exclaimed. "We have at the head of it a Western man with Eastern notions, and we have at the other end an Eastern man with Western character, the statesman and the cowboy, the accomplished man of affairs and the heroic fighter. The man who has proved great as a President, and the fighter who has proved great as governor. We leave this old town simply to keep on shouting and working to make it unanimous for McKinley and Roosevelt." The Exposition hall crowd went wild with loud agreement.

Then DePew recalled the Cuban conflict and the ships in Santiago Harbor. "On board those transports were 20,000 soldiers that had gone away from our shores to liberate another race, to fulfill no obligations but that of humanity. On the ship *Yucatan* was that famous regiment of Rough Riders of the far West and Mississippi Valley. In command of that regiment was that fearless young American, student, scholar, plainsman, historian, statesman, soldier, of the Middle West by adoption, of New York by birth. That fleet sailing around the point, coming to the place of landing, stood off the harbor, two years ago tomorrow, and the navy bombarded that shore to make a place for landing, and no man who lives, who was in that campaign as an officer, as a soldier, or as a camp follower, can fail to recall the spectacle; and if he closes his eyes he can see the awful scenes in that campaign in June and July, 1898.... And the leader of one of those regiments in that campaign shall be the name that I shall place before this convention for the office of Vice President of the United States.

"McKinley, a young soldier, and coming out a major; McKinley, a congressman, and making a tariff; McKinley, a President, elected because he represented the protection of American industries; and McKinley, after four years' development, in peace, in war, in prosperity and in adversity, the greatest President save one or two that this country has ever had, and the greatest ruler in Christendom today. So with Colonel Roosevelt; we call him Teddy.

"He was a child of New York, of New York City, the place that you gentlemen from the West think means 'coupons, clubs, and eternal damnation for everyone.' Teddy, this child of Fifth Avenue, he was a child of the clubs; he was the child of the exclusiveness of Harvard College, and he went West and became a cowboy; and then he went to the Navy Department and became an assistant secretary. He gave an order, and the old chiefs of bureaus came to him and said: 'Why, colonel, there is no authority and no requisition to burn this powder.' 'Well,' said the colonel, 'we have got to get ready when war comes,' and powder was manufactured to be burned. And the burning of that powder sank Cervera's fleet outside Santiago Harbor, and the fleet in Manila Bay.

"At Santiago a modest voice was heard, exceedingly polite, addressing a militia regiment, laying upon the ground, while the Spanish bullets were flying over them. This voice said: 'Get one side, gentlemen, please, one side, gentlemen, please that my men can get out.' And when this polite man got his men out in the open, where they could face the bayonet and face the bullet, there was a transformation, and the transformation was that the dude had become a cowboy, the cowboy had become a soldier, the soldier had become a hero, and rushing up the hill, pistol in hand, the polite man shouted to the militiamen lying down: 'Give them hell boys. Give them hell!'" As the old New York Senator fell silent, the entire convention hall broke loose again with ecstatic cheers for their political hero, their nominee for Vice President, Theodore Roosevelt. And the band played the convention favorite, "There'll Be A Hot Time In The Old Town Tonight."

The roll call of the states for Vice President proceeded with cheers from each delegation as they cast their allotted votes, each tally seconded by cheers from the entire convention. In the end, New York was the only state not to record unanimous endorsement of McKinley's new second. Theodore Roosevelt would not vote for himself as long as the entire convention was casting its all but unanimous ballot for him. No less than the unified voice of the people could propel Theodore Roosevelt to public service. The hero was swept away by the throng that surrounded him and lifted him to the portals of national significance. The Twelfth

Republican National Convention had just unwittingly nominated its second President of the United States for the first term of the twentieth century.

Republicans from every state and territory fell in line for McKinley and Roosevelt, and "Four More Years Of The Full Lunch Pail." When McKinley's personal friend George Perkins called the White House the following day, he told them, "Everyone feels very happy this morning over the nomination." Even Hanna was reconciled. But in defeating him, the "Young Lions" had made headway against the "Old Guard." Hanna consoled himself that at least the political veterans were still in charge and everyone was united behind the ticket that promised victory in the fall.

Back in his Fifth Avenue Hotel, Senator Thomas Platt, Roscoe Conkling's successor as New York State's Republican boss, told reporters, "I'm glad we had our way, I mean, the people had their way." Both phrases were accurate. Platt had been endangered by the unpredictable actions of the reforming Governor, and the Senator's plan, as directed by some of the state's political interests and corporations that Roosevelt was investigating, was to get him out of New York politics. Platt and Quay had done that. But the people wanted their hero, and so they also had him.

Roosevelt himself was not so sure who had won. He had wanted a second term as governor, but in the end believed he could be thwarted by Platt. He also thought he would be placed on the shelf as Vice President. Still, he had beaten Hanna, and all the other Washingtonians who had seemed amused that he had declared so many times during the year that he was not a candidate.

Now Lodge cautioned Roosevelt that he must appear "everywhere as the champion of the President." Lodge added, "Fortunately his policies on the great questions are our policy. He is doing admirably so far as I can see in all directions, and especially in the difficulties in China, and I am anxious that your advocacy of him should appear in every thing you say.... This is going to be of immense importance to us four years hence...."

Upon notification of the convention's will, McKinley extended warm greetings to Roosevelt and welcomed him to the ticket. Yet he wondered aloud to friends how Roosevelt would be able "to sit still long enough to preside over the Senate." That afternoon train cars filled with delegates and well-wishers traveled from Philadelphia to Washington to celebrate the renomination at the White House. Party leaders, delegates, friends from Ohio all crowded around McKinley to offer their congratulations. As the party died down, the President took Charles Dawes, who had acted as a Presidential intermediary with Roosevelt, to the cabinet room and assured him that he believed "all has come out for the best."

McKinley sent Hanna a note of thanks, for "the courage and sagacity of true leadership...." Hanna wrote back, "Well it was a nice little scrap at Philadelphia, not exactly to my liking with my hands tied behind me. However we got through in good shape and the ticket is all right. Your duty to the country is to live for four years from next March."

After enough hesitation to make his friend nervous, McKinley again appointed Hanna to direct the national campaign. Both McKinley and Hanna knew the pitfalls of over-confidence. Both knew that no election was a certain thing. In 1896, Hanna had run a fierce campaign to defeat the emotionally-charged prairie fire set by William Jennings Bryan, "the boy orator of the Platte," whose anti-Eastern banking "Cross of Gold" speech had electrified the nation. "You shall not press down upon the brow of labor this crown of thrones," he had dramatically intoned inside the Chicago Wigwam during the Democracy's 1896 convention. "You shall not crucify mankind on a cross of gold," he had bellowed as he extended his arm in sympathetic union with the bankrupted farmers and unemployed working men whose livelihood had been lost in the wreck of economic speculation and tight money bank policy.

Hanna had thrown everything at Bryan to stop him. Everywhere Republican stump speakers made charges calling the Democrat a demagogue, buffoon, home-spun economist, and from the nation's church altars, ministers made the accusation of "anti-Christ" against the eloquent young political missionary. In 1896, Bryan had made thousands of speeches from the back of his railroad car to crowds in the tens of thousands, and to small gatherings along the rail path where his train halted so he could address them. McKinley ran a front-porch campaign from his home in Canton, Ohio, where he was instructed by Hanna to say as little as possible. The campaign had been rugged, but in the end, it was the conservative American people, who gave the silent McKinley their vote. McKinley totaled 271 electoral votes to Bryan's 176.

In the election's wake, the discovery of new gold deposits in North America, along with the expansion of currency that followed, and McKinley's success in firing up the economy, set the nation to rising like a phoenix out of the worst depression yet and almost made the gold/silver debate moot, although it retained some of its emotional overtones even in the 1900 contest.

On the fourth of July, 1900, in Kansas City, the Democracy gathered, reunified after their internecine battle at the 1896 convention when "Gold Democrats" had refused to vote for a "Silver" nominee and had boycotted Bryan's campaign. This time William Jennings Bryan, who was at his Lincoln, Nebraska, home during the convention, was unanimously endorsed by all 936 delegates, while 20,000 spectators cheered. His 1896 antagonist, New York Senator David B. Hill, gave Bryan's seconding speech, also indicating a unified party. President Cleveland's second Vice President, Adlai E. Stevenson, of Illinois, who was also a silverite, was again nominated for the post.

The Democratic delegates, boiling in the Kansas City heat, expanded on Bryan's radical 1896 silver platform to include an attack on McKinley's "imperialistic war." The Democratic platform asserted, "We hold that the Constitution follows the flag, and denounce the doctrine that an executive or Congress deriving their existence and their powers from the Constitution can exercise lawful authority beyond it or in violation of it. We assert that no nation can long endure half Republic and half empire, and we warn the American people that imperialism abroad will lead quickly and inevitably to despotism at home."

The Bryan Democracy added, "We are not opposed to territorial expansion when it takes a desirable territory which can be erected into the states in the Union, and whose people are willing and fit to become American citizens. We favor trade expansion by every peaceful and legitimate means. But we are unalterably opposed to seizing or purchasing distant islands to be governed outside the Constitution, and whose people can never become citizens...."

The Democratic platform of 1900 observed, "...the burning issue of imperialism growing out of the Spanish war involves the very existence of the Republic and the destruction of our free institutions. We regard it as the paramount issue of the campaign...." The platform also called for a canal across Nicaragua, instead of the route across the Panama Isthmus proposed by Republicans.

Bryan had volunteered for the war in Cuba, and like Roosevelt became a colonel. But he was caught in a malaria-infested post in Florida instead of on San Juan Hill. Still the Bryan Democracy declared, "We oppose militarism. It means conquest abroad and oppression at home. It means the strong arm which has ever been fatal to free institutions.... This Republic has no place for a vast military establishment, a sure forerunner to compulsory military service or conscription. When the nation is in danger, the volunteer soldier is his country's best defender."

On the question of the trusts, the platform pledged "the Democratic party to an unceasing warfare in nation, state, and city against private monopoly in every form. Existing laws against trusts must be enforced and more stringent ones must be enacted.... Tariff laws should be amended by putting the products of trusts upon the free list, to prevent monopoly under the plea of protection." And as in 1896, Democrats endorsed bimetallism, and the minting of silver coins at a value ratio of 16 to 1 to gold. There was still substantial resistance to this plank, particularly among Eastern delegates. However, Bryan threatened to refuse nomination if it failed. The pro-silver amendment passed by only a single vote in committee.

The Bryan Democracy also called forth progressive reforms such as the creation of a Department of Labor, in contrast to the Republican suggestion for a Department of Commerce; and the popular election of Senators directly by voters, taking the power away from the bosses in the state legislatures and opening the Senate, which was seen as a rich man's club, to the direct voice of the people.

A confident and conscientious McKinley was determined to make no campaign at all, but rather to attend exclusively to the affairs of the Presidency. For the first time, he thought, since the Civil War, a President represented all sections of the nation. He was content to let the American people vote upon his record. He delivered but one speech all summer, and that was his formal acceptance of the notification of his nomination, delivered on July 12, from the porch of his Canton, Ohio, home. Senator Lodge, chairman of the notification committee, led a large delegation from Washington, that joined McKinley's friends and well-wishers in the blistering heat. The President promised "prosperity at home and prestige abroad." He singled out a sound currency as shown in his gold policy as the number one campaign issue, not imperialism, as Bryan had done. The Democratic recommendations of 1896, had been defeated by McKinley's successful policies as evidenced by 1900. As the Boxer movement grew, he promised to maintain the open door and protection of Americans in China. He defended the actions of American expansion with the example of Porto Rico, and insisted "there would be no scuttle" of his policy in the Philippine war against insurgents.

American voters were still paying the taxes on his wars in Cuba and the Philippines, wars that sparked deep controversy and disgust in some quarters. Speaker of the House, Thomas Brackett Reed, for example, left Congress in protest over the shabby war profiteering. The forgotten war was filled with unpleasant horrors and Aguinaldo's rebels were still active. Yet with just as many voters, McKinley's military policies infused them with patriotism and pride. He justified making rebels submit to American sovereignty before independence to show that America was not weak. McKinley called the imperialism charges absurd. The party of Lincoln had liberated tens of millions from colonial domination and would give them the democratic institutions for law and order. As McKinley said in South Carolina during the spring, "It is no longer a question of expansion with us; we have expanded. If there is any question at all, it is a question of contracting; and who is going to contract?"

McKinley led an informal luncheon after his speech, and was a witty and urbane host for his guests. The people all over the land were charmed with McKinley's sincerity and simplicity of purpose. At the dawn of a new century, he represented American optimism and opportunity, and his friends and colleagues cheered his brief remarks and lingered long afterward to enjoy a beautiful summer day in the Middlewestern splendor of turn-of-the-century Canton. The President had spoken and would not speak again. "Now I am President of the whole people, and while I am a candidate again, I feel that the proprieties demand that the President should refrain from making a political canvass in his own behalf, and I shall not engage in speech-making this year, save one or two when I will speak on national questions rather than partisan politics." He greeted guests all summer and kept in touch with the government back in Washington by telephone. He took Hanna's "stand pat" advice to heart.

In the absence of an active Presidential candidate, Hanna had a void to fill, and he didn't find it in the apathetic and overly-confident ranks of the Republican party that summer. But the electoral task was not as great or as uncertain as 1896, for the nation no longer faced starvation, but mass abundance, and Bryan's issue of imperialism was intellectual, while his program of economic reform four years earlier had been emotional.

To Hanna, gold, not silver, had brought back prosperity. McKinley was the prophet of profit; Bryan the false messiah of alarm and doom. Still there was an unfulfilled movement of labor that threatened disorder. The cities were havens of democratic machines that could turn out votes. The citizen of New York, Chicago, Baltimore, Indianapolis, Buffalo, San Francisco, Denver, Kansas City, and Jersey City were now controlled by Democratic mayors. And, the Silverite and one Populist party had endorsed and would work for Bryan. (The other Populist party endorsed Wharton Barker of Pennsylvania, and the best-selling author Ignatius Donnelly, of Minnesota, for Vice President. The Socialist party nominated Eugene V. Debs, of Indiana, President; Job Harriman, Vice President.) The newly coalesced American Federation of Labor also would get out a vote for Bryan. But Hanna was confident that simple repetition of the old slogan, "A Full Lunch Pail," would appeal to all voters in November. And of course he expected to receive abundant contributions from corporations that Republican party policies so carefully protected.

McKinley headed a Republican party that was no longer the anti-slavery party, but one that identified pro-business with the gospel of freedom. The martyrs had led one movement, the millionaires the other. In the Democratic press, McKinley was caricatured as child of the trusts. The Republican press was as strong in its denunciations. "Mr. Bryan starts out on his second race for the Presidency still the head of a rabble half fanatical, half demonic," wrote Horace Greeley's old assistant, Whitelaw Reid, editor of the New York *Tribune.*

But Senator Henry M. Teller, of Colorado, observed, "If there is a man in the United States today who comes near to Abraham Lincoln, that man is William Jennings Bryan." Bryan's nomination acceptance speech was given in Indianapolis at Military Park in early August when he spoke before 40,000 supporters. The Democratic candidate charged McKinley with trying to "civilize with dynamite and proselyte with the sword." He called for immediate independence for the Philippines and mocked the idea that the United States would educate Filipinos, "lest they learn to read the Declaration of Independence and the Constitution of the United States." He warned, "God himself... never made a race of people so low in the scales of civilization or intelligence that it welcomes a foreign master." And he evangelized, saying, "The Command, 'Go ye into the world and preach the Gospel to every creature' has no Gatling gun attachment." Rather, Bryan called on his nation to become "the supreme moral factor in the world's progress and accepted arbiter of the world's disputes...."

The "Bryan special," his 12-car train filled with jubilant campaigners, made its way across the nation, drawing huge crowds wherever he spoke. Bryan's attacks worried McKinley. He felt that the failure of General Arthur MacArthur's amnesty offer to the Philippine rebels resulted from Democratic campaign rhetoric. The problem was compounded by the fact that the army was scheduled to revert to a regular force of just 28,000, down from 60,000, on July 1, 1901. The war with its steady casualties, McKinley was afraid, could lead to his defeat. By mid-summer, fears of a Democratic victory were in evidence and an economic panic was set off by business fears of a Bryan victory.

But as the campaign developed the issue of imperialism failed to take hold in the public's mind as questions of domestic economics loomed larger. Over the summer, as he delivered his speeches, reduced in number from 1896, Bryan moved his focus to the questions of inequity and the monopolistic trusts. Unlike 1896, most Eastern Democrats embraced Bryan. In October, Bryan launched a 17-city speaking tour, in which he traveled 16,000 miles and gave 600 speeches. He mended fences with Richard Croker, Tammany Hall's boss, who in turn hosted a mammoth Madison Square rally where he mocked McKinley's "Full Dinner Pail," saying the Republicans regarded the workingman as "all stomach, without heart or heard... like a hog."

Hanna, who divided his organizational time between New York and Chicago, collected $2.5 million from Wall Street to conduct the canvass and oil the machinery of state electioneering. Hanna wrote the President, "We are filling the doubtful states with spellbinders and ploughing the fence corners." With McKinley staying home at Canton, Roosevelt took to the stump and attracted crowds almost as large as Bryan's. His train shadowed the route taken by the eloquent Democrat, and Teddy gave them a fist-thumping, pro-McKinley, Americanism speech wherever he stopped. His voice crackled often in high falsetto, and he lost it all together at the end of the canvas, but still the crowds cheered him. When one spectator first saw the exuberant Roosevelt flashing his famous teeth and bounding about, he asked, "Is he drunk?" His companion, replied, "Oh no. He needs no whiskey to feel that way. He intoxicates himself by his own enthusiasm." Roosevelt attracted more attention than McKinley.

As in 1896, manufacturers again warned their workers not to come to work the day after the election if Bryan won, that their operations would be suspended. Contracts again carried "Bryan clauses," which made them void should the Democrat prove victorious. Bryan responded, "I believe the time has come when corporations should be compelled to keep its hand out of politics and tend to the business for which it was organized. I am not willing that the independence of the citizens should be destroyed."

"Wake up!" Hanna warned the trusts as Bryan's attacks became more passionate. And for the first time, the old political professional, Hanna, took to the speaker's platform and in his unassuming, everyday manner charmed the crowds that came out to see the man the Democracy described as the devil himself. Hanna's train made its way across the disenchanted West through small farming and ranching stops where he spoke sincerely and persuasively. "Let well enough alone," he pleaded. At one stop where a platform collapsed under him, he laughingly remarked, "This was, I think, a Democratic platform." At election time Hanna helped McKinley take back Bryan's Nebraska, Kansas, Wyoming, Utah, South Dakota, and Washington for the Republican sound money cause. (Sound money indeed; Hanna gave Standard Oil a $50,000 refund on its campaign donation.) Republicans spent $5 million to $500,000 for the Democracy.

On election night, the bands played outside the President's Canton home. Thousands gathered around his porch as he said a few words of thanks. In the end, McKinley bettered his 1896 margin of victory. His 1900 total reached 7,218,491 to Bryan's 6,356,734; an increase of over 100,000 over 1896, and he posted an Electoral Vote of 292 to Bryan's 155.

Hanna wired his friend. "God bless and keep you for the patriotic purposes to which you have dedicated your life." The President wrote back that Hanna's service to the party and the country was "incalculable." Dawes wrote, "The President seems more impressed with his responsibilities than his triumph." McKinley was satisfied. "I can no longer be called the President of a party; I am now the President of the whole people."

In spite of his initial fears, Roosevelt was to be Vice President.

He wrote a friend, "I do not expect to go any further in politics." When the inauguration came around, Senator Platt told friends, "Yes, I'm going to Washington to see Theodore Roosevelt take the (death) veil." But on inauguration day, March 4, 1901, Roosevelt again stole some small portion of the spotlight. On that rainy day, the crowds cried out his name and the newspaper correspondents wrote profiles of the Vice President. He ended up presiding over the Senate for only five days that spring.

On September 6, 1901, McKinley visited the Temple of Music at the Pan-American Exposition in Buffalo, New York. The day before he had delivered an important speech on domestic and foreign policy. He was in a festive mood, now that his words had been so welcomed. He looked forward to standing in a receiving line to greet his public, as he loved to do. He was the people's President, and was eager to meet and talk with them, to learn their problems, and address their issues. Half-way through the 20-minute greeting session, a deranged anarchist, Leon Czolgosz, shot McKinley with two bullets and one lodged in his abdomen. An African-American named James B. Parker grabbed the assassin's gun and prevented a third shot. The first U.S. President of the twentieth century lingered in pain for a little more than a week before dying on September 14, and "that damned cowboy," as Hanna called Roosevelt, became President of the United States of America, the second one nominated by the Philadelphia Presidential convention of 1900.

The 1936 Democratic National Convention: Rendezvous With Destiny

Convention-at-a-Glance

Event: Twenty-Seventh Democratic National Convention
Date: June 23-27, 1936
Location: Municipal Auditorium, Thirty-fourth Street and Civic Center Boulevard; Franklin Field, University of Pennsylvania
Philadelphia Mayor: S. Davis Wilson, Republican
Philadelphia's Population: 1,931,334 (1940)
Convention Permanent Chairman: Senator Joseph T. Robinson, Arkansas
Number of Delegates: 1100
Number Needed to Nominate: A majority; Two-thirds Rule repealed
Candidate for Renomination: President Franklin Delano Roosevelt, New York
Presidential Nominee: President Franklin Delano Roosevelt
Age at Nomination: 54
Number of Ballots: None; by acclamation
Vice Presidential Nominee: Vice President John Nance Garner, Texas
Largest Audience: 100,000 (Franklin Field)
Platform Positions: Endorsement of the New Deal; protection of the family and the home; establishment of a democracy of opportunity for all the people; aid to those overtaken by disaster
Campaign Slogan: "A Rendezvous with Destiny"
Popular Convention Song: "Happy Days Are Here Again"
Campaign Song: "Go And Win With Roosevelt"

President Franklin Delano Roosevelt
1936 Democratic Presidential
Nominee

Vice President John Nance Garner
1936 Democratic Vice Presidential
Nominee

1936

The 1936 Democratic Convention: Rendezvous With Destiny

At 1 P.M. Tuesday, June 23, 1936, the chairman of the Democratic National Committee, James A. Farley, of New York, called to order the Twenty-Seventh Democratic National Convention, the first Democratic national convention ever to meet in Philadelphia. Delegates gathered in the large art deco Municipal Auditorium at Thirty-fourth Street and Civic Center Boulevard in West Philadelphia. The massive, domed-ceiling building, designed by Philip H. Johnson, had opened in 1931, and dwarfed the neo-classical Exposition Auditorium where President McKinley had been nominated in 1900 that stood next door, now called the Commercial Museum. Despite the depths of depression, the city fathers had managed to raise $200,000 to bring the convention to town, and even accommodated Democrats by suspending the "Blue Laws" against the sale of alcohol on Sunday. After all, it was the Democrats who brought an end to Prohibition in 1933.

The Most Reverend Hugh L. Lamb, auxiliary Bishop of the Diocese of Philadelphia, blessed the gathering "in this solemn hour" as it sought to "nominate a captain for that ship of state and to chart a course which will bring the vessel, with its precious cargo of human lives, safely into the harbor of peace and prosperity."

Then Chairman Farley directed the convention "to stand for just one minute in solemn tribute to the memory of a great American, Will Rogers." Rogers had entertained the Democratic convention and national radio audience four years earlier in Chicago. Then after a robust singing of the national anthem and a chorus of "America the Beautiful," led by the Philco Men's Glee Club, the delegates were welcomed by Philadelphia's Republican mayor, S. Davis Wilson, a likeable but unpredictable administrator who was fond of intoxicants. Wilson had been a Democrat, but won election as a Republican. Some of the delegates had flown into the new municipal airport that he had named after himself.

"Philadelphia embraces you in a heartfelt welcome," exclaimed Mayor Wilson. "We are proud to be your hosts on the occasion of this great and momentous conclave.... Every resource of this great city has been concentrated to the end that your stay will be comfortable and satisfying." The mayor said, "We are giving you the cool weather we promised you.... Everyone in America knows Philadelphia as the City of Brotherly Love and we are planning to give you a practical demonstration of that fact.... It is hoped that you will drive through our beautiful Fairmount Park, the largest in the world, where you will see such wonders as the famous Wissahickon Creek.... We expect you to visit the many historic shrines for which our city is famous... that you will pause for a moment in Independence Hall, the home of the Liberty Bell; in Carpenter's Hall; the Betsy Ross House, birthplace of the American flag; and breathe for a little while the atmosphere wherein the first great minds of America struggled with the responsibilities of government." He also urged visits to the classic Parkway, the Rodin Museum, the Fels Planetarium, and the Franklin Institute. He pointed out that Philadelphia, 90 miles from the sea, could boost the largest inland harbor where the mighty Delaware and Schuykill rivers met, with 267 wharfs and the Philadelphia Navy Yard.

"You cannot but be interested in a city which was the first capitol of the United States," he told them, "where the first Continental Congress met, where the immortal Declaration of Independence was written, signed, and proclaimed to the world, and the Constitution adopted." Mayor Wilson reminded the Democratic delegates that, "Philadelphia was Penn's haven for the oppressed, where men and women could worship in whatever manner they desired. Philadelphia was not only the pioneer city of the nation, it has been a city of firsts, since Penn's 'Greene Towne' was established 254 years ago, and it has maintained its enviable position as a leader through the years, centuries, down to the present. Franklin made it a home of science, literature, and philosophy; and while it has safeguarded that heritage, it developed along many other fields of endeavor and is now known throughout the world as the Workshop of the World and the City of Homes."

Mayor Wilson's civic speech avoided the fact that he had run against Roosevelt's record in his election of 1935 with the financial backing of Sun Oil owner Joseph N. Pew, Jr., saying the New Deal must be "utterly repudiated." But with Philadelphians in desperate straits during the depression, Mayor Wilson accepted millions in federal funds to give jobs to 40,000 Philadelphians and for Works Progress Administration (WPA) projects, including to improve roads in Fairmont Park and city streets, to build airport runways and 900 public housing buildings, to improve the Navy Yard, and to rehabilitate 25 miles of blighted housing.

When Mayor Davis finished, Chairman Farley asked everyone to smile for the official convention portrait of the opening, but the camera and lights malfunctioned, so Farley began his official address. "Ladies and gentlemen [this was the first national convention in Philadelphia in which women were allowed to participate as delegates], in inaugurating this convention, I am conscious of a great responsibility. The occasion which brings us together is one of the most momentous in the history of our country. The continuance of the New Deal is the issue." Here Farley was interrupted with thunderous and prolonged applause, which sparked the band to play the Roosevelt theme song, "Happy Days Are Here Again," with the whole auditorium of delegates and spectators pitching in. "The question is, shall we continue the New Deal, which has rescued our country from disaster and despair, or shall the government be turned back to the old dealers who wrecked it?" He was stopped by applause again. "There you have the issue stripped of all camouflage."

"Fortunately for us and the country, we know now that the old dealers stand right where they have always stood. The convention at Cleveland [that nominated Republican Alfred Landon, governor of Kansas] both in manner and method, revealed once more that the old habits are not abandoned.... I merely wish to impress on all of you the significance of the task to which we are committing ourselves.... The consequences of the coming election are vital to the future of this nation. Because of their gravity, no one of us dares do less than his utmost toward swelling the majority that will testify to the national desire that the processes of recovery, initiated and carried by Franklin D. Roosevelt, shall not be interrupted." Farley was met again with a wave of cheers and the convention theme song as the entire body stood in ovation for their Democratic President. "That verdict must be so overwhelming, so conclusive, so compelling, that nobody can doubt that the country is united in its determination that there shall be no backward steps in our progress. Our party will remain in power so long as its ideals and purposes do not deviate from the straight path of public service. We are a fortunate party; first, in the high patriotism and caliber of our President; second, in that we are on the right side, both morally and economically."

Farley updated the delegates and the nation listening to the convention on radio to the progress made by the New Deal Democracy. "Through the masterful work of the candidates of the 1932 convention and the Congress which was elected in sympathy with them, our country has been lifted out of the worst depression in our history and onto the fair highway that leads to permanent prosperity." Then he unmasked his party's opponents, "As soon as the huge financial interests that have been the backbone of every Republican administration had been rescued from the depths of loss and again began to make money, they exerted their pressure, furnished the funds, and engaged in a crusade of vituperation and detraction in an effort to destroy the faith of the people in the President.... But he was insisting the fortunes for the few and poverty for the many did not spell prosperity, and they, feeling themselves threatened with deprivation of unearned and uneconomic favors and privileges they had enjoyed for so long, inaugurated the movement for a return of the old system of everything to them and nothing for the plain people.

"Then it was that the minority party orators and the newspapers controlled by the big interests began telling our people that Franklin D. Roosevelt sought to be a dictator," Farley intoned. "Then it was that the laws of Congress had been enacted, and for which many of the Senators and Representatives of their own party had voted, were denounced as being intended to make our country a socialistic and communistic state... that they were all the product of dreamers and visionaries."

Of the Republican convention in Cleveland, Farley proclaimed, "By their platform they would have assured our victory, I believe, even had our national organization remained dormant during the whole pre-convention period.... Our friends, the enemy, had an opportunity to be sincere. If they had any regard for consistency, they would have renamed Herbert Hoover, who represents the classical attitude of their party...." But, Farley concluded, "Good government is good politics. That was true when Jefferson founded our party and the formula has not changed. Circumstances and conditions change. The immortal principles that have made us the freest, most secure people in the world remain changeless.... For three years, this has been a people's government. It is our job to keep it a people's government." Roars filled the hall.

"Behind the Republican ticket is the crew of the du Pont Liberty League and their allies, which have so far financed every undercover agency that has disgraced American politics with their appeal to race prejudice, religious intolerance, and personalities so gross they had to be repudiated even by the regular Republican organization. They will continue to disown these snaky assaults and to seek to profit by them. But the leaguers will never gain the prize." The convention cheered.

"The real New Deal, sane and orderly, not the wild, visionary, socialistic or communistic creation of its enemy's imagination, will sail on serenely to the goal of complete recovery, and at its helm, the calm, capable, and courageous commander, Franklin D. Roosevelt." The poetry of Farley's oration sent the convention into a 30-minute demonstration of support for their President and his national chairman. When the commotion ceased, the body adjourned to begin the tasks of committees to formally organize the convention.

The second session of the 1936 Democratic National Convention convened at 9 P.M. that evening. After a blessing and rendition of "America" by Miss Kitty Carlisle, Governor George H. Earle III, of Pennsylvania, addressed the assemblage. "As the Governor of the Commonwealth of Pennsylvania and as a Democrat, I am happy to welcome you here on this historical occasion. It is fitting that you should come to this city, the birthplace of American liberty, to rededicate the party of Thomas Jefferson to those principles of liberty and equality immortalized in the Declaration of Independence." Earle, speaking on behalf of those bonded to economic serfdom, declared, "We have political liberty in this great nation of ours, but until we have economic liberty we shall not have attained the great objectives of the founding fathers.... Chattel slavery was destroyed, but on its ashes there has arisen in our nation an even greater evil; wage slavery. Today there are great masses of our people who have even less liberty than the slave 100 years ago."

Earle denounced the romantic cover attached to the phrase "rugged individualism," and charged, "It is revolting to consider that these groups mask their selfish greed in such language while they destroy the liberty of the toiling masses of our people." The crowd applauded the Pennsylvania governor. "The worst enemies of capitalism are its so-called capitalists.... They are bent on the destruction of the nation because they are too-short sighted, too selfish to realize that the economic serfdom which they seek to perpetuate means inevitable economic decay."

The governor confessed, "Four years ago I was a Republican. All my life I had been a Republican. My grandfather was a Republican. My father, Thomas Earle, was the Vice Presidential candidate of the Liberal party out of which the Republican party grew. I left the Republican party because it no longer represented the principles and ideals of its founder, the immortal Abraham Lincoln. I left the Republican party because its leadership was controlled by the forces of predatory wealth.... In common with millions of other Republicans in this country, I followed the leadership of America's great progressives and gave my support to the Democratic party...."

The governor then told a folksy story. "One of Pennsylvania's old-time Republican bosses once laid down a rule of political action which perfectly illustrates the strategy of our opponents. He said, 'If you have a good candidate and a bad platform, stress the candidate and forget the platform; if you have a bad candidate and a good platform, forget the candidate and stress the platform; but if you have neither good platform nor good candidate, then wrap yourself in the Constitution and wave the American flag.'" The delegates laughed at this bit of political wisdom and its apparent connection to their Republican opponents.

Earle continued, "The Republican leadership has adopted as its slogan, 'Three long years.' They haven't been so long that our people have forgotten the state of the nation three years ago." He elicited cheers for his cleverness. "Three long years ago every bank in the United States was closed. Three long years ago hundreds of thousands of our self-respecting citizens stood in bread lines. Three long years ago farm riots spread like prairie fires through our great agricultural Midwest.... Three long years ago, our industry was prostrated, commerce was virtually stagnant. Three long years ago security markets were demoralized. Three long years ago more than 13 million of our population were unemployed. Three long years ago millions of our home owners, small business men, and farmers lost their properties through sheriff sales. Three long years ago our entire nation, economically and spiritually, was at the lowest ebb in history. Three long years, but why go on." The band played and the cheers rose in appreciation of Governor Earle's summary of the situation.

" 'Lest we forget,' forget the chaos and demoralization of Republican misrule and the little short of miraculous recovery that this nation has achieved under the leadership of that great humanitarian, that great American who picked up the torch from the trenches of despair and carried us over the top to recovery, Franklin Delano Roosevelt." The President's name set off another lengthy demonstration replete with bands and banners before the governor continued: "The Democratic party is our nation's main bulwark today against the advancing armies of big business fascism... it will have on its side the great liberals of both parties, and the millions of citizens of both parties who believe in fair play, in social justice, in the rights of labor, and in the ideals of human brotherhood embodied in our frame of government.

"Today," the governor concluded, "as never before in our history, we must fight to destroy those subversive influences which have seized control of the party of Abraham Lincoln and now are waging a war to the death for control of our government. If we do not, most surely they will destroy us all." Engulfed in applause, Governor Earle left the podium.

A few announcements followed, including that the next morning a Bryan Memorial Breakfast was scheduled at the Pennsylvania Athletic Club with Ambassador Josephus Daniels presiding. (Bryan, the party's three-time Presidential nominee and Woodrow Wilson's first Secretary of State, had died in 1925.) Then the call of the convention was read, including the recommendation that half of all delegates-at-large in state delegations be women. The official photograph was finally taken.

James Farley then announced that Senator Alben W. Barkley, of Kentucky, would serve as temporary chairman. Barkley, a favorite spellbinder who had been picked to deliver the keynote, spoke for most of an hour, but few of his Democratic listeners were wearied by his remarks. "We are assembled here, not merely to defend, but to proclaim the New Deal as the surest highway to that 'life, liberty, and the pursuit of happiness' to which Thomas Jefferson devoted his life and Franklin D. Roosevelt is consecrating every fiber of his immortal spirit."

"We come to this convention in the name of a Democracy which is national in its historic background, in its approach and willingness to deal in a national way with problems that are national in their scope. We recognize the complexity of modern life." He then outlined in detail the history of misery that accumulated as depression deadened the nation. ''The impact of the crash was so terrific and convulsive that through terror men cried out in the anguish of their souls at the loss of their life's savings and their economic independence. Industrial production had declined to 53 percent of normal, while industrial employment declined to 61 percent. The purring wheels of production were silent, and smokestacks were silhouetted against the heavens like monuments on a deserted battlefield.

"Led on by the sirens of speculative excess and the false signals flashed from the doors of the treasury and the executive mansion, millions of men and women found themselves stunned by the falling debris of worthless securities foisted on them by investment pirates. Archaic and unethical methods of business competition obtained illegitimate profits regardless of merit and strangled smaller units of production and distribution. Sweatshops, long hours, low wages, unwholesome working conditions, and the physical and mental degradation of children remained the crowning infamy of portions of American industry.... Three long years of Republican superiority found local charity and relief everywhere collapsing and millions of human beings were begging for bread, raiment, and shelter, and uncounted numbers of them found sleep only by the roadside or upon park benches, from which they crawled with the rising sun like dogs from a kennel."

Senator Barkley's sonorous voice kept his crowd in his grasp, "Three long years of normalcy, and they had wiped out half the values accumulated in this nation since Christopher Columbus and half the total income of the United States.... And then came Franklin Roosevelt." A frenzy overtook the delegates on the convention floor at the name of the man who had led them from the valley of despair. Then Barkley outlined the achievements of the New Deal. "There is not an American who does not know what happened then. Faith returned. Confidence revived. National courage rose like the sun at dawn.... While under Mr. Hoover more than 7,000 banks closed their doors permanently,... thus far in the good year of 1936, not a single national bank in the United States has closed its doors in the faces of the people." Then he recounted the decade-old trouble of falling farm prices. But Roosevelt's "Agricultural Adjustment Act was the fulfillment of a Democratic pledge to farmers of the nation... and the prices of farm products were increased, sometimes doubled and trebled, and more than three billion dollars was added to the annual income of agriculture."

Barkley's speech displayed a mastery of numbers and statistics outlining the rebounding economy. The Works Progress Administration (WPA) had employed 3.5 million, mostly from the relief rolls and built 30,000 "worthy projects of public need.... There has been no such volume of recovery in so short a time in the whole history of the world as occurred here in the first six months of 1933. It paused momentarily in 1934; but it has gone steadily upward with no sustained recession. It has included every form of human activity.... Farm prices, up 50 percent; factory pay roll, up 59 percent; industrial earnings, up 35 percent; bank deposits, up 33 percent; automobile production, up 30 percent; decline in commercial failures, down 66 percent.... But there are human values far beyond these figures....

"May I conclude with this quotation," Barkley rhetorically queried. "'No greater thing could come to our land today than a revival of the spirit of religion; a revival that would seep through the homes of the nation and stir the hearts of men and women of all faiths to a realization of their belief in God and their dedication to his will for themselves and for the world. I doubt if there is any problem, social, political, or economic, that would not melt before the fire of such a spiritual awakening.'" Then Senator Barkley concluded his keynote address, "The American people are not afraid to follow. They will follow the man who spoke those words. He is the present and the next President of the United States, Franklin Delano Roosevelt." A 15-minute demonstration followed Barkley's marathon speech and finally settled down at the approach of midnight. The convention then adjourned until noon the following day.

It wasn't until past one in the afternoon that the Democratic assembly started again. Returning delegates were blessed then entertained with glee club versions of "Dixie" and "Anchors Aweigh." Secretary of State Cordell Hull, moved, "That by a rising vote of thanks this convention convey to the eminent Senator from Kentucky its deep appreciation of the brilliant, inspiring, and statesman-like qualities of his address last night." His resolution was loudly and unanimously affirmed by the appreciative delegates.

The convention then adopted the rules of the House of Representatives to govern its deliberations. Paul V. McNutt, Governor of Indiana, called for a reading of the roll of states for committee positions, and that was done. Senator Robert F. Wagner, of New York, was appointed chairman of the Committee on Platform and Resolutions, on which Matthew H. McCloskey, Jr., of Pennsylvania, also sat. Eddie Dowling, of New York, chairman of the Stage and Screen Committee, then introduced Princess Lushanya Mobley, "an Indian girl from Oklahoma," who sang "By the Waters of the Minnetonka," while the Committee on Rules, the Committee on Credentials, the Committee on Permanent Organization, all were meeting in the convention hall building.

Dowling introduced several radio commentators, including Harry Hershfield, H. V. Kaltenborn, Gabriel Heatter, John B. Kennedy, Boake Carter, "one of the greatest of all," Lowell Thomas, and Bob Trout, "up in the control booth." Hershfield told a quick joke. "You know, I've been to many conventions, and listened to many speeches, and I have come to this conclusion: there are three sides to every story, his, yours, and the

Philadelphia Mayor S. Davis Wilson puts up convention decorations on Broad Street. Philadelphia's City Hall topped with the statue of William Penn is in the background. Associated Press. The Historical Society of Pennsylvania (HSP).

truth." The delegates laughed. Dowling next introduced several entertainers, including Major Bowes, a radio show talent scout, Bob Mack, who sang "Without a Song," and Miss Charlotte Ridley. Then he welcomed Hattie W. Caraway, of Arkansas, the second woman to serve in the United States Senate, who bowed. (Rebecca Felton, of Georgia, was first.) Dowling, was like a vaudeville master of ceremonies, calling out names and telling jokes, while elsewhere in the building the committees ground onward with their work.

Philadelphia had barely voted to retain Herbert Hoover in 1932. The Democratic party was surging back to prominence. John L. Kelly, the handsome former brickmaker and top-flight sculler was chairman of the recently revived Philadelphia Democratic Committee. He had narrowly lost in the last mayor's race but was building the foundation for the party that would control Philadelphia during the second half of the century. (His six-year-old daughter, Grace would become a dazzling star of the silver screen and Princess of Europe's small principality of Monaco.) Kelly noted that the Republican convention in Cleveland gave former-President Hoover a 15-minute ovation when he arrived, but a 32-minute salute when he left. Then he assured his Democratic friends that, "We are still going to win in a walk with Roosevelt." The convention listlessly recessed at 3:15 P.M., to reconvene that evening, Wednesday, June 24, 1936.

After a prayer by Reverend Doctor Ivan Murray Rose, and a rendition of "Happy Days Are Here Again," more songs were sung. Mrs. John Galleher, of Virginia, spoke to delegates about "the young people in the Democratic party.... I mean practically every young man and every young woman in this country." The featured speaker of the evening was Senate Majority Leader, Joseph Robinson, of Arkansas, the convention's permanent chairman. He too entertained delegates with statistics of the nation before and after Roosevelt. He catalogued the specific actions of Congress. "The Cleveland platform denounces the Democratic party for policies and measures which have been adopted during the Roosevelt administration for the promotion of national recovery. Many Republican members in both branches of the Congress, suggesting no substitute, voted for the passage of the legislation because they, as did Democratic members of Congress, recognized the extreme and unusual conditions which made extraordinary action imperative. This is true of the most important laws held unconstitutional by the Supreme Court, including the National Recovery Act, the agricultural adjustment law, and the Guffey coal measure."

Robinson then cut apart different sections of the opponent's platform. "The principal danger to the liberties, both of the individual and the masses, exists in the power of monopolies and trusts, which, under the last three Republican administrations, thrived and prospered with

146

respect to both production and distribution. Nothing significant to check them was done during any of the Republican administrations.... It is at once amusing and shocking to witness this pretended devotion to sacred causes by the delegates to the Cleveland covention, while they paraded and danced to the thrilling strains and inspiring sentiments of the Republican campaign song, 'Oh Susanna, Don't You Cry'." He was interrupted with applause and laughter.

Robinson concluded with a look at the candidate Roosevelt faced in November. "William Allen White, sponsor of the Republican candidate, Governor Landon, characterized his favorite in an article as 'the dumb, smiling enigma, who has America guessing.' That is not my characterization. It is the statement of the candidate's closest friend.... We advance to the battle of 1936 confident that the voters of this nation will not turn back to the defeated and disheartened leadership which abandoned them when the need for service, loyalty, and courage was the greatest ever known." A ten-minute demonstration followed Senator Robinson's remarks and then the second day's crowd emptied into the Philadelphia night. (But those staying at the Bellevue-Stratford, the Democratic headquarters, faced difficulties getting a late-night snack since all the employees were on strike.)

On Thursday morning, June 25, 1936, the Municipal Auditorium slowly stirred back to life. Amid the usual songs, the Credentials Committee reported back no disputes and their document was accepted by voice vote before adjourning. Delegates were back in their seats by nine that evening for the sixth session, with Permanent Chairman Joseph T. Robinson presiding. He reminded delegates to visit the Exposition of National Progress displayed in the Exhibition Hall next to the convention, the building where McKinley and T. Roosevelt were nominated in 1900. George Waverly Briggs, of Texas, invited delegates to participate in a celebration of the one hundredth anniversary of independence of the Lone Star State. "Upon this hallowed ground of Philadelphia, where the American Union was cradled, it is an appropriate gesture to the majestic figures of the heroic past for the representatives of the party of Jefferson and Jackson who are assembled here once more to confide its destiny to the superb guidance of Roosevelt and Garner."

His appeal was followed by another by Frank Wickhem, of South Dakota, pledging the support of the Young Democratic Clubs of America to the reelection of their leader. "I say to you that young people will never go back. We are going to go forward with Roosevelt. We are going to give him a bigger majority in '36 than we gave him in '32."

Congressman Arthur W. Mitchell, of Illinois, followed. "This administration came into power with the distinct understanding that the forgotten man should be remembered, and that government should function not only for the rich and powerful, but for the hungry and helpless. It was dedicated to the task of helping the underprivileged, in which group millions of American citizens find themselves today. No thinking American was surprised a few years ago when a former Republican Vice President went to the Republican President and from the coffers of our treasury received a so-called loan of $90 million for what was said to have been a defunct bank. This is the way the Republican party does things. That party always lends a listening, attentive, and sympathetic ear to the cries and the requests of the rich and the privileged; not so the Democratic party. It is the party of the common people and stands for a square deal for all the people."

Representative Mitchell continued: "One of the most startling events in the recent political life of this nation was an humble happening in the delta of Mississippi shortly after this administration came to power. Sylvester Harris, a Negro farmer, living near Columbus, Mississippi, in some way heard that this was a humanitarian administration, which had as a part of its program the lending of money to distressed homeowners. This poor Negro, unlettered, dressed in overalls, sold a cow from his farm, and with the price of the cow, called President Franklin Roosevelt at the White House, and said to him: 'I am about to lose my farm through foreclosure of a mortgage. I have no money with which to pay the mortgage. I understand that this government, through you, will help people in my condition. Will you not help me?' Within less than 30 days, money with which to pay this mortgage had been provided through the activities of the party, and this man was once more a happy farmer, a happy and contented husband and father, a satisfied and progressive American citizen, realizing in his heart that under the Democratic party, this is a government that reaches down and helps the forgotten man, the underprivileged citizen, be they white or black....

"There was a time when the late Frederick Douglass said 'that in as far as the Negro is concerned, the Republican party is the ship and all else is the sea.' That might have been true in his day, but certainly it is not true today. The Republican party may be the ship, but I say to you, the ship is on fire, and like the 'Morro Castle,' is burning to the water's edge. The safety of my people consists in taking a life belt and plunging into the sea. By so doing, there is hope through the renewed agencies of the Democratic party. The so-called generous attitude of the Republican party toward the Negro ended 30 years ago. The Grand Old Party long since divested from its ancient doctrine of human rights in quest of material prosperity."

When he concluded, Mitchell was roundly applauded. Then the chairman introduced the report of the Committee on Rules and Order of Business, offered by Senator Bennett (Champ) Clark, of Missouri, who called for a change in nominating procedure that had divided the 1932 convention. His committee had unanimously resolved, "That all questions, including the nomination of candidates for President of the United States of America and Vice President of the United States, shall be determined by a majority vote of the delegates to the convention, and the rule heretofore existing in Democratic conventions requiring a two-thirds vote in such cases is hereby specifically abrogated."

The two-thirds rule had caused many a fierce convention fight to nominate candidates that the Democratic party fully supported. As recently as the 1924 Democratic convention in New York City, the rule had forced 103 ballots to nominate John W. Davis. And the fight to abolish the two-thirds rule had almost cost Roosevelt his nomination in 1932. FDR was charged with trying to change the rules of the game while it was in progress. Senator Clark said, "There have been no suggestions of personality, Mr. Chairman, either present or past. None of the great men who in past years have been candidates for the Democratic nomination for President... could in any way be reflected upon by the action of this convention in subjecting Democratic procedure to the Jeffersonian principle of the rule of the majority.... Mr. Chairman... whatever reason there may have been for the two-thirds rule, in my judgement passed with the Civil War, and the two-thirds rule should have been abolished with the abolition of slavery." Now Roosevelt's effort was accepted enthusiastically by the body that came to renominate him. The Rules Committee also put a 20-minute limit on nominating speeches, 5 minutes on seconding speeches, and 30 minutes on floor debate on any issue.

Senator Robert F. Wagner, chairman of the Committee on Platform and Resolutions then stepped forward to read the 1936 positions of the Roosevelt Democracy. "We hold this truth self-evident, that the test of a representative government is its ability to promote the safety and happiness of the people," Wagner began. "We hold this truth to be self-evident, that 12 years of Republican leadership left our nation sorely stricken in body, mind, and spirit; and the last three years of Democratic leadership have put it back on the road to restored health and prosperity. We hold this truth self-evident, that 12 years of Republican surrender to the dictatorship of a privileged few have been supplanted by a Democratic leadership which has returned the people themselves to the places of authority, and has revived in them new faith and restored the hope which they had almost lost...."

Wagner continued, "We hold this truth to be self-evident, that government in a modern civilization has inescapable obligations to its citizens, among which are 1) Protection of the family and the home; 2) Establishment of a democracy of opportunity for all the people; 3) Aid to those overtaken by disaster. These obligations, neglected during 12 years of the old leadership, have once more been recognized by American government. Under the new leadership, they will never be neglected."

Wagner then elaborated points under each category. Democrats, he said, had safeguarded savings and investment; built the foundation for old age and social security through the Social Security Act; protected consumers; fostered rural electrification; saved more than two million homes from foreclosure and set up machinery to provide decent housing to people of meager means, and to provide just treatment for veterans.

The 1936 Democratic platform also proclaimed, "We have taken the farmers off the road to ruin" by reducing indebtedness and doubling the net income of farmers. It pledged to continue to improve soil conservation and domestic allotment programs; and to work for more farm cooperatives, and the retirement of submarginal land. Democrats under Roosevelt had also "given the army of America's industrial workers something more substantial than the Republicans' dinner pail full of promises. We have increased the worker's pay and shortened his hours; we have undertaken to put an end to the sweated labor of his wife and children; we have written into the law of the land his right to collective bargaining and self-organization free from the interferences of employers; we have provided the federal machinery for the peaceful settlement of labor disputes."

Democrats claimed equal progress for business. "We have taken the American businessman out of the red. We have saved his bank and given it a sounder foundation; we have extended credit; we have lowered interest rates; we have undertaken to free him from the ravages of cut-throat competition. The American businessman has been returned to the road to freedom and prosperity. We will keep him on that road."

But the platform was not generous to megabusiness. "Monopolies and the concentration of economic power, the creation of Republican rule and privilege, continue to be the master of the producer, and the exploiter of the consumer, and the enemy of the independent operator.... We pledge vigorously and fearlessly to enforce the criminal and civil provisions of the existing anti-trust laws, and to the extent that their effectiveness has been weakened by new corporate devices or judicial constructions, we propose by law to restore their efficacy in stamping out monopolistic practices and the concentration of economic power."

The 1936 Democratic platform declared, "We believe that unemployment is a national problem, and that it is an inescapable obligation of our government to meet it in a national way. Due to our stimulation of business, more than five million people have been reemployed; and we shall continue to maintain that the first objective of a program of economic security is maximum employment in private industry at adequate wages. Where business fails to supply such employment we believe that work at prevailing wages should be provided in cooperation with state and local governments on useful public projects, to the end that the national wealth may be increased, the skill and energy of the worker may be utilized, his morale maintained, and the unemployed assured the opportunity to earn the necessities of life."

Democrats also pledged to work within the constitutional limits of law, but to offer amendments to the Constitution in cases where problems needed to be solved. And they pledged "the immediate extension of the merit system of government promotion through the classified Civil Service." On the question of foreign policy, which would become the paramount concern of the nation by the time of the next convention, the 1936 platform asserted a "policy of the good neighbor" and settlement of all problems through peaceful means. "We shall continue to observe true neutrality in the disputes of others; to be prepared, resolutely to resist aggression against ourselves; to work for peace and to take the profits out of war; to guard ourselves against being drawn, by political commitments, international banking, or private trading, into any war which may develop anywhere." The party also promised to increase foreign trade, to seek to lower "tariff barriers, quotas, and embargoes which have been raised against our exports of agricultural and industrial products; but to continue as in the past to give adequate protection to our farmers and manufacturers against unfair competition or the dumping on our shores of commodities and goods produced abroad by cheap labor or subsidized by foreign governments."

Senator Wagner concluded, "The issue in this election is plain. The American people are called upon to choose between a Republican administration that has and would again regiment them in the service of privileged groups and a Democratic administration dedicated to the establishment of equal opportunity for all our people." Chairman Robinson called for the vote, and the 1936 Democratic platform was unanimously adopted by the large, cheering body of delegates.

Chairman Robinson next introduced Pennsylvania's first Democratic Senator in 60 years, Joseph F. Guffey, who proclaimed Saturday, June 27, 1936, as President Roosevelt Day. The proclamation was followed by a brief tribute to the deceased Senator from Florida, Duncan U. Fletcher. Then the delegates heard some encouraging words from Congressman Guy T. Helvering, of Kansas, who read a telegram from Sedgewick County, showing that over 1,000 Republicans had changed their party affiliation to join the Democratic party that spring. "In addition thereto, since the nomination of Governor Landon, of Kansas, in this one county alone, 101 changes of party affiliation from Republican to Democratic and 24 from Democratic to Republican." Helvering added, "Ladies and gentlemen, I wish to state that this is going on in every county in our state, and when November rolls around in the great column of Democratic states will be aligned the state wherein lives the candidate of Mr. Hearst and the Liberty League, but it will be on the Democratic side."

George Marshall followed that moment of levity with a resolution to extend suffrage to residents of the District of Columbia. The resolution passed on voice vote. Then the session concluded with resolutions thanking Albert Greenfield, John B. Kelly, S. Davis Wilson, and all the citizens of Philadelphia who had put the convention together. The sixth session adjourned at 11:30 that evening.

Friday, June 26, 1936, was dedicated to nominating speeches. Chairman Robinson gaveled the delegates to order at nearly one in the afternoon. After a prayer by Rabbi William H. Fineshriber, the call of the roll for nominations for President of the United States began. Alabama, the first state called, yielded to New York, home of President Roosevelt, and Judge John E. Mack, a lifelong friend of the President, advanced to the rostrum. "Mr. Chairman and delegates to the Democratic National Convention, we meet again," the judge who first nominated Roosevelt for New York governor and President bellowed. "Four years ago we met at a period of great concern, a period of depression and dissatisfaction, and a period of widespread alarm as to our farming and business prospects and the future of our country as a whole. At that time, the convention promised an earnest, sincere, and determined effort, under the leadership of a man whose courage was unquestioned, to bring about a recovery from the ills accentuated and increased by Republican uncertainty and instability.

"We now meet after three years of such effort. We meet to account for our stewardship, and to give to the people the man best calculated to succeed in carrying out and continuing the rehabilitation so quickly begun and so successfully carried out. I am here to nominate such a man. Probably because of my intimate knowledge of this man and his early history, I have been selected for the honor of presenting him to you," the New York judge continued. "We were raised as boys in adjoining towns, but with different horizons. My horizon was the Hudson Valley; his the universe. I was his senior in years. As a Democratic office holder, I presented his name as our candidate for state senator in 1910. Believing I knew him better than most of his constituents, I told them that this young man was ready to carry out the heritage of his birth, to give his time and his life for the benefit of his state and his country.

"His district was almost hopelessly Republican. With his usual perseverance and courage, he stumped it in the company of Dick Connell, a much older man, the Democratic candidate for Congress. Dick had been the perennial Democratic candidate in this Republican district. Whenever he came to a little old red country schoolhouse, he went in and made a speech on patriotism to the pupils and teacher, and he whispered to his younger co-candidate, 'You know, if I live long enough for these children to grow up, they will vote for me and in time elect me.' This vision grew into a reality in 1910 because the congressman and senator were both swept into office.

"From the beginning, our nominee, although coming from a distinguished family, fought the fight of the common people, and against the domination of the railroads, then at the height of their power. He opposed the influence of the financial interests in politics and in government. He showed a complete understanding of the farmers who had just come through a period of depression and farm foreclosures. He opposed the efforts of the Chamber of Commerce in his district to freeze out industries which paid their employees a living wage. He opposed the blacklist, secretly managed by manufacturers' associations."

The old judge beamed; "When this young man arrived in Albany, he found that a leader of his own party was about to send to Washington as United States Senator, a man definitely tied up with a powerful and selfish traction interest. He immediately took up the fight against this betrayal of the people's trust. He continued it with such determination and unflinching courage that the nomination was blocked and there was selected as United States Senator a lawyer and judge of unquestioned probity and integrity." Here, finally, the audience which had been intently interested in their leader's biography, burst into applause for his early idealism. "The triumphant reelection of our nominee in 1912 was proof of the confidence the people of his district had in him, and a recognition of his leadership in the state senate. It was also a demonstration of the fact that he represented not any particular interest, but the entire people.

"His service in the New York Legislature directed the attention of the nation to this young man. He was invited to become Assistant Secretary of the Navy by President Woodrow Wilson, a post formerly filled by his illustrious cousin. Here again were shown his determination and ability to get at the bottom of things. He familiarized himself with every detail of the navy. He covered and became familiar with the needs of every part of the country, and took an active part in the World War both here and in Europe.

"At San Francisco in 1920, his party recognized his fighting ability by nominating this young man for the office of Vice President. His brave fight and his noteworthy loyalty to his chief are now history. Outstanding above all in that campaign was his sportsmanship in defeat. 'He could take it.'" The convention agreed with an ovation.

"Then, in 1921, came the sudden affliction which seemed to all of us would forever remove this young man from pubic life. We did not know in those days that Providence was only preparing him for the greater work that the future had in store for him. I had not then studied Emerson's essay on 'Compensation.' No one can have full sympathy for the misfortunes of others until and unless he has suffered too. All of the suffering through which he has gone has broadened his heart, has given him a greater capacity for sympathy and understanding of human needs of all kinds. It prepared him for the stricken nation which was placed in his hands on the fourth of March, 1933. It prepared him for the emergency and radical surgery necessary to rid the body corporate of the disease which beset it. As early evidence of this sympathy, he undertook the assistance of crippled children that they might receive the benefit of greater efforts to make their lives a bit more happy and more complete.

"During all these years, the home life of this young man remained typically American. He lived in his home at Hyde Park. He managed the farm, happy with his trees and fields. Years ago he started soil conservation on the rough portions of his own farm by the planting of evergreens. It was one of the earliest examples of the proper use of land. He maintained the same friendly contact with his neighbors and with the people in his own home county, alive to their personal problems and to general local business affairs, content in the friendship of his Dutchess County friends.

"Happy in the knowledge that he was pulling his own weight in the boat, in 1928 he came back to public life in New York State, not because of any personal political ambition of his own, but solely in answer to the call of friendship. He came to 1932 with a background of four successful years as governor of the Empire State. Despite an opposition majority in the legislative body, his every nomination had been confirmed, and nearly every important proposition submitted by him was ultimately approved and put into legislative form. In his own state, as governor, he came to be known as the champion of the liberties of the plain people.

"In 1932, not only the Democratic party, but the entire country was on the lookout for a man of broad vision, one conscious that the prosperity of the United States depended upon the well-being of the entire people and not of any special class. It had at last become apparent that the great banking and financial and business interests had through mismanagement, lack of foresight, and lack of prudence brought the temple down upon their own heads." Here applause accompanied the judge's observation.

"When the crash came, neither the bankers, nor big business, nor the administration which had given them aid and comfort, had any workable suggestions for relief. It is true that some aid was extended to certain favored banks and institutions, but the chief wail we heard was 'prosperity was just around the corner.' The people had no confidence. Six thousand banks had failed. Bankruptcy was rampant throughout the land. The country, led by the Democratic party, turned to this young Galahad for relief, for aid, and for help.

"As a result, on March 4, 1933, there came to the City of Washington as chief executive of the United States, a man with this splendid background and thorough training, filled with relentless

154

Inside Philadelphia's Municipal Auditorium after FDR's unanimous renomination. Associated Press. The Historical Society of Pennsylvania (HSP).

determination to rejuvenate the nation, to break down special privilege, and to place this country on a permanently sound and stable footing. He surrounded himself in his cabinet with the most able and progressive representatives of the Union. He did not wait for prosperity to come around the corner. He knew that the best defense to depression was an attack. He saw that unless something was done at once starvation would soon face the United States. With the aid of his splendid cabinet, with the aid of the Democratic Congress, and with the aid of the forward-looking, country-loving, and far-sighted Progressives and Republicans, he proceeded to place this country on its feet."

Roosevelt's old friend was sincerely passionate in his delivery. "We have blazed a path to prosperity and security. Our faces are towards progress. We shall not turn back in this contest between greed and humanity." The convention was on its feet. "Our friendly enemies, friendly until the approaching election, cheerful until the approaching election, suddenly discovered that the nation is going to the dogs. Whence come these cries? Not from the farm owners and home owners whose properties have been saved from foreclosure." The delegates and spectators roared approval. "Not from the million and a half boys who have received employment in the CCC camps. Not from the millions who have received employment through the instrumentalities of relief and public works agencies. Not from the suffering farmers whose purchasing power is being restored." Again applause buoyed the New Yorker as he forged forward with his sketch of Roosevelt administration achievements.

"Not from the citizens of that vast section of the country where lives and property are being preserved by flood control." Judge Mack paused for more applause from those water border districts. "Nor from the millions now receiving electrical energy at a fair rate because of the effort of the T.V.A., the Federal Power Authority, and other instrumentalities of the government." Again cheers swelled in the auditorium. "Not from the millions whose future is assured by the Social Security Act. Not from the millions of depositors whose savings in banks are guaranteed by the Federal Deposit Insurance Corporation." The applause echoed again. "Not from the small merchants and shopkeepers. Not from those having investments providing moderate living incomes. Not from the millions of workers for whose benefit we have endeavored to ensure a living wage." The mighty applause redoubled.

"From where then arise the cries of anger and the vicious attacks? From those who themselves brought about the great depression. From the great financial interests whose high-powered salesmen induced foreign countries unnecessarily to plunge themselves into debt and unload their bonds on trusting American investors, bonds many of which are now in default and practically worthless. From the same great financial interests that pyramided company upon company for the purpose of rooking the financial public by watering down and cheating the consuming public by inflated prices." The convention cheered. "All of these great financial interests at the outset led in the acclaim for the courage of our leader and his splendid attempts to afford relief. Why this ungratefulness now? Why these complaints?

"Every American knows the answer. These classes of privilege have seen the handwriting on the wall. They know that under this administration the power and influences over government which their wealth had given them is now gone. They know, from the new laws supervising holding companies and regulating the sale of securities, from the Social Security Act, and from the new tax laws, along with a score of other measures, that the control of legislation has passed from their hands to the people themselves." The judge's wisdom appealed to the clapping auditorium. "The issue is now whether the people are going to retain that control of the process of government or whether they are going to turn it back to this same small group whose destructive abuse of their former power was responsible for all our troubles. We are ready for the issue. We have ended starvation, bread lines, and soup kitchens. And we have brought this country through the greatest depression ever known." The judge was wildly cheered.

"With increasing national income and increasing national prosperity, we are moving forward. The credit for all this improvement is due to our leader, his splendid cabinet, and the splendid Congress which backed him to the last ditch. He is willing to take responsibility. He fears not those who are dissatisfied, nor do we fear criticism. The great masses of the people of the United States are well aware of our condition in 1933, and our condition in 1936." He received more support.

"With our decks cleared for battle, with justice and right and progress with us, we are ready for more action under the inspirited leadership of that great American whose name I give you as your candidate for President, no longer a citizen merely of one state, but a son of all the 48 states, Franklin Delano Roosevelt." So great was the energy the old judge invoked in his partisan audience and so great was the pride that the social achievements of their nominee elicited in their hearts, that a 70-minute demonstration, which rung from the highest balcony to the platform, transformed the Municipal Auditorium into a house of bedlam. When the storm died down, Chairman Robinson, announced that this demonstration had broken the record of all previous convention demonstrations, (so far as he measured them), and also broke a primitive applause-o-meter set up to measure response.

Robinson then recognized a delegate from Alabama who made the first of many seconding speeches for FDR from every state in the Union. Governor Bib Graves added a little levity to an old metaphor, "When our party took over the car of state, it had slid off the road and was mired in the ditch. It was dark, without a light or a spark; the battery was dead. First of all, we put in a live battery. Immediately the lights came on and showed the way; the engine worked; the car got on the road and headed for home."

Mrs. Samuel White, of Arizona, proclaimed, "On behalf of the State of Arizona and on behalf of the pioneer women of the West, I am proud to second the nomination of Democracy's good Samaritan, Franklin D. Roosevelt." Senator Hattie W. Caraway, of Arkansas, said, "This man's high attributes of courage, vision, and sincere belief in the rights of the people to equal consideration in all things has been so clearly demonstrated from the day he declared a bank holiday, thus saving us from financial chaos, to this day...." Senator William G. McAdoo, of California, who had been a Presidential contender in the 1920s, introduced Mrs. Lucretia Del Valle Grady. She pointed out that the Sunshine State, "...in 1932 had a 400,000 Republican majority; and now California has a 500,000 Democratic lead."

Alva B. Adams, of Colorado, joked, "Mr. Landon is a neighbor of Colorado, and we think so much of him as a neighbor we are going to keep him as a neighbor and keep him in Kansas." Roosevelt's Attorney General, Homer Cummings, seconded Roosevelt for Connecticut: "When the history of this era is written, in the cool and contemplative days of a later period far removed from the animosities and misunderstandings of the present time, President Roosevelt will be more and more clearly revealed not only as a friend of human justice and progress, but as the protector and defender of our accredited form of government which, by his genius, he has vindicated." John Biggs, Jr., seconded the President for Delaware. N. G. Robertson, of Florida, noted, "This man, whose voice has captivated the world, this man who is a man of destiny, this man who stands out in every American heart, this man is to be our next President."

Marion H. Allen, of Georgia, said, "As a spokesman of the delegation from the youngest of the 13 original colonies, from the state that has never wavered in its loyalty and support of the Democratic party and its nominee; from the adopted home of that man who represents the ideals of Jefferson and Jackson and who is the ideal American... I have the honor and privilege to second the nomination of the most fearless, the most constructive, the most admired, and the most beloved American." Mrs. Frank D. Johnesse, of Idaho, said, "Under our American form of government, we now return to the voters for their verdict." Governor Henry Horner, noted, "We of Illinois did not wait for this convention to let the nation know the high regard in which we hold Franklin Roosevelt. The sentiment of Illinois was eloquently expressed at our recent primary, when 2,600,000 Illinois voters went to the polls to cast the greatest primary vote in the history of our state... for four more years of progress and recovery."

The permanent chairman then introduced Indiana Governor Paul V. McNutt, "that white-plumed knight of Democracy," who declared, "Indiana, once the battleground of the nation, but now a citadel of Democracy, is here to pledge that leader unfaltering loyalty and united support. Who opposes that leader? The socialists, the communists, the fascists, the reactionary Republicans, and that last infirmity of political minds, the Liberty League, taken together an unholy alliance of bourbons and bolsheviki, oppose him. That is one reason so many real Americans are for him. These political enemies are resorting to fake alarms in order to confuse the people." McNutt also provided the audience with a couplet they could use on the campaign trail, "Back on the rocks, with Landon and Knox."

Lieutenant Governor Nelson G. Kraschel, said, "Iowa is deeply indebted to Franklin Roosevelt for restoring hope to the hearts of our people." Senator George McGill, of Kansas, assured the auditorium and national radio listeners, "Let there be no fear, the great agricultural states of the Middle West, including, if you please, the State of Kansas, will not be misled, but throughout the upcoming campaign and at the election in November will be found marching and fighting under the banner of our great humanitarian President and notwithstanding bitter attacks at Belshazzar feasts under the guise of the Liberty League where none but multi-millionaires attend, and notwithstanding the attacks of bitter partisan critics, the American people will reward a faithful servant."

Kentucky Governor A. B. (Happy) Chandler, said, "In the name of the generation who lost its youth in 1917 because of a great war, and in the name of the generation who lost both youth and opportunity because of the Hoover panic, I appeal to the men and women of this convention and of the United States to remain steadfast in their faith and confidence in the man that we nominate today.... The story of the New Deal is the story of a miracle." From Louisiana came the second of Senator-elect Allen J. Ellender. F. Harold Dubord, of Maine, bellowed, "Let me say to you, my colleagues, at this time that in September the Pine Tree State, by a resounding Democratic victory, will send a clarion call of courage and prophecy to all America." Senator Millard "Glad" Tydings, of Maryland, added his voice to the rising roll of seconds for Roosevelt. Governor James M. Curley, of Massachusetts, counseled, "Fellow Democrats and friends of the radio audience, it is both fitting and proper that the Democracy should convene in Pennsylvania for the renomination of the present standard bearer. There is no section of America, with the possible exception of my own beloved Bay State, where freedom had its baptism of blood and where the courage to dare and die in the sacred name of liberty had its inception than in Pennsylvania."

Frank A. Picard, of Michigan, announced, "Michigan's nearly

five million of human beings appreciate the New Deal. Its thousands of automobile workers, the men in the shops as well as those meeting the customer, recognize what Franklin D. Roosevelt did for them, and gradually it is dawning upon the leaders of that great industry that the complexion of their balance sheets having changed from red to black is not due to the fickle waverings of the indicators on the wheels of chance. They are about to admit that this is the result of a matchless, systematic, definite plan under a severe but sympathetic administration that has made it possible for them to head the parade in the return to prosperity. In 1932 the automobile industry had no jobs for their own workmen; in 1936 they gave millions as an extra bonus to those workmen who are today employed."

The Honorable John Regan, of Minnesota, chimed in, "Minnesota, always a leader in progressive thought, feels it a great privilege to second the nomination of President Franklin D. Roosevelt. The liberal thought of the Northwest has found its greatest exponent in the warmth and leadership of his courageous human heart." Mrs. Anna Dickie Oleson, of Minnesota, was one of the few in this vast convention, to even mention the great issue which would soon confront the nation: Europe. "As we look toward Europe we see the people in the throes of fascism and communism. America is a free land. There is freedom of the press, freedom of speech, freedom of assemblage. A great new courage has come over the people. It is 'Forward with Roosevelt,' to the greatest era that America has ever known. On behalf of the women of the Northwest and the women of Minnesota, I rise to second the nomination of the greatest humanitarian and the greatest President since Lincoln; Franklin Delano Roosevelt."

Governor Hugh L. White, of Mississippi, spoke on behalf of "the greatest leader of our time." James P. Aylward, of Missouri, quoted poet Josiah Gilbert Holland, "A time like this requires strong minds, great hearts, true faith, and ready hands." Dr. T. J. B. Shanley, of Montana, laughed that in the West "even the opposition party will tell you that they haven't a chance." James C. Quigley, of Nebraska, was happy to second FDR because he was, "the first President since the days of Thomas Jefferson, who could see West of the Mississippi River."

By 5:30 Friday afternoon, the string of seconding speeches had wearied the delegates who were restless and hungry. So after Robert Roltner sang the new campaign song, "Go and Win With Roosevelt," and "Home on the Range" the convention recessed until 8:30 that evening and thousands of spectators went foraging on their own range.

At 9 P.M., June 26, 1936, Permanent Chairman Joseph T. Robinson banged the gavel again and slowly quieted the thousands of talking voices. After a prayer by Dr. Nathan R. Melhorn, the parade of seconding speeches continued with new energy. William S. Boyle, of

Nevada; James J. Powers, of New Hampshire; Mrs. Mary Norton, of New Jersey; Governor Clyde Tingley, of New Mexico; Senator Josiah Bailey, of North Carolina; Harry Lashkowitz, of North Dakota; Governor Martin L. Davey, of Ohio; Scott Ferris, of Oklahoma; Mrs. Nanny Wood Honeyman, of Oregon; Governor Herbert Henry Lehman, of New York; all made eloquent appeals to the auditorium and national audiences.

Mrs. Emma Guffey Miller, sister of Senator Guffey, spoke for Pennsylvania. "Fellow Democrats and independent Republicans. For 16 years I have watched the mental and spiritual growth of Franklin Roosevelt. In 1920, when women were enfranchised, I allied myself with the Democratic party.... As our Vice Presidential candidate that year we named Franklin Delano Roosevelt, and wherever he went during the campaign he was marked out by his radiant manhood, his thoughtfulness, his good humor, and his unfaltering courage in the face of an overwhelming opposition." Miller reviewed his career, his New Deal achievements, and the new opposition attacking him. She asked, "Who would change Franklin Roosevelt for the unknown and untried Republican candidate? Why, only the retreating remnants of a once proud party now captained by the embittered owner of a yellow press." (She referred to William Randolph Hearst.)

The seconding parade brought to the rostrum even more distinguished state and local Democratic politicians in celebration of their leader. Governor Theodore Francis Green, of Rhode Island; Governor Olin D. Johnston, of South Carolina; Governor Tom Berry, of South Dakota; Senator Kenneth McKellar, of Tennessee; Senator Tom Connally, of Texas; Utah's secretary of state, Dr. J. M. Schaffer; Cleon Perkins, head of the Young Democrats, of Vermont; Virginia's Speaker of the House of Delegates, Ashton Dovell; Roy B. Misener, of Washington; Senator M. M. Neeley, of West Virginia; Charles E. Broughton, of Wisconsin; and L. G. Flannery, of Wyoming.

Then came speeches from territories and districts: Frank Murphy, governor general of the Philippine Islands; Anthony J. Dimond, of Alaska; John Walsh, of the District of Columbia; William H. Heen, of Hawaii; F. Vall-Spinosa, of Puerto Rico; Mrs. L. O. Keen, of the Canal Zone; and Joseph Alexander, of the Virgin Islands.

The audience by now was anxious for action. The speeches had marched on past midnight. Finally, Tom Berry, of South Dakota, was recognized by the chair and moved "that the rules be suspended and the Honorable Franklin Delano Roosevelt be declared the nominee for President of the United States by acclamation." The chair called for the question and the vote and indeed Roosevelt was made the nominee, by wild acclamation that lasted another 30 minutes, until the convention adjourned at 12:55 A.M. and exhausted delegates poured into the streets of Philadelphia, headed for their hotel rooms.

The convention's fifth day, Saturday, June 27, 1936, started early, at 9:25 in the morning. After the prayer by Reverend Frank W. Ruth, of Bernville, Pennsylvania, and a rendition of another campaign song, "We're All For You," sung by Charles Gould, and a number of resolutions of affirmation to President Roosevelt, and thanks to the Permanent Chairman Robinson, party chair James A. Farley, and to others including the broadcasting systems, James Farley offered a brief tribute to Colonel Louis McHenry Howe, "a gallant warrior in a cause that is actuating us all. Four years ago he performed a great part in the labors that brought about the return of Democracy to our government. To his shrewd, untiring, and intelligent directing effort was due in no small degree the election of Franklin D. Roosevelt in 1932." The convention rose in a minute of silence in memory of Roosevelt's former political strategist. Appointments to the Democratic National Committee followed, including those of Pennsylvania Governor George H. Earle and Mrs. Emma Guffey Miller.

Then Senator James Byrnes, of South Carolina, approached the podium and said, "Mr. Chairman, I move that the rules be suspended and that the chairman be authorized to recognize delegates for the purpose of placing in nomination candidates for the Vice Presidency and for the purpose of seconding such nominations. The motion carried and Governor James V. Allred, of Texas, rose to renominate Vice President John Nance Garner, of Texas. "Already fitting tribute has been paid to our beloved President. It now becomes my high honor, my privilege, and pleasure to remind you of the life, the character, and the ability of one of the greatest Vice Presidents in our history.... Thirty-four years ago he was elected to Congress from a Texas district geographically bigger than the State of New York. Modern writers have correctly likened him to Lincoln.... He has lifted the dignity of the Vice President's office from a post, the principal duties of which were social and perfunctory, to one of transcendent importance in the administration. His ability, his uncanny judgment, his forthrightness, have made him an indispensable member of the cabinet, one though without portfolio. Unquestionably, he has been the President's right hand in much of the legislation and relationships with Congress. His sound horse sense, the general stability of his character, his service as Speaker and as Vice President has compelled the tribute of the nation. The country is now as proud of him as Texas has always been.... I am honored to present in nomination for the high office of Vice President of the United States, the name of our beloved John Nance Garner, of Texas." A ten-minute demonstration followed Governor Allred's oration.

After seconding speeches from Senator James F. Byrnes, of South Carolina, and Congressman John F. Carew, of New York, Pennsylvania's lieutenant governor, Thomas Kennedy, who was also secretary and treasurer of the United Mine Workers, saluted Garner and promised that "the great Keystone State of Pennsylvania will aid in the victory by turning in a substantial majority for the reelection of the Democratic ticket."

More seconding speeches came from Congressman Fred M. Vinson, of Kentucky; Senator Bennett (Champ) Clark, of Missouri; Miss Thelma Parkinson, of New Jersey; Mr. Emil Hurja, of Michigan; Congressman Wesley E. Disney, of Oklahoma; Clifford C. Anglim, of California; Miss Helen N. Hanson, of Maine; Miss Josephine Colgan, of Montana; William Stanley, of Maryland; Minter L. Wilson, of West Virginia; Mrs. Benjamin Ableman, of Delaware; former Senator J. Thomas Heflin, of Alabama; and Garner's protégé, Congressman Sam Rayburn, of Texas. Senator James F. Byrnes then approached the podium to "move that the rules be suspended, and that the Honorable John Nance Garner be nominated for Vice President by acclamation," which he was.

Final resolutions of appreciation to officers of the convention and the host city were extended. Albert M. Greenfield, chairman of the All-Philadelphia Citizens Committee, proclaimed, "Never since General Howe took possession of Philadelphia with his British Redcoats has Philadelphia surrendered so completely to an organized army as it has to you.... Our All-Philadelphia Citizens Committee, composed of both Republicans and Democrats, spared no effort to extend to you hospitality and entertainment.... Take with you when you leave a few adjectives that belong to Philadelphia: Philadelphia is snappy; Philadelphia is vigorous; Philadelphia is progressive, alive, enthusiastic; Philadelphia is up and coming; in short, Philadelphia is everything we mean in that grand word, 'American.' We bid you farewell as you go out into your formations to fight the good fight."

With all business taken care of, at 2:20 P.M., James A. Farley declared, "And it is now a pleasure for me to move that this convention do now adjourn sine die." Delegates and spectators filed out, only to reassemble that night at Franklin Field, the nearby, red-brick football stadium on the campus of the University of Pennsylvania that had been built in 1922 and hosted some great gridiron rivalries, for the official Vice Presidential and Presidential notification of nomination and acceptance speeches.

That evening, Chairman Farley called the excited gathering of nearly 100,000 supporters to order at 9:45 P.M. Lily Pons sang the "Star Spangled Banner" and Episcopal Bishop Tate led a prayer. Vice President Garner was officially notified of his nomination by Senator Pat Harrison, of Mississippi. The Vice President then gave his acceptance speech, declaring, "We are now, as it were, midway in our course. Great as are the things which have been accomplished to bring order out of chaos in which we found the country in March, 1933, much remains to be done.

There must be no return to the conceptions denominated by the old deal. And what do we mean by the old deal? We mean a political system which fosters an economic order giving special privilege to a few favored ones through the sacrifices of the many. By the New Deal we mean simply an adaptation of the laws of the country so that the greatest good will come to the greatest number...." When he completed his speech, the applause of the giant field filled with delegates and spectators rose in prolonged ovation.

President Roosevelt was notified of his nomination by the convention's Permanent Chairman Robinson. The President then addressed the huge throng, along with a national radio audience listening and news-reel cameras rolling. His voice was strong and clear, filled with the confidence that had rallied the nation during its darkest hour. "Senator Robinson, members of the Democratic convention, my friends here and in every community throughout the land. We meet at a time of great moment to the future of the nation, an occasion to be dedicated to the simple and sincere expression of an attitude toward problems, the determination of which will profoundly affect America.

"I come not only as the leader of a party, not only as a candidate for high office, but as one upon whom many critical hours have imposed and still impose a grave responsibility." The President was interrupted with enthusiastic applause. "For the sympathy, for the help and confidence with which Americans have sustained me in my task I am grateful. For their loyalty, I salute the members of our great party, in and out of official life in every part of the Union. I salute, too, those of other parties, especially those in the Congress who on so many occasions put partisanship aside. I thank the governors of the several states, their legislatures, their state and local officials who participated unselfishly and regardless of party in our efforts to achieve recovery and destroy abuses. Above all I thank the millions of Americans who have borne disaster bravely and have dared to smile through the storm." His audience cheered him on.

"America will not forget these recent years, will not forget that the rescue was not a mere party task, it was the concern of us all. In our strength we rose together, rallied our energies together, applied the old rules of common sense, and together survived. In those days we feared fear. That is why we fought fear. And today, my friends, we have won against the most dangerous of our foes. We have conquered fear." The field filled with cheers. "But I cannot, with candor, tell you that all is well with the world. Clouds of suspicion, tides of ill will and intolerance gather darkly in many places. In our own land we enjoy indeed a fullness of life greater than that of most nations. But the rush of modern civilization itself has raised for us new difficulties, new problems which must be solved if we are to preserve to the United States the political and economic freedom for which Washington and Jefferson planned and fought.

"Philadelphia is a good city in which to write American history. This is fitting ground on which to reaffirm the faith of our fathers; to pledge ourselves to restore to the people wider freedom; to give to 1936 as the founders gave to 1776, an American way of life." Roosevelt was stopped by loud waves of clapping. "That very word 'freedom' in itself and of necessity, suggests freedom from some restraining power. In 1776 we sought freedom from the tyranny of political autocracy; from the eighteenth-century royalists who held special privileges from the crown. It was to perpetuate their privilege that they governed without the consent of the governed; that they denied the right of free assembly and free speech; that they restricted the worship of God; that they put the average man's property and the average man's life in pawn to the mercenaries of dynastic power; that they regimented the people.

"And it was to win freedom from tyranny of political autocracy that the American Revolution was fought. That victory gave the business of governing into the hands of the average man who won the right with his neighbors to make and order his own destiny through his own government. Political tyranny was wiped out at Philadelphia on July 4, 1776." The audience stood to cheer their President and his affirmation of their freedom.

"Since that struggle, however, man's inventive genius released new forces in our land; forces which reordered the lives of our people. The age of machinery, of railroads, of steam and electricity; the telegraph and the radio; mass production, mass distribution; all of these combined to bring forward a new civilization and with it a new problem for those who would remain free. For out of this modern civilization economic royalists carved new dynasties. New kingdoms were built upon concentration of control over material things. Through new uses of corporations, banks, and securities, new machinery of industry and agriculture, of labor and capital, all undreamed of by the fathers, the whole structure of modern life was impressed into this royal service.

"There was no place among this royalty for our many thousands of small businessmen and merchants who sought to make a worthy use of the American system of initiative and profit. They were no more free than the worker or the farmer. Even honest and progressive-minded men of wealth, aware of their obligation to their generation, could never know just where they fitted into this dynastic scheme of things. It was natural, and, perhaps, human that the privileged princes of these new economic dynasties, thirsting for power, reached out for control over government itself. They created a new despotism and wrapped it in the robes of legal sanction. In its service new mercenaries sought to regiment the people, their labor and their properties. And as a result, the average man once more confronts the problem that faced the Minutemen." The President's remarks sparked more support from those who packed the outdoor stadium seats and the field itself.

"The hours men and women worked, the wages they received, the conditions of their labor; these had passed beyond the control of the people, and were imposed by this new industrial dictatorship. The savings of the average family, the capital of the small businessman, the investments set aside for old age, other people's money, these were tools which the new economic royalty used to dig itself in." More turmoil swept across Franklin Field. "Those who tilled the soil no longer reaped the rewards which were their right. The small measure of their gains was decreed by men in distant cities. Throughout the nation, opportunity was limited by monopoly. Individual initiative was crushed in the cogs of a great machine. The field open for free business was more and more restricted. Private enterprise became too private. It became privileged enterprise, not free enterprise.

"An old English judge once said, 'Neccesitous men are not free men.' Liberty requires opportunity to make a living, a living decent according to the standard of the time, a living which gives man not only enough to live by, but something to live for. For too many of us the political equality we once had won was meaningless in the face of economic inequality. A small group had concentrated into their own hands an almost complete control over other people's property, other people's money, other people's labor, other people's lives. For too many of us life was no longer free; liberty no longer real; men could no longer follow the pursuit of happiness.

"Against economic tyranny such as this, the citizen could only appeal to the organized power of government. The collapse of 1929 showed up the despotism for what it was. The election of 1932 was the people's mandate to end it. And under that mandate it is being ended." The President again paused before the chorus of support before continuing.

"The royalists of the economic order have conceded that political freedom was the business of the government, but they have maintained that economic slavery was nobody's business. They granted that the government could protect the citizen in his right to vote but they denied that the government could do anything to protect the citizen in his right to work and live. Today, my friends, we stand committed to the proposition that freedom is not a half-and-half affair. If the average citizen is guaranteed equal opportunity in the polling place, he must have equal opportunity in the market place.

"These economic royalists complain that we seek to overthrow the institutions of America. What they really complain of is that we seek to take away their power. Our allegiance to American institutions requires the overthrow of this kind of power. In vain they seek to hide behind the flag and the Constitution. In their blindness, they forget what the flag and the Constitution stand for. Now, as always, the flag and the Constitution stand for democracy, not tyranny; for freedom, not subjection; and against a dictatorship by mob rule and the over-privileged alike. . . . But the resolute enemy within our gates is ever ready to beat down our words unless in greater courage we will fight for them.

"For more than three years we have fought for them. This convention in every word and deed has pledged that fight will go on. The defeats and victories of these years have given to us as people a new understanding of our government and of ourselves. Never since the early days of the New England town meetings have the affairs of government been so widely discussed and so clearly appreciated. It has been brought home to us that the only effective guide for the safety of this most worldly of worlds is moral principle. We do not see faith, hope, and charity as unattainable ideals, but we use them as stout supports of a nation fighting the fight for freedom in a modern civilization.

"Faith, in the soundness of democracy in the midst of dictatorships. Hope, renewed because we know so well the progress we have made. Charity, in the true spirit of that grand old word. For charity literally translated from the original means love, the love that understands, that does not merely share the wealth of the giver, but in true sympathy and wisdom helps men understand themselves. We seek not merely to make government a mechanical implement, but to give it the vibrant personal character that is the embodiment of human charity.

". . . It is a sobering thing to be a servant of this great cause. We try in our daily work to remember that the cause belongs not to us but to the people. The standard is not in the hands of you and me alone. It is carried by America. We seek daily to profit from experience, to learn to do better as our task proceeds. Governments can err. Presidents do make mistakes, but the immortal Dante tells us that divine justice weighs the sins of the cold-blooded and the sins of the warm-hearted on different scales." Again the President received the applause of adulation. "Better the occasional faults of a government that lives in a spirit of charity than the consistent omissions of a government frozen in the ice of its own indifference.

"There is a mysterious cycle in human events. To some generations much is given. Of others, much is expected. This generation of Americans has a rendezvous with destiny. In this world of ours in other lands, there are some people who, in times past, have lived and fought for freedom, and seem to have grown too weary to carry on the fight. They have sold their heritage of freedom for the illusion of a living. They have yielded their democracy.

"I believe in my heart that only our success can stir their ancient hope. They begin to know that here, in America, we are waging a great war. It is not alone a war against want and destitution and economic demoralization. It is more than that. It is a war for the survival of democracy. We are fighting to save a great and precious form of government for ourselves and for the world. I accept the commission you have tendered me. I join with you. I am enlisted for the duration of the war."

As President Roosevelt concluded, the immense Franklin Field, named after a wise Philadelphia patriot, filled with an ovation so great that it split the darkness of the night and lit the way to an overwhelming victory in November. When five months later the popular vote was counted, Franklin Delano Roosevelt had garnered 27,757,333 votes, or 60.8 percent of the nation's active democracy, to Alfred Landon's 16,684,231, or 36.5 percent. In the Electoral College, the count was an astonishing 531 votes for FDR and only 8 for Landon. This time, Philadelphia gave the President a victory by a 209,876 vote margin. All of the city's congressional representatives were now Democrats, and Democrats grabbed control of both houses of the Pennsylvania legislature. Indeed, as its President had declared, America had a "rendezvous with destiny."

The 1940 Republican National Convention: "Miracle in Philadelphia"

Convention-at-a-Glance

Event: Twenty-Second Republican National Convention
Date: June 24-28, 1940
Location: Convention Hall, Thirty-fourth Street and Civic Center Boulevard
Philadelphia Mayor: Robert E. Lamberton, Republican
Philadelphia's Population: 1,931,334
Convention Permanent Chairman: Congressman Joseph W. Martin, Jr., Massachusetts
Number of Delegates: 1,000, plus 1,000 alternates
Number Needed to Nominate: A majority
Candidates for Nomination: Senator Styles Bridges, New Hampshire; Governor Harlan J. Bushfield, South Dakota; Thomas Edmund Dewey, New York; Frank Ernest Gannett, New York; Governor Arthur H. James, Pennsylvania; Hanford MacNider, of Iowa; Senator Charles Linza McNary, Oregon; Senator Robert Alphonso Taft, Ohio; Senator Arthur Hendrick Vandenberg, Michigan; Wendell Lewis Willkie, New York
Presidential Nominee: Wendell Lewis Willkie
Age at Nomination: 48
Number of Ballots: Six
Vice Presidential Nominee: Senator Charles Linza McNary, Oregon
Largest Audience: 17,000
Platform Positions: Attack on New Deal programs that injured business and industry, failed to end unemployment, and created dependency on government; attack on President Roosevelt's attempted usurpation of power from Congress and the Supreme Court; his arrogance in running for an unprecedented third term; his failure to militarily prepare the nation for defense and his attempt to rush the U.S. into the European war; opposition to involvement in foreign wars. "The Republican party stands for Americanism, preparedness, and peace."
Campaign Slogan: "Win With Willkie"
Campaign Song: "Heigh-ho, Heigh-ho. It's Back to Work We Go"

Wendell Lewis Willkie
1940 Republican Presidential
Nominee

1940

The 1940 Republican Convention: Miracle in Philadelphia

On Monday, June 24, 1940, at eleven o'clock in the morning, the Twenty-Second Republican National Convention, one of the most unpredictable in convention history, was called to order by John Hamilton, of Kansas, chairman of the Republican National Committee, who had been Presidential candidate Alf Landon's campaign manager in 1936. Delegates gathered in West Philadelphia in Convention Hall, the recently renamed Municipal Auditorium where President Roosevelt had been renominated for a second term four years before.

The gavel fell during one of the bleakest moments in world history. Earlier that spring, Hitler had invaded Denmark and Norway. In May 1940, the Nazis had overrun Belgium, Luxembourg, Holland, and France. A month before the delegates gathered, 350,000 British and French soldiers in full retreat were backed up to the English Channel where most made a daring escape at Dunkirk. The future of the world seemed to hang in the balance.

At the invitation of the chair, Clyde Barrie led 15,000 delegates and spectators at Convention Hall in an emotional rendition of "America" and Reverend Dr. Albert Joseph McCartney, of Washington, D. C., blessed the assembly. Then Philadelphia Mayor Robert E. Lamberton, a Republican, greeted his Republican brethren as they found their seats in Convention Hall decorated with red, white, and blue bunting. (Control of the city government during the Depression remained with the Republicans. Philadelphia's Republican mayor was a former sheriff who would die in office after 19 months of service.) The interior of the hall was designed with a sense of intimacy as delegates on the floor were surrounded by two tiers of Republican supporters. Lamberton said:

"We hope that all of the time you are here you will feel that you are among friends. We really want to be your friends. Philadelphia is known as the city of Brotherly Love, and from an experience of 50 years I can attest that the people of Philadelphia are friendly people. We have among our citizens persons of every race and every creed, but we live in a spirit of peaceful tolerance. No matter what our ancestry we are Americans first, last, and all of the time. And from a political view point, you will be among friends. Philadelphia has a Republican mayor and Pennsylvania has a Republican governor. This city has not elected a Democratic mayor within my memory and Pennsylvania in that time has elected a Democratic governor but once.

"You have returned to the city where the first national convention of the Republican party was held in 1856. The nation needed the Republican party then. The Republican party saved the Union. There are many of us who feel that the nation needs the Republican party even more today, in order that the American system of government may be saved. There is a heavy responsibility resting on your shoulders. May God give you strength and wisdom in your deliberations."

After the reading of the official call for the convention, Minnesota Governor Harold Edward Stassen, just 33 years old, was unanimously elected temporary chairman and took the gavel. Then committee appointments were made by the chair. The Committee on Credentials and the Committee on Rules and Order of Business were assigned meeting space at the grand Bellevue-Stratford Hotel on South Broad Street which served as the party's headquarters, while others met in Convention Hall. The proceedings were being covered by the three radio networks of the country and many local stations. Additionally, the 1940 Republican convention was the first ever televised to the nation. (TV was introduced to the public at the 1939 New York World's Fair.) Relatively few households owned a TV set and pictures were small and fuzzy, but NBC pioneered convention coverage with four cameras and broadcast events to 50,000 viewers in New York City, the Northeast, and as far West as Tulsa. Television cities were linked by coaxial cable. (The first gavel-to-gavel coverage of Presidential conventions took place in Chicago in 1952.)

With committee assignments completed, the convention adjourned early to start committee work. Then at 4:30 P.M., the delegates reconvened at Philadelphia's Independence Hall for an open-air "Americanism-Patriotism Session" and an address by National Chairman Hamilton. "I salute you on this spot sanctified by the wisdom of the founding fathers," the Kansas orator began. "One hundred and sixty-four years have passed since the symbol of freedom which rests here first sent its peals of liberty around the world. There was no cable then, no radio to flash its message to the far ends of the earth in a twinkle of an eye. But just as surely, it penetrated wherever, in any language, word was writ or spoken.

"Alas," Hamilton bellowed, "How the world today is being robbed of the truth taught by the men who created our Republic. Are we also, here in the land of democracy's birth, failing to uphold the principles that for a century-and-a-half enlightened the world and heartened mankind? The world is witnessing a terrible demonstration of how quickly the hard-won rights of man can be destroyed. We begin to see that we have been too complacent; we have felt too secure; taken too much for granted, both hard-earned liberties and the bounties of nature which we inherited.

"If we have not duly appreciated this matchless wealth, if we have given little thought to the possible loss of this rich heritage, we are today suffering a sudden and rude awakening. Individual liberty and opportunity are gone in much of the world; the rights of man, slowly built up over a thousand years, have vanished. But here and now the representatives of a great political force in the history of our country are gathered before this historic shrine, dedicated to the rule of law and the rights of man. These delegates and alternates 2,000 strong, from every section of the nation, meet to make free choice of a leader whom they intend to elevate to the Presidency by the free votes of American citizens. It is a privilege remaining to few peoples today.

"The action of our convention will be upon the high plane which holds that 'he serves his party best who serves the country best.' Our exercises here today are conducted under the title 'Americanism and Patriotism.' It is an inspiring combination. In the light of history, and in the spirit of the great convention which is enjoying the hospitality of this historic city, permit me to make our theme a natural trinity; Americanism, Patriotism, Republicanism." The delegates leaped to their feet and gave Hamilton and his message long and spirited support.

When the crowd settled, Hamilton continued. "This is the first time our Liberty Bell has ever been heard by the people of America from the Atlantic to the Pacific, from the Mexican border to Canada. It will be struck 13 times in honor of the 13 original states. The bell, which as you know is cracked [The breach occurred when it was first rung in Philadelphia. The crack was repaired and then cracked again when it was rung all day after the death of George Washington] will be tapped as it rests in Independence Hall with a special rubber mallet by Miss Margaretta Sergeant Duana, 11 years of age, a direct descendent of Benjamin Franklin. Present with us here are Mayor Lamberton, of Philadelphia, Mrs. Worthington Scranton, chairman of the women's division of the Philadelphia citizens committee for the Republican National Convention, and Mr. C. Brewster Rhoads, chairman of the Philadelphia citizens committee."

As the hallowed Liberty Bell struck its 13 tolls, the vast assemblage that filled Independence Plaza rose and stood with bowed heads. (The Bell would be next rung after the Normandy invasion in 1944.) Richard Crooks then sang "The Cradle of Freedom," before Mayor Lamberton again addressed the convention. "Ladies and gentlemen.... Here walked George Washington. Here walked Thomas Jefferson. Here walked Benjamin Franklin. On this spot in 1776 the Declaration of Independence was signed, that great document which declares that all men are created equal. On this spot in 1787 the convention met which drew up the immortal Constitution, the bulwark of our political and individual liberties. Here the Liberty Bell rang out in 1776 and here the Liberty Bell still stands, the Mecca of thousands of our people who come here each year to rededicate themselves to the American principles of government."

When the mayor completed his remarks, he introduced former Senator George Wharton Pepper, "the foremost citizen of Philadelphia today." (Pepper, a great barrister, had gone to the Senate in 1922 replacing Boies Penrose but was beaten in the Republican primary in 1926 by Philadelphia boss William S. Vare.) Pepper recounted the work of the founding fathers, and then tried to set the tone for the convention. "Had they failed, our representative democracy would not have been brought to birth. If we fail it cannot survive.... During those sessions rumors were current throughout the land that the convention would recommend to the people a monarchial form of government with a king at its head.... In those days people instinctively turned to Benjamin Franklin when they needed light on any subject. As soon therefore as the sage appeared upon the steps of this historic building, a woman... asked, 'Well, doctor, what have we got, a Republic or a monarch?' Listen Americans, all of you, to his reply: 'A Republic, if you can keep it.'

"For 144 years we did keep it a Republic, most of the time as a matter of course. Even during the World War, when all power centered for a while in Washington, we felt that no doubt when the war was over that power would revert automatically to the states and to the people. Within the last seven years, however, we have come to realize more clearly than ever before why wise old Dr. Franklin issued the solemn warning....

"During the past seven years we have seen at Washington a peace-time concentration of power almost as great as anything we have known in war, and this not as a momentary concession to a passing emergency but as a pattern of government seriously commended to us for all future time. We have watched an unprecedented development of executive power until the point has been reached at which it is scarcely an exaggeration to say that it is the President who must be asked if one wants to know what the Congress is going to do and what the Court is going to decide. We have seen the power of life and death over American enterprise lodged in the hands of men and women who not only themselves have never been elected to office but who would not dare to appear before any American electorate. We have watched the quenching of American business initiative. We have attended the funerals of once great and prosperous enterprises, and we have noted that outstanding among recent pieces of federal legislation is an extension of the Bankruptcy Act....

Pepper declared, "Have we allowed our Republic to slip from our grasp: is there still time to recapture and keep it? As I look into your faces I sense your answer: it is 'Yes,' spoken from the heart...." Then the former Senator reviewed the distressing situation in Europe. "What the implications of national defense may be no man can foresee. Aid to Great Britain and France, or to Great Britain alone, may easily prove to be not merely an office of friendship but a measure of self-preservation. The circumstance that war has been declared by Canada, our good friend and neighbor, against both Germany and Italy, makes it timely for us to reaffirm the Monroe Doctrine, and if necessary, to fight for its vindication.

"But whatever happens, we must be prepared; and adequate preparedness can be accomplished only by the Republican party. The failure of the Democratic administration in time of peace is a poor passport to public confidence in time of peril. That administration has poured out our money like water; we must not allow it to do the like with the blood of our sons...." As Pepper concluded, the crowd rose to its feet, applauding and waving American flags, hats, and state banners. Then Richard Crooks led the crowd in the enthusiastic rendition of "America," before a final benediction, led by the Right Reverend J. Carroll McCormick, D.D., Chancellor of the Archdiocese of Philadelphia. Then at 5:45 P.M., the convention was recessed for the second time.

The third session of the first day of the 1940 Republican National Convention reconvened at Convention Hall at 9:30 P.M. with every seat in the vast hall occupied. Dennis Cardinal Dougherty, Archbishop of Philadelphia gave another invocation. Then the Philadelphia Symphony Orchestra, under the direction of Victor Bey, played the "Ballad for Americans."

The keynote address that evening was delivered by the temporary chairman of the convention, Governor Harold E. Stassen, of Minnesota, the youngest man ever to give a keynote to a Republican convention. Stassen began his hour-and-a-half oration, "Our forefathers created here a great lighthouse of liberty. They showed a new way for men to live. At last men and women could stand erect. They were free; free to think for themselves, to speak, and to work, and to worship for themselves. Free to use their hands and their brains to build homes for themselves. And free to choose from among themselves their own rulers....

"Their task was well done. Let us strive to do as well in this our time of crisis. For once again the black shadow of despotism falls over the world. Fellow Republican delegates, even as we meet, lights are going out in Europe. Blackouts of dictatorships take the place of lighthouses of free men. It is our grave responsibility to keep burning brightly the light of liberty. If we meet the challenge before us, we will here nominate a man the people of these United States will make their President next November." Again applause punctuated his words.

Then Stassen turned his guns on President Roosevelt. "Our army chief of staff reports a tragic lack of preparedness for our own defense. All about us moves the discouraging evidence that we still have ten million unemployed men and women. A heavy blanket of $45 billions of indebtedness weighs down over all of our people. Back on the farms millions of rural families face their burdens with shrunken incomes....

"We need more than millions of men and women willing to spring to defense of the country," the Minnesota governor declared. "We need the physical and mechanical means of answering the challenge of those who seek to turn the great benefits of machine development into a mechanical Frankenstein of destruction. We must develop our air force to take its place beside the army and navy. We need large quantities of the most modern aeroplanes and anti-aircraft guns, the most modern ships, and coast defense.... We must be constantly alert in research and invention of the means of defense against new weapons of aggression...."

Then Stassen attacked the Democratic defense record. He charged, "During these seven years cruel acts of aggression occurred in rapid succession. With full knowledge of these dangerous developments what did our national leadership do to meet these threats?... We are too woefully weak to give the Allies that material assistance this nation wants to give them.... We can be thankful today that the overwhelming demand of the people drove him, begrudgingly, to turn some portions of the task over to tried and experience men of industry who gladly stepped forward to aid their country....

"The most dangerous example of the wrong way to prepare was the startling proposal of the President last week that all boys and girls in this country between the ages of 18 and 20 be compelled by the government to enter federal training camps. That was the method of Hitler, Mussolini, and Stalin. It is not the American way." Cries of "No, it is not!" resounded through Convention Hall. "Dare the nation continue for the next four years under such leadership?" Stassen was answered with shouts of "No, no." Stassen continued, "For too long a time we have talked boldly of quarantining aggressors in order to protect other nations and now find we are not even prepared to protect ourselves." A cry went up of, "That sure is true."

While Stassen didn't mention it, Republicans were also angered by Roosevelt's most immediate response to the war threat. Two days before the convention, FDR had pulled a political coup by appointing two of the party's luminaries to his cabinet. He made Republican internationalist, Henry L. Stimson, Secretary of War, and Chicago *Daily News* publisher Frank Knox, the Republican party's 1936 Vice Presidential candidate, Secretary of the Navy. Knox had been a Rough Rider with Teddy Roosevelt. Stimson had served as President Taft's Secretary of War and President Hoover's Secretary of State and was a critic of FDR. The GOP's hierarchy was livid at FDR and had virtually written Knox and Stimson out of the Republican party.

Stassen had another warning. "Our citizens also know that we must defend against the fifth column. They have heard and read the almost unbelievable stories of boring from within, of treachery, and of treason in one nation after another. They have seen how this fifth column of traitors within has joined hands with enemies from without, to cause the speedy downfall and ruthless destruction of sturdy little nations. They have observed how men have taken advantage of the liberties of democracy to aid in cutting out the very heart of freedom itself. We must prepare our defense against similar actions here, carefully and vigorously but without any ill-considered witch hunts.... First and foremost, there must be a determination that no one supporting communism, Naziism, or fascism should be permitted on the public payrolls of this nation." At this, delegates jumped to their feet cheering and waving American flags.

In fact, unbeknownst to Stassen and the Republicans gathered to hear him that night, the Nazi underground was active in Philadelphia. Months before the convention, the German Foreign Ministry had organized to influence the convention's outcome and insure the nomination of an isolationist candidate and platform to keep the U.S. out of the European war. Germany's charge d'affaires in Washington, Dr. Hans Thomsen, and master-spy George Sylvester Viereck, working under the cover of a Munich journalist in Washington, were coordinating the subversive effort.

Their propaganda blitz included a covert $3,000 effort to aid the unwitting isolationist congressman from New York, Hamilton Fish, Jr., grandson of President Ulysses S. Grant's Secretary of State, to bring 50 isolationist Congressmen to Philadelphia to influence the Committee on Resolutions which was writing the party's plank on European involvement. They also planned to support full-page advertisements in papers around the nation to arouse public opinion in favor of the appeasement plank. In fact, Fish signed a Tuesday, June 25th ad that ran in several papers across the country urging delegates to "Stop the March to War! Stop the Interventionists and Warmongers!"

At the rostrum, Stassen continued, "Second, we must encourage the great trade union movement manned as it is by loyal American citizens, to divest its organizations, in its own way, of all officers and organizers who are sympathetic to either fascism, communism, or Naziism." The crowd cheered Stassen again. "Third, we must unmask and expose those un-American organizations that are now parading under false fronts." Stassen charged through the cheers. "Fourth, we must proceed vigorously to seek out and punish by due process every violation of law committed by the fifth column."

Stassen attacked the Democratic response to the perceived internal threat. "Members of the Democratic party itself cried out against these subversive activities, only to find themselves derided and belittled from the highest places and to find directed at them a vicious purge, ruthlessly using all peace-time weapons of a powerful administration in endeavoring to line them up against the wall for political oblivion. No, the New Deal cannot lead our advance on this front."

Then Stassen moved his war-metaphored argument to questions of free enterprise. "For too long a time American enterprise has been subjected to the strafing of dive-bombing demagogues. To advance upon the domestic field we must unite our forces. The flames of industrial warfare, of strikes and lockouts and violence, have levied the staggering toll of 80 million days of labor in the past five years.... The New Deal has helped to stoke these flames of industrial warfare....

"We must recognize that government should furnish a cushion against the sharper fluctuations of this economic system, but it cannot successfully furnish a bed upon which society can go to sleep. We must recognize that we gain together and we lose together.... The inefficiency of our government is a travesty in a land that has developed such a magnificent efficiency in private endeavor.... To whom shall we entrust leadership on this front? Shall it be to those who have added almost 400,000 men and women to the public payrolls of their political army, but have added only a few thousand to the payrolls of our regular army?" The audience shouted back, "No, no!" Stassen added, "Or to those who tried to pack the Supreme Court of these United States?" Again, loud shouts of "No!" echoed through the hall.

"Have we been too harsh in our judgement? No, in fact, we have not even referred to the strong self-indictment of the obvious effort to break down one of our bulwarks of freedom by violating the third-term tradition. The saddest chapter of the last four years has been that the national administration, instead of keeping its eyes, statesmanlike, upon the welfare of the people of this nation, has turned its political gaze upon a third term. This un-American desire for a third term completely undermines their forthrightness in meeting all our issues...."

Stassen's voice rose as he reached his conclusion. "Fellow delegates. If we could reverse the magic of radio tonight, if we could turn the millions of radio receiving sets throughout this land into microphones, and if we could turn our microphones here in this great convention hall into a receiving set, we would hear an overwhelming message sweeping in on us. It would be a cry for a statesmanlike leadership to make America strong and our way of life secure. Shall we rise to meet this challenge?" The convention hall was filled with shouts of "Yes, yes!"

As Stassen stepped away from the microphone, delegates and alternates stood on their chairs to cheer and wave flags and throw their hats in the air. Then the convention adjourned at 11:26 P.M., delegates exhausted from a long first day. But the 1940 Republican party had a new confidence that at last it could defeat Franklin D. Roosevelt and regain its historic role of leadership.

On Tuesday, June 25, 1940, the Republicans reconvened at 11 A.M. with Temporary Chairman Stassen at the podium. After the morning prayer by Paul H. Andreen, Th.D., of Cokato, Minnesota, and the national anthem sung by Muriel Dickson of the Metropolitan Opera Company, Edward N. Barnard, of Michigan, reported that the Committee on Credentials had "sustained the ruling of the national committee in all respects" and presented the permanent roll of delegates. G. Mason Owlett, of Pennsylvania, read the report on Permanent Organization, which recommended Congressman Joseph W. Martin, Jr., of Massachusetts, as the convention's permanent chairman, along with Charles L. Brown, of Pennsylvania, as one of the vice presidents.

Congressman Martin was then escorted to the platform to deliver the morning address, which was scheduled to begin as soon as the convention was joined by the national radio audience. Martin, who had served from the fourteenth district in Massachusetts for 16 years, began his remarks as the permanent chairman, to prolonged applause.

"I shall try earnestly to perform the duties of the convention chairmanship in a way to justify your confidence." Then the chairman launched into his message. "We are here to rally all patriots in a crusade for Americanism. Our party is commanded by epochal events in the history of mankind to give vitality and power once more to the fundamental inspirations and traditions of our national life. Ours is the task to rescue our beloved America from the bogs of failure and futility. We are challenged to defend and preserve the basic values of life, liberty, and human freedom in a world paralyzed and broken by the ravages of dictatorship, hatred, and war....

"The founding fathers gathered in this city in a period of national crisis. So do we today assemble in Philadelphia in a period of grave national trial, indeed, a period of world crisis. The early patriots came here to form a nation. We come here today to protect and preserve that nation." Martin was interrupted by loud applause. "We have watched with anxious eyes the liberties and rights of ancient peoples vanish almost overnight. We have seen with heavy hearts our own nation, for seven years, drifting toward one-man government and national bankruptcy.

These twin evils were greatly feared by the founding fathers. They sought in every possible way in their deliberations in this very city to guard against them. All that is precious to us, all that makes life attractive and promising, personal liberty, equal rights, equal justice, constitutional government, these are in danger of being extinguished....

"All fifth columnists must be rooted out and thrown out. Trojan horses must be barred from our government. We must not permit political liberty to be used as a mask for plotters against the American system. The Constitution must not be used to destroy the Constitution.... We want an America at peace with the world; an America untainted by hatreds and fears. Following the paths of party tradition, the Republicans in Congress have consistently supported proposals to make the military and economic defenses of the nation adequate. As long ago as April, 1939, we appointed a special committee of House Republicans to study our national defense. The proposals of that committee were ignored by the administration. To provide an adequate defense at this time enormous sums of money must be spent. It will mean taxes which will reach painfully into every household in this land. Many of those taxes should not be necessary now. They would not be if the administration had not in the last few years failed in its responsibility to protect the savings and the substance of the American people....

"We have had seven years of blundering and contradictory policies. We have had a nightmare of experimentation and spending. We have had national planning without a plan. We have had managed economy with neither management nor economy. Vast sums of money, sums too vast to be comprehended by the human mind, have been scattered about with reckless abandon. Under the cloak of emergency and distress the American people have been ruinously exploited. Today the administration is bewildered by the effects of its own irresponsible conduct....

"Now what do we find after seven years of spending and promising? The depression continues. Demands for relief are greater than ever. Millions are still without jobs. If it were not for the war, business would be in the midst of a panic more severe than anything we ever had before. The public treasury is empty. The debt limit of $45 billions will soon be passed. Enormous taxes are in the offing. The record is a somber story of failure and futility and broken promises.

"And there is much reason to believe we may yet wake up to find we have been pushed into war. That is the record of the New Deal. That record will never be approved by the American people. They will repudiate it next November. America wants to get back to sanity, progress, and peace. Peace at home. Peace abroad."

When Martin stepped back from the rostrum to listen to the ovation, he smiled at the sea of waving flags. He was then presented a gavel by Judge Benjamin S. DeBoice, of Illinois. "This gavel is made from black walnut taken from the interior finish of the Edwards home in Springfield, Illinois, where Abraham Lincoln courted and married Mary Todd. The head of the gavel was a part of the staircase in that home and the wood has no doubt frequently felt the caress of Lincoln's hand...." Martin responded, "I am sure that the spirit of Lincoln will be the spirit of this convention...."

The Rules Committee then submitted its report, after which the convention recessed until 9 P.M. During that period, the Resolutions Committee continued to meet and struggle between the isolationists and interventionists views on how to position the party platform in response to the European war. Alf Landon served as chairman of the committee. He favored aid to Great Britain so it could better defend itself, but not U.S. participation in the war. Senator Henry Cabot Lodge, Jr., of Massachusetts, was leading the isolationist faction, as his father had led the fight against U.S. involvement in the League of Nations after the First World War.

Meanwhile, in the downtown hotels candidates and their supporters were lobbying delegates for support. No one had a majority yet. Thomas Edmund Dewey came into the convention as the leader, having won overwhelming victories in nine of the ten primaries in which his name appeared. He worked out of his suite of rooms at the Hotel Walton. The 38-year-old Dewey, always impeccably dressed, was the strong favorite going into the convention. His public popularity resulted from an impressive anti-racketeering and gang-busting record of prosecution as U.S. Attorney for the Southern District of New York. He had only narrowly lost the New York Governor's race in 1938. Dewey's strategy was to say as little as possible and keep his backers in line for an early knockout. He didn't take the recent boom for the political amateur Wendell Willkie very seriously. When asked if he would accept the second spot on the 1940 ticket, he glared at the reporter who dared to ask him about it, "I hope that question is totally academic." Dewey's advantage of youth and vigor in the primaries now was beginning to seem like a liability as the nation faced the uncertain threat of war.

Senator Robert Alphonso Taft, elected from Ohio in 1938 and leader of the party's conservative wing, had rented 102 rooms at the Benjamin Franklin. Taft, son of President William Howard Taft, had a long record of state political success before moving to Washington and was the favorite of the Republican organization and his fellow members of Congress. Political insiders and reporters thought he would be the victor if he could withstand Dewey's early charge. Beyond the Buckeye State, he had support in the party's "rotten boroughs" of the South, particularly in Texas. He was actively courting Pennsylvania's 72 votes which were committed to favorite son Governor James. Taft thought

Willkie had strength, but the strength of a demagogue, not a true Republican. As the champion of main street Republicans, he saw Willkie as a front for Wall Street and the powerful utilities. Taft had been loyal to Herbert Hoover, so he was optimistic that he could corner California's delegates after they were ceremonially cast for the former President. Taft expected to win on the fourth ballot. Hoover himself harbored hopes that the convention would turn to him when it deadlocked between Dewey, Taft, and Vandenberg.

Arthur Hendrick Vandenberg, of Michigan, had been in the U.S. Senate since 1928 and was a leader of the isolationist block of Republicans. He operated out of 48 rooms at the Adelphia. Senator Vandenberg, who had been an early favorite before Dewey knocked him out in the primaries, was also counting on a deadlock in this "completely free and open convention," and anticipated a sixth-ballot victory. Vandenberg and Dewey had conferred on ways to stop Willkie. But each was too vain to accept the second spot on the ticket in exchange for an alliance, even though Vandenberg assured Dewey he only wanted the office for one term and then would turn it over to his junior partner. Dewey turned aside the Senator's suggestion that they flip a coin to decide who would head the ticket. "Everybody is mad at everybody here except me," the Michigan Senator reasoned. He discounted a brokered convention. "The only smoke-filled room will be in Chicago, and the smoke will come from one long cigarette holder," he joked, referring to Roosevelt.

In contrast, the convention dark horse who was coming on strong in the stretch was Wendell Lewis Willkie, of New York. Willkie was the only one of the candidates who was not an isolationist. As was typical of his homespun style, he had reserved just two sixteenth-floor rooms at the Benjamin Franklin for his headquarters, and was staying with his wife in a friend's suite at the Warwick. His supporters were left to fend for themselves and were scattered about town. Willkie, 48 years old, was cocky and confident. The civil liberties lawyer's roots were in Indiana, but he had become nationally known for saving the Commonwealth and Southern Corporation, a utility company that had almost gone bankrupt in 1929. Willkie arrived in Philadelphia on Saturday afternoon without a campaign staff or fund. He jousted with reporters at the Thirtieth Street Station. "Ask me any damn thing in the world and I'll answer it," he dared them. "Nothing is off the record. So shoot." He insisted, "This is a wide open convention" and rashly predicted victory on the "fourth or fifth ballot." Few took him that seriously.

As late as May 8, Dewey led the Gallup Poll with 67 percent; Vandenberg scored just 14 percent, Taft 12 percent, and Willkie 3 percent. But by mid-June, once the Willkie boom had started, Dewey had fallen to 52 percent and Willkie had surged to second place with the public, scoring 17 percent. Willkie quipped, "I would like to think it means I'm a hell of a fellow. But I think it means I represent a trend or am ahead of a trend." That trend might be that Willkie was the only non-isolationist among the potential Republican nominees. By convention week, Dewey had slipped to 47 percent and Willkie had jumped to 29 percent, Taft and Vandenberg pulled only 8 percent, while former President Hoover was favored by 6 percent.

Oren Root's Willkie Club volunteers distributed tens of thousands of copies of Willkie's articles and editorials throughout the lobbies of Philadelphia hotels that became convention homes to the visiting delegates. Willkie was the talk of the town. *Time* magazine's June 24, 1940, issue had featured "The Story of Wendell Willkie." He smiled out from the cover of *U.S. News* and was topic one of the *Saturday Evening Post* June 22 issue, published right on Independence Square. Willkie also was endorsed by a number of influential newspapers, including the Scripps-Howard chain. Willkie even wrote an article for *Look* magazine, "Roosevelt Should Run in '40." He wanted to knock off the champ.

All four Presidential campaigns were frantically trying to persuade uncommitted delegates and those committed to favorite sons to support their candidates. All four candidates were confident that they could win, given the right scenario.

That evening, Convention Hall was packed when the permanent chairman called for the sergeant at arms to clear the aisles. Bishop John Andrew Gregg, of the African Methodist Episcopal Church in Kansas City, gave the invocation before the audience joined Margaret Speaks in singing "God Bless America." The evening's highlight was an address by former President Herbert Clark Hoover, who harbored vague hopes that he might be drafted by the convention. Hoover looked tanned and fit. The band played an enthusiastic rendition of "California Here I Come" as he stepped to the rostrum, accompanied by Pennsylvania Governor Arthur James and the former President's son, Allan.

Hoover's speech began with dramatic flair and drew great applause. "We are here faced with the task of saving America for free men. Two-thirds of the world has become the stamping ground of militant despotism.... Even in America our system of liberty has been weakened." But many delegates yelled, "Louder, louder," Hoover's microphone seemed muffled.

After describing the bleak situation overseas, the former President outlined for his party "seven stern tasks" that faced the nation. "First. We must restore and revitalize liberty in America. Second. We must restore and rebuild morals in government. Third. We must restore decent life and living to one-third of our farmers and workers, who have been chronically submerged by the New Deal. Fourth. We must restore competence to government. Fifth. We must prepare this nation to defend the Western Hemisphere. Sixth. We must develop and maintain foreign policies that keep us out of these wars unless we are attacked. We should facilitate all nations fighting for their freedom in procuring materials and munitions, but subject to definite limitations which keep us out of war. Seventh. We must recall our people from the flabbiness of the New Deal. We must reestablish stamina, character, and ideals. We must regenerate hope and confidence in America." He then launched into lengthy explanations of each of the tasks he had set out for the nation.

But with the defective microphone blunting his message many delegates paid scant attention and the calls of "louder" continued. President Hoover finally concluded, "The New Deal has contributed to sapping our stamina and making us soft. In quest of security we have retreated from liberty. In quest of reform we have abandoned justice and stirred class hate. In quest of relief we have injured self-reliance. In quest of an easy way out we have lessened the vision of America. The road of regeneration is burdensome and hard. It is straight and simple. It is a road paved with work and with sacrifice and consecration to the indefinable spirit that is America....

"If man is merely one of the herd, running with the pack, Stalin is right, Hitler is right, and God help us for our follies and our greeds, the New Deal is right. But if man is an inviolable human soul, possessed of dignity, endowed with unalienable rights, America is right. And this is a war that Americans dare not lose.... Republicans!" the former President shouted, "You go into battle for the greatest cause entrusted to the government of mankind. With steadfastness to these ideals, you can put this house in order. You can defend this nation. You can demonstrate that self-governing, free people can solve the problems imposed by the industrial revolution. You can restore employment and agriculture and end their sufferings. You can wipe out coercion and corruption. You can make this a classless country devoted to equality for all. You can build up humane measures of security, of increasing standards of living for all of the people. You can remove their fears. You can inspire their devotion to American ideals. You can, and you will, hold aloft to the confused world the lamp of liberty. Republicans! Are you prepared to fight?"

Their answer was loud and long cheering and flag waving, and even after several songs from the band, as Hoover took a final bow, the audience rose again in mass to loudly hail their former leader for an ovation lasting ten minutes. Then, at 11:05 P.M., Chairman Martin adjourned the session.

But after his speech, Hoover was disappointed and angry about the sound system and ordered pictures of the microphone from the convention's first day to compare with the one he had used. His backers charged, "It was deliberately rigged." Later, it was rumored that Willkie strategist Samuel F. Pryor, of Connecticut, who handled convention arrangements, had made a switch. Hoover's men might have been particularly sensitive to the tactic, since they had cut the microphone off from an opponent at the 1932 Chicago convention when they feared a sudden stampede for former President Calvin Coolidge to take over from Hoover who had been discredited by the economic crash. The 1940 switch might have been a retaliation, or perhaps it never occurred. In any case, Hoover had failed to sway the convention in the direction of his dark horse candidacy.

The convention's third day, Wednesday, June 26, 1940, was dedicated to adoption of the Republican platform and nominations for President. The morning session was devoted to announcements, and recessed early. But now the most dangerous moment for the convention and its delegates took place. Just before the evening session when nominations were scheduled to begin, Martin and Hamilton were informed by Pennsylvania state police and Philadelphia detectives that a terrorist plot to bomb Convention Hall had been uncovered. Evidently, a police infiltrator had already blunted one effort to place several homemade bombs in Convention Hall and busy hotel lobbies. No one knew for certain how many conspirators were lurking about ready to inflict deadly damage. Two bombs were defused before the evening session and two conspirators, Adolph Heller and Bernard Rush, were taken quietly into custody. Whether they had Nazi or some other connections was never learned. (The two conspirators were convicted in 1941 of possession of a bomb, but the case was later overturned and dropped for lack of evidence.) The police were uncertain whether others were on the loose, ready to attack that night or the next day. But Martin and Hamilton decided to keep the plot secret in order not to panic the convention. In a state of high alert, police guarded the grounds and the proceedings went on without public disruption.

That afternoon, when the delegates reconvened at 4:45 P.M. Herbert K. Hyde, of Oklahoma, read the report of the Committee on Resolutions. The 1940 Republican party platform began with a frontal attack on the Roosevelt Administration. "The New Deal administration has failed America. It has failed by seducing our people to become continuously dependent upon government, thus weakening their morale and quenching the traditional American spirit. It has failed by viciously attacking our industrial system and sapping its strength and vigor. It has failed by attempting to send Congress home during the world's most tragic hour, so that we might be eased into the war by word or deed during the absence of our elected representatives from Washington. It has failed by disclosing military details of our equipment to foreign powers over the protests by the heads of our armed defense. It has failed by ignoring the lessons of fact concerning modern, mechanized, armed defense. In these and countless other ways the New Deal administration has either deliberately deceived the American people or proved itself incompetent longer to handle the affairs of our government.

"The zero hour is here. America must prepare at once to defend our shores, our homes, our lives, and our most cherished ideals. To establish a first line of defense we must place in official positions men of faith who put America first and who are determined that her governmental and economic system be kept unimpaired. Our national defense must be so strong that no unfriendly power shall ever set foot on American soil. To assure this strength our national economy, the true basis of America's defense, must be free of unwarranted government interference. Only a strong and sufficiently prepared America can speak words of reassurance and hope to the liberty-loving peoples of the world."

On the issue of war, the 1940 platform further declared, "The Republican party is firmly opposed to involving this nation in foreign war. We are still suffering from the ill effects of the last World War, a war which cost us a $24 billion increase in our nation debt, billions of uncollectible foreign debt, and the complete upset of our economic system, in addition to the loss of human life and irreparable damage to the health of thousands of our boys.... The Republican party stands for Americanism, preparedness, and peace. We accordingly fasten upon the New Deal full responsibility for our unpreparedness and for the consequent danger of involvement in war." This is the plank that had caused so much committee wrangling; it had been resolved with ample ambiguity.

On the issue of employment, the 1940 Republicans asserted, "The New Deal's failure to solve the problem of unemployment and revive opportunity for our youth presents a major challenge to representative government and free enterprise. We propose to recreate opportunity for the youth of America and put our idle millions back to work in private industry, business, and agriculture. We propose to eliminate needless administrative restrictions, thus restoring lost motion to the wheels of individual enterprise."

The Republican platform also called for taking "waste, discrimination, and politics" out of relief programs. On Social Security, it favored "the extension of necessary old age benefits on an ear-marked pay-as-you-go basis to the extent that the revenues raised for this purpose will permit. And it called for continuation of unemployment compensation administered by the states "with a minimum of federal control." On the question of labor relations, the platform noted, "The Republican party has always protected the American worker. We shall maintain labor's right of free organization and collective bargaining." But it called for amending the National Labor Relations Act "in fairness to employers and all groups of employees so as to provide true freedom for, and orderliness in self-organization and collective bargaining."

On the question of agriculture, the 1940 Republicans declared, "We shall foster government refinancing, where necessary, of the heavy federal farm debt load through an agency segregated from cooperative credit.... We advocate a foreign trade policy which will end one-man tariff making, afford protection to farm products, regain our export market, and assure an American price level for the domestically consumed portion of our export crops." But the party also noted, "We are threatened by unfair competition in world markets and by the invasion of our home markets, especially by the products of state-controlled foreign economies. We believe in tariff protection for agriculture, labor, and industry as essential to our American standard of living.... We shall explore every possibility of reopening the channels of international trade through negotiations so conducted as to produce genuine reciprocity and expand our exports." And the GOP promised "adequate assistance to rural communities suffering disasters from flood, drought, and other natural causes."

On monetary issues, the Republican platform of 1940 argued, "The Congress should reclaim its constitutional powers over money and withdraw the President's arbitrary authority to manipulate the currency, establish bimetallism, issue irredeemable paper money, and debase gold and silver coinage." On taxation, it noted, "Public spending has trebled under the New Deal, while tax burdens have doubled.... We shall not use the taxing power as an instrument of punishment or to secure objectives not otherwise obtainable under existing law."

On the economic position of women, the 1940 Republicans asserted, "We favor submission by Congress to the states of an amendment to the Constitution providing equal rights for men and women." And the party further pledged, "that our American citizens of Negro descent shall be given a square deal in the economic and political life of this nation. Discrimination in the Civil Service, the army, navy, and all other branches of government must cease. To enjoy the full benefits of life, liberty, and the pursuit of happiness, universal suffrage must be made effective for the Negro citizen. Mob violence shocks the conscience of the nation and legislation to curb this evil should be enacted."

The Republican party also called for deportation of aliens "who seek to change by force or violence the American form of government." And it asserted, "Statehood is a logical aspiration for the people of Puerto Rico who were made citizens of the United States by Congress 1917." Republicans also opposed any censorship on radio. And the party condemned "the New Deal attempts to destroy the confidence of our people in private insurance institutions." Finally, the 1940 Republican platform said, "To insure against the overthrow of our American system of government, we favor an amendment to the Constitution providing that no person shall be President of the United States for more than two terms."

When Mr. Hyde finished his reading of the platform, he moved its adoption. His motion was seconded by C. Wayland "Curly" Brooks, the Republican Senate nominee from Illinois, who expressed some reservations. "We were shocked, as you were, at the knowledge and realization of the last few weeks that the march of mechanized monsters threatened liberty throughout the world.... Therefore we came with rather definite thoughts. We came with the thought that the voice of this convention to the people of America should be, above all, that we stand for America first, and for preparedness to defend this country against any and every form of attack. We have spoken rather bluntly out there in the Middle West when we said we believed in this tragic hour the blood of America, consisting of the blood of the nationalities of the people of the world who had learned to live in entire harmony with each other, that the blood of America belonged to America to the last drop and should not be shed in any foreign war." This idea received great applause in the hall.

Brooks continued, "We came prepared to write rather bluntly that thought. I yielded to the gentlemen of the Resolutions Committee, who showed me that even though they were not using that language, that the spirit of that thought, that the elasticity of our thinking, was indicated in this platform, and therefore I say the platform should be adopted unanimously, without a single objection, at this convention."

After Brooks finished, the platform was further seconded by two stringent isolationists, Senator Henry Cabot Lodge, Jr., of Massachusetts, Congressman Hamilton Fish, of New York, and by Earle T. Fiddler, of Puerto Rico, all of whom made brief statements of support. Then, as Brooks had recommended, the platform was unanimously adopted by voice vote.

Immediately after the platform's passage, Chairman Martin opened the floor to nominations for President and the call of roll of the states. But first he reminded them that nominating speeches were to be limited to 30 minutes. In the first Republican convention, and in the second that nominated Lincoln, nominating speeches had lasted no longer than a sentence or two. That tradition had yielded to one of elaborate oratory. When Alabama was called in 1940, it yielded to New York and John Lord O'Brian rose to nominate its favorite, Thomas E. Dewey.

"Fellow delegates, fellow Republicans, fellow Americans: Everything we in this country hold dear stands in peril today. Weakened and disunited, our country is confronted by a world in flames. Never have its problems been more serious. Never has the Republican party been faced with graver responsibilities. Upon the character of the leader we are about to select may depend not only the fate of our children but the very future of civilization." O'Brian was interrupted by a wave of applause.

"The leader whom I am about to nominate has for years identified himself with those deep, underlying moral forces which silently, but so powerfully, determine the course of our destiny. His leadership has been tested in the never-ending battle against the enemies of those moral forces. His courage and sound judgment have been proven by a record of high achievement. He is a leader who can unite the divergent interests of our citizens into one great common purpose. And, above all, he can be trusted to keep us out of war....

"Few realize what a dramatic epic his life has been and how consistently it embodies the great American tradition. His ancestors were among those dauntless men who landed at Salem, Massachusetts, in 1630. His grandfather was one of those who under the oaks at Jackson, Michigan, in 1854, founded the Republican party. The man himself was born in the small Michigan village of Owosso. There he spent the formative years of his life. In 1925, like many another youth coming in from the West before him, he began to practice law in New York City. Only six years later, at the age of 29, he became Chief Assistant United States Attorney for the Southern District of New York, in charge of a staff of 60 lawyers....

"His record in handling civil cases alone would have made him an outstanding public servant. But the duties of that office also brought him face to face with the most powerful and the numerous groups of organized criminals in the world. So far-reaching were their ramifications, so powerful were their alliances with corrupt officials, that prosecuting officers had long since despaired of convicting them. They had begun to regard these racketeers as all but immune to prosecution. But to this young man from Michigan every seemingly impossible undertaking was only one more challenge, and in the end, one more triumph." Here O'Brian was stopped by thunderous applause.

"So outstanding was his work that in 1933, when his chief resigned, the nine federal judges unanimously appointed him United States Attorney for the largest and most important federal district in the country. At 31 he was the youngest man who had ever held that powerful post. His success in administering the office is best attested by what followed. In the spring of 1935, in response to public protests and outcries of resentment against the inefficiency of the Tammany District Attorney for the County of New York, the governor was obliged to name a special prosecutor....

"June 24, 1935, marked the turning point in the history of the largest American city.... Boldly undertaking a task which skeptics viewed as impossible, he organized the forces for the defense of society.... What followed is history known to every citizen. It is a classic of American achievement. A city of nearly seven million people seemed powerless to deal with a veritable army of criminals. All of you remember the loan shark rackets, the policy rackets, the poultry and restaurant rackets, the infamous Luciano and his gang, the incredible brutes Lepke and Gurrah, who preyed on labor unions and employers alike, the unholy alliances between criminals and corrupt politicians like Tammany chieftain, Hines, dispenser of New Deal patronage.

"Everyone remembers the smashing prosecutions that brought relief and safety to the victims, small businessmen, and workers. These and hundreds of other prosecutions affected the affairs and the lives of thousands of people. This man's achievement as a prosecutor has been unequaled. More than that, this man's accomplishment has gone beyond the mere prosecution of wrong-doers. He has instituted a system under which prominent lawyers appear without fee to represent penniless defendants. He has brought about the reconstruction of thousands of old tenement houses that had been fire-traps. As a result of his work the people of New York have been saved from extortion by food racketeers to an amount estimated by the commissioner of markets at $50 million a year.

"For nine years he has been fighting against the forces of organized crime.... Step by step he broke their power. One by one he convicted their leaders, millionaire policy kings, common gangsters practicing methods of unheard-of torture and cruelty, dishonest and powerful political leaders, corrupt public officials, and finally faithless members of the judiciary. One by one he and his men brought them all down; not merely scores, but hundreds of them."

O'Brian then turned to Dewey's political record; how in 1938, he became the Republican party nominee for Governor of New York. "The odds against him were overwhelming. No Republican had been elected governor in 18 years. Only two years earlier, in 1936, the state had gone Democratic by more than a million votes. Yet he waged a vigorous campaign that won the admiration of the whole country. The New Deal's greatest orators, including the President himself, had to be rushed from Washington to stave off the threatened defeat of the entrenched Democratic machine. But the Republican candidate received more than 2,300,000 votes, more votes than New York State ever gave a Republican candidate for President. He carried every county in the state except Albany County and the City of New York. In a total vote of nearly five million, he came within 65,000 votes of winning. And 100,000 of those who voted against him were communists. His vote-getting ability restored the Republican party to top place of the ballot for the first time since 1922. And it will be there next November.... Make no mistake. If he cannot carry the State of New York, no other Republican can...."

O'Brian reached his crescendo. "Such a leader we offer you.... Here is a man who can make us a united nation. With earnestness and confidence we ask you to nominate as the Republican candidate for President, the nation's favorite son, Thomas E. Dewey, of New York."

O'Brian's speech set off a wild demonstration. The New York standard was paraded around the hall, followed by Michigan's and standards of a number of other states. Delegates held aloft large photographs and a six-foot tall painting of the mustached Dewey, others waved placards reading "Dewey for President," "Dewey Wins Votes," "Dewey Can Beat Roosevelt," "Tom Dewey is a Vote-Getter," and Dewey umbrellas were opened and twirled for all to see.

After a time, Chairman Martin called for order which eventually was restored. Dewey was then seconded by Dr. Lester H. Clee, of New Jersey, William E. King, of Illinois, Albert J. O'Melia, of Wisconsin, and Mrs. M. E. Norris, of Washington.

The roll call of states then continued with Arizona, which yielded to former Senator, now Congressman, James W. Wadsworth, of New York, who in 1920 had been among a small number of Senators who in the smoke-filled rooms 408-410 of the Blackstone Hotel in Chicago had hand-picked their colleague, Senator Warren G. Harding, to break a deadlocked convention to become the Republican nominee. This time Wadsworth stood up for another dark horse.

"No one will deny that the American people look to this convention with intense interest and concern," the former Senator began. "The ever-growing multitude, which understands the menace to our free institutions inherent in the New Deal and the menace to our national security arising from events abroad of which we are not the master, is looking to this convention, hoping and praying that its performance will be creditable.... The names of several men are under discussion in connection with this Presidential nomination. They are good men, all of them, men of honor and understanding, men of good records, entitled to our respect....

"Some of you may have learned of my adherence to a neighbor of mine in western New York, with whom I have been well acquainted for many years, and in whose character and abilities I have great confidence. His friends have asked me to place him in nomination. I do so gladly. For this Presidential nomination, I propose Frank Gannett." Gannett was the big spender among the 1940 candidates, having spent over half a million dollars from his own pocket. One lavish expense was the troupe of elephants marching in front of Convention Hall that evening.

"Like so many others who have risen to leadership in this country," Wadsworth continued, "Gannett was born on a farm. It was a hilltop farm in south-central New York. Frankly, it was a hard-scrabble farm and the family just managed to scrape along by the hardest kind of work. The youngest at the age of nine started earning pennies to help himself and his family. His first great objective was the obtaining of an education. To get it he had to work every step of the way clear through his graduation from Cornell University. Incidently, his ratings in scholarship upon graduation broke all previous records."

Wadsworth recounted highlights of Gannett's career; how upon graduation Cornell University's president took him to the Philippines as his private secretary in 1899; how after the insurrection was quelled, the new territorial governor and future President of the United States, William Howard Taft, had tried to retain him; how Gannett chose instead to work on an Ithaca, New York newspaper for $15 a week; how he struck out on his own and became owner and publisher of the third largest string of newspapers in the country. "His is a performance peculiar to America, the land of opportunity," Wadsworth extolled. "His papers, all of them, are clean and decent, and their policies sanely progressive.... It is not strange that a man with such a record of experience and success should take an active interest in public affairs. He has done so for years, and far more than the average businessman has studied the problems of government."

Wadsworth recalled how Gannett had responded to the request of the late Senator Borah to fight President Roosevelt's attempt to "pack" the Supreme Court. "With tremendous energy he put together a nationwide organization to fight the Supreme Court-packing bill. His messages of warning reached every nook and corner in the country.... Frank Gannett contributed most to the defeat of that bill." The audience loudly applauded his effort. When Wadsworth concluded, a demonstration of several minutes followed, before Gannett was seconded by Miss Adele Arbo, of California, John W. Evans, of Minnesota, Judge William M. McCrea, of Utah, and James H. Crummey, of Georgia.

Then the roll call of states picked up again with Arkansas, which yielded to Grove Patterson, of Ohio, publisher of the Toledo *Blade*, who put forth one of the two favorites for the nomination, Senator Robert Alphonso Taft, son of President William Howard Taft. "Ohio, mother of Presidents, brings to this convention a great American. He has a constructive program. He has knowledge and experience in international affairs. He has imagination and courage. He is an amazing vote-getter.... His program is built to turn back a tragic march toward an 'equalitarian destitution,' this barefooted crusade in which the New Deal is attempting to lead us all to a secure poverty. Millions of Americans who have been given government by sound, rather than sound government, can be pointed on the road to definite and permanent economic recovery only by policies in which they have faith, policies personified by a man to whom they can give utter confidence and full measure of devotion. Ohio presents this man.

"He is no newcomer to the stage of public affairs." Patterson's comment was aimed at Wendell Willkie who had never held public office. "He is 50 years old. Twenty years ago he was elected and re-elected to the Ohio legislature and to the house, to the speakership, to the state senate. In his mastery of the puzzle of taxation, his sensitive understanding of the workingman's problems, his comprehension of the economic need of the average man, his record remains today, distinguished in the annals of Ohio. With a genius for study, he has from youth given a painstaking devotion to political, economic, and social issues.

"When he became a candidate for the Presidency he held high, for all to see, against whatever darkness or confusion, his basic program. As to the policies which afflict America he strikes straight out at crackpot demagoguery, class warfare, the microphone promise of the millennium, the million-dollar-per-hour spending of your money, the primeless pump of the bottomless well, quack remedies for chronic ills, the concentration of power in a bureaucracy, the tank attack on business, and the experiment with a Russianized economic system. He describes the Russian economic system in a single sentence. It is a whole nation on WPA. Russia cannot distribute wealth. Russia can only distribute poverty.

"Constructively, he has presented his plan for abolishing the control of big and little business by bureaucratic commissions. Constructively, he has shown the nation how a billion dollars a year can be saved to the taxpayers by ending unwarranted spending. Constructively, he has planned subsidies for the American farmer which are not based upon the destruction of crops and livestock in a hungry world. Constructively, he has shown the nation how the WPA can be taken out of politics, and relief administered with economy, through local communities.... He is a man with a program. He stands for something.

Patterson then outlined Taft's international experience as counsel for the American Relief Administration "to bring economic and social order out of the chaos which followed the disaster of World War number one." Of the impending crisis in Europe, Patterson pointed out that Taft had "early advocated repeal of the arms embargo, because it favored aggressor nations against peaceful nations.... He held unswervingly to his principles while bitter opponents were attacking the neutrality bill. Seventy thousand letters came to his office, nearly all in opposition to his position. It was characteristic of his proverbial courage that he did not change his mind. Subsequent events proved him right. His program was, and his program today is, that of a man who knows his way abroad....

"If our candidate is not the best backslapper," Patterson joked, "he has the best backbone." The convention laughed. "He has the courage to be himself. He has not the art of the demagogue or the wiles of the trickster. But he has the brains to conceive, the mind to execute, and a heart that is unafraid. In the highest significance of the word, he is a statesman.... He insists that the public is entitled to his views on every public matter. He has never shunned a responsibility, never dodged an issue. With it all, he is a gentle and friendly man. Those who know him best are the most acutely aware of his warm, personal qualities, his never-failing kindliness and consideration for others, his simple family life, his devotion to wife and four sturdy sons....

"We say he is an amazing vote-getter.... The State of Ohio had been going Democratic. President Roosevelt carried it in 1936 by 600,000 votes. Just two years later came the campaign for a United States Senator.... All the ingenuity of the New Deal high command was centered upon retention of the Ohio seat in the Senate. What happened?... The more than 600,000 Roosevelt majority of only two years before had been turned into a majority of almost 200,000 for a man who opposed the Roosevelt policies and who had this amazing capacity to convince voters of the rightness of his own program.... Is he a voter-getter?" Delegates shouted back, "Yes."

"The American people have become desperately tired of crooning, of glamour unsupported by achievement, of defense pretense instead of defense preparation. They are ready for clear thinking, expression unafraid, honest conviction honestly expressed. Confronted by the bewildering problems of this day, there is no substitute for knowing what to do. In the storm and stress of life, there is no substitute for having the courage to do it. Our candidate, by natural habit and experience, faces hard facts with tranquility and without fear. He knows what to do and is not afraid.

"I have said that he is a gentle and a friendly person. He is more than that. He is what we call out our way, as common as an old shoe. Perhaps that is one of the main reasons we are so enthusiastically for him. That is the main reason we so genuinely love him. He is easy and approachable. His farm and city neighbors say he is the most unselfish man they know. He hates a high hat, literally and spiritually.... Because we are profoundly convinced that in this crisis the government needs, as it has not needed in our times, a realistic mind; because we are profoundly convinced that these times need the brave serenity, the almost divine imperturbability of the great emancipator, we plead for your confirmation of the leadership of one who possesses in such satisfying measure those qualities of mind and spirit which the hour so acutely demands.

"Fellow delegates..." Patterson passionately concluded, "Ohio, mother of Presidents, brings to this convention its distinguished son, a great American, Senator Robert A. Taft."

At the end of Patterson's comments the convention roared with wild celebration. Balloons were dropped from the rafters. The Ohio standard was marched around the hall, followed by those of many other states, along with large photographs of Senator Taft. Signs reading "Taft the Statesman," "Taft will Win," "As Ohio Goes so goes the Nation," "Out of the Wilderness with Taft," "Pick a Man who is big and strong, who knows what is right and won't do wrong, Bob Taft," "The Best Man for the Biggest Job, Bob Taft," and many others joined the parade through the aisles.

Congressman George H. Bender, from Cleveland, Ohio, shouted, "Three cheers for a winner," and the convention cheered three times. Then Bender yelled, "Three cheers for our next President," and again the convention joined him. The crowd called out, "We want Taft," "We want Taft."

When Chairman Martin attempted to restore order, the "We want Taft" cries resounded again and again on the floor. Whereupon R. B. Creager, of Texas, shouted, "Ladies and gentlemen of the convention. Will you please be quiet. Let us give the other fellow a chance, not that it will amount to anything, but let us give him a chance. Please sit down." Finally, enough calm was restored for Senator Warren R. Austin, of Vermont, to give a Taft seconding speech. He was followed by the seconding speeches of Mrs. A. G. Natwick, of Washington, Judge King Swope, of Kentucky, and Herman H. Langworthy, of Missouri.

The roll call of states resumed. California passed; Colorado passed; Connecticut passed; Delaware passed; Florida passed; Georgia passed; Idaho passed; Illinois passed. Then Mr. Bobbitt, of Indiana, introduced Congressman Charles A. Halleck of the Hoosier State. Halleck had been deluged with hate mail from isolationists and right-wing extremists since he had endorsed the candidate he was about to nominate. The 39-year-old Halleck took two shots of scotch, then charged onto the platform.

"Mr. Chairman, fellow delegates, men and women of America," he began. "This is a free and independent convention of a great political party. It is one convention in which the delegates are going to choose the candidate. It is representative government in action. It is proof that democracy is yet alive and efficient. If anyone were to ask me what job in this convention I would like best to have, I would choose the job I have right now. I would say, I want to place in nomination before this independent body the name of the next President of the United States, Wendell Lewis Willkie."

Halleck had defied tradition in uttering the nominee's name first. A strong chorus of "boos" rang out on the floor, but in an instant, the galleries surrounding the delegates on the floor responded with fury. The isolated cheers of "We want Willkie," that had been ignored on Monday and Tuesday, were amplified five thousand times. The "boos" were swallowed in the turbulent chant that rocked Convention Hall: "We want Willkie. We want Willkie. We want Willkie."

The same Samuel Pryor who was suspected of rigging Hoover's microphone, was in charge of accommodations and credentials. He had secretly distributed the bulk of gallery spectator tickets to members of the 2,000 Willkie for President Clubs that had spread across the nation during the last two months since Willkie had announced his availability. Until then, the tickets had been appropriately under the protection of Pinkerton guards. But the guards couldn't prevent Pryor from short-changing the Dewey and Taft supporters by half. Willkie enthusiasts even outnumbered backers of Pennsylvania's favorite son, Governor Arthur James. And the standing-room section at gate 23 had been opened to the capacity flood of Willkie boosters. (In 1860, fake tickets to the Second Republican National Convention had been given to Lincoln supporters who stampeded the convention for him.)

"I nominate Wendell Willkie because, better than any man I know, he can build this country back to prosperity," Halleck continued. "I nominate him because, better than any man I know, he can keep us out of war. As a veteran who served in France he knows the horror of war at first hand. He is against war. And he can scare these dictators by building the greatest defense system on earth. I nominate him because he is the strongest campaigner that the people of this country have seen in a generation. He can win next November. He has licked Franklin Roosevelt once. [Halleck referred to their fight over private utilities.] He can do it again.

"I nominate him because if he were elected he would make a President that his country would be proud of; because every one of you would be proud to say to your children and grandchildren, I helped to put that man in the White House. I nominate him because he understands business." [Willkie was president of the Commonwealth and Southern Corporation.] "He is one of the most successful managers in the country. Because he understands labor. He has 30 contracts with established unions, both A.F. of L. and C.I.O. Because he understands agriculture. He has worked on farms and he owns five in Indiana. He will pull these groups together. He will never make a deal, domestic or foreign, that will be unfair to any one of them."

Halleck continued, encouraged by the cheers that answered his rhetoric. "I nominate this man because he knows what an organization is; because, out of his own experience, he knows how to work with, through, and for an organization. I nominate him because he is a Republican who will stand by his party, win, lose, or draw. And in presenting this nomination I ask only one thing. I ask that this proposition be decided on its merits. That is the way I want it decided. That is the way my candidate wants it decided. And that is the way the people want it decided." Here the delegates applauded as one. "And let me tell you this from my candidate, from all his supporters, and from myself. Whoever

Wendell L. Willkie and his wife, Edith, inside Convention Hall after receiving the 1940 Republican Presidential Nomination. Acme Photos. The Historical Society of Pennsylvania (HSP).

you select to lead this party to victory next November, you will find us in there pitching to assure that victory.

"Back in Indiana where he was born, this man had a nickname. They called him 'Win' Willkie. Indiana had the right idea about him from the beginning. Put yourself back in that little old town of Elwood 48 years ago. There was a boom in natural gas. They had so much gas they never turned out the lights. Then the gas ran out and everybody in town went broke. Why, this man Willkie knew about public utilities before Franklin D. Roosevelt had hardly heard of Indiana. And I will say this: It will be better to have a public utility president than a President who has no public utility." The crowd roared with laughter.

"Win's father and mother were both lawyers. They loved books, they loved ideas, and they loved freedom. [His family had a library with nearly 7,000 volumes.] That is what they taught their children. Win is an Indiana boy. He went to Indiana University. He was admitted to the Indiana bar. He went to war from Indiana. And he married the librarian of Rushville, an Indiana girl. He got to work right early. When he was 11, he went into business with one of his older brothers. Later he harvested wheat in Minnesota. He dressed tools in the oil fields of Texas. He operated a cement-blocking machine in Wyoming. He ran a boom-town hotel in Colorado. And he bummed his way out to California in a freight car to pick vegetables. He is familiar with every region of the United States, mostly because he has worked there. He knows the land and its history. He learned history in Indiana. He taught history at a school in Kansas. And he made history in the valley of Tennessee. He knows the East Coast and the Alleghenies; the broad plains and the Rocky Mountains; the West Coast and the southern coast. He can see all that in his mind's eye. In all those areas he has been the friend of the people. Today he is hailed in all those areas by the people. And my proposition is that we put him to work for the people.

"As he says, he left Indiana because the competition got too tough. But I will tell you why he left. He left because of an irresistible urge to test himself against the toughest jobs that are to be found in this great enterprise that we call the United States. He left Indiana to face, time after time, the challenge of a free, hardworking, competitive system. He met that challenge at the bar. And you of Ohio can remember him as one of the most brilliant lawyers in Akron for more than ten years. [Willkie worked for Firestone Tire and Rubber Company.] He met that challenge in industry; and you of Georgia, of Michigan, of Ohio, of Indiana, of Illinois, of Pennsylvania, of South Carolina, of Alabama, of Mississippi, of Florida know him as one who has produced more electricity for less money than any major operator in the land. He met that challenge when he stood up almost alone against the New Deal on an issue involving the rights of all of us to do business, and won it. And he is meeting that challenge today by standing without compromise for the simple, homely principles of liberty.

"Mr. Chairman, and fellow delegates, in this day of trial, when we stand in doubt before the terrible events of Europe; when we stand in danger, our arms bound by the restrictions of a hostile government in Washington, our minds poisoned by political philosophies that we can only dread, I submit that this man who has thrust himself into every corner of American life, from the wheat fields to the skyscrapers of Manhattan, and from the Indiana bar to the committee rooms of Congress, that this man Wendell Willkie is the man we need for the defense and rehabilitation of our American life." Again loud cheers of "We want Willkie" filled the hall.

"The people of this country are worried and perplexed. They want the wheels of industry to turn, they want bigger farm incomes, they want a better break for labor, they want to give new opportunity to those who are now unemployed. Above all they want to defend this country from aggression. I submit, Mr. Chairman, that this is the man the people are looking for. If any man can do that job, Wendell Willkie can." The spectator galleries resumed their chant.

"I have heard it said, and we have all heard it said, that he is unavailable to our party because he is a business man. Worse, he has made a success of that business and himself. Are we to understand from this proposition, Mr. Chairman, that any man is barred from our deliberations who has been an American success?" Cries of "No!" answered Halleck.

"What should that Indiana boy have done when he accepted the challenges that came his way? Shall we say that a man must refuse to enter American industry in order to become a leader of this nation? Is that the stand the Republican party is prepared to take? Fellow delegates, that is New Deal propaganda. I have a boy 11 years old. He is ambitious. And some day I want him to make a contribution to his country. What path shall I tell my boy to follow? Shall I say to him: 'Son, if you want to get anywhere in this world for heaven's sake don't succeed in business. If you get an offer to head up a big industrial company, don't accept it! If you have a chance to increase our American standard of living by producing more goods for less cost, don't take that chance! Because if you do the Republican party won't accept you'?

"Or shall I say to that boy: 'I know a man born in Indiana just like you. His dad didn't have any more dough than I've got. He didn't have any better opportunity than you've got. But that fellow got a chance to run one of America's big enterprises. He took that chance. He succeeded at it. And I want you to do likewise.' You bet I am going to tell my boy that. I am not going to fill him full of New Deal propaganda. I am going to fill him full of the old fight.

"Let's look at the record. On January 1, 1933, this man I am giving you became the president of a business with assets of over a billion dollars, employing 25,000 men and women in ten states. This company was operating at a deficit. Its morale was low. On March 4, 1933, four months later, Franklin D. Roosevelt took office as President of the United States. Our country was also operating at a deficit. The national debt was $23 billion. Industry and agriculture were demoralized.

"Now what is the picture? Why, the enterprise entrusted to Franklin Roosevelt is worse off. The national debt is crossing $45 billion. We still have at least nine million unemployed; labor dissatisfied; business without hope; and the country unprepared for the international crisis facing it. But what happened to the job that America gave Willkie seven years ago? He hit it like a ton of bricks. The company is making a profit today. It has built new plants. It has expanded. It has cut its prices and raised its output. While Roosevelt was promising the more abundant life, Willkie was delivering it. He raised the standard of living of every school teacher, factory worker, and farmer on his lines. While Roosevelt was unbalancing an eight-billion-dollar budget, Willkie was helping to balance the $800 family budgets of his customers.

"I tell you that balancing those $800 budgets is the immediate goal of the Republican party. My man has helped to balance them in ten states. Let's let him try it in 48." Boisterous applause and cries echoed through the hall. "Or do you believe with the New Deal that there is no hope?" Halleck was answered with shouts of "No!" "Do you believe that the growth of this country is finished?" Again he heard the cries of "No!" "Do you believe that the family budgets can never be balanced, the family incomes never increased? If you believe these things don't nominate my man.

"For I tell you that this man is going to fight. He believes that this country will grow, that those budgets are going to be balanced and those incomes increased. If you nominate him, that is what he will fight for, and that will be a fight to tear a man's heart out! I am not kidding you. This is one of the serious moments in American history. We are not gathered here merely to confer a title of honor, or to distribute rewards. I say we are here to save this country from disintegration. We have gathered to assign the most stupendous job on the American record! We are not rewarding anybody. He whom we choose here will age more rapidly than we. He will never again enjoy life as he has enjoyed it in the past. The scars of the fight that lies ahead of him will be with him forever. The people of this country have risen up in overwhelming numbers to tell you this. They have risen up to tell you that they want this fighter, this man Willkie.

"How do I know this? Again, the record is my proof. A year ago a few personal friends began saying that this man ought to be President.

He turned them off with courteous and friendly gestures. Six months ago he was known as an occasional contributor to national magazines. Three months ago a few individuals who made no pretense at a knowledge of politics set out to see what they could do. And then, less than nine weeks ago, the first Willkie for President Club was started. And a great uprising of the people began! In less than nine weeks, by voluntary effort, without a political organization, and with no campaign fund, this man has been taken up by the people in every walk of life and in every corner of the land. And as one who believes in the democratic process and the Republican party, I am confident that you delegates will not ignore that demand.

"I have heard it said that we, the delegates to the Republican National Convention, would never nominate this man because he is too recently a Democrat. [Willkie was a delegate to the 1924 Democratic convention working for Al Smith over William Gibbs McAdoo who had Ku Klux Klan backing.] Is the Republican party a closed corporation? Do you have to be born in it? In 1936 my candidate became a Republican by conviction. He voted that year for the ticket that we nominated in Cleveland. In 1938 he demonstrated his conviction by enrolling in the Republican party. Mr. Chairman, we do not run the Republican party on the basis of seniority. Let it never be said that we bar from our deliberations a man who is one of us, a man who believes in us, a man in whom millions of our people, members of our party, already fervently believe....

"He can win because millions now enrolled in the Democratic party crave those blessings, denied to them by their own party. They will vote for Willkie. When this man appears before the country in a real campaign, the whole blessed nation will vote for him. I tell you we will have a Republican stampede." Scores of delegates and thousands of spectators exploded into loud cheers that lasted several minutes. "I know what I am talking about. I have been here in Philadelphia for two weeks riding in front of a tidal wave the like of which has never been known in national politics. I have felt the surge of the people beneath me.

"I have seen a vision. I see now as I have never seen before that a great battle has broken out upon the earth! It is a battle between slavery and freedom. We have talked about economic competition and industrial competition. But I see now a more desperate competition, a competition between two different ways of life; the totalitarian and the free. Fellow delegates, to win that competition we must be strong. Only the strong can be free. If Hitler can build a stronger system than ours, we shall lose that competition to Hitler. Our way of life will be liquidated. Already the New Deal, impotent to compete against the rising totalitarians, has made a move toward drafting the manhood and womanhood of this country. This is exactly the opposite direction from the one in which we ought to move. The only way we can compete against a competition is to make our own system work in its own way better than the competitor's system.

"This is my vision. Millions of people in this country have seen it, and millions more will follow. We, the people, want a man whose personal loyalty has met the test of thousands upon thousands to whom he has freely given it. But above all, we the people, want a strong man to defend our freedom; A man who can liberate us from the grip of depression; A man who can save us by building the greatest defense system in history; A man who can awaken our energies to create for us a new world. Mr. Chairman, I am just a young congressman from Indiana, but in six years I have seen them all. And when I stand in the presence of this man in this crisis I say to myself; 'There is a man big enough to be President of the United States: Wendell Lewis Willkie.'"

When Congressman Halleck completed his oration, pandemonium broke out. In the commotion, the Indiana standard led a parade of state standards as the deafening chant of "We want Willkie" thundered throughout the hall, repeated over and over, far surpassing the demonstrations that had been staged for Dewey and Taft. Willkie himself had planned no floor demonstration, just as he had no campaign manager and had raised no campaign funds. But a spontaneous demonstration began from the front where the Indiana delegation of his home state sat and spread through New Jersey and Connecticut. Their state standards were thrust into the air. Amid the confusion a fist fight flared up in the New York delegation between Syracuse Mayor Rolland B. Marvin, a recent Willkie convert, and a Dewey delegate from the Bronx, Frank Bruschi, as they struggled for the Empire State standard of Willkie's adopted home. Then another delegate from the Bronx tackled the mayor before delegation chairman, Judge William F. Bleakley, also a Dewey man, broke it up. The New York standard joined the wild march for Willkie. Not since the Rough Rider days of Theodore Roosevelt and the violent "ball bat" state conventions leading up to the Republican National Convention of 1912 in Chicago had such passion been exhibited by delegates and spectators.

But the delegates were not just being stampeded by the galleries. All week and until the end of the convention, the postal service and Western Union delivered a million letters and telegrams in favor of Willkie. The deluge was coordinated by the 2,000 Willkie Clubs that had been organized in two months by Oren Root, grandson of Teddy Roosevelt's Secretary of War and later State. The outpouring was unprecedented and the cumulative effect of this sudden outburst on the delegates and the national radio audience astounding.

When at last the permanent chairman pleaded for order, he was shouted down with even more fervent cries of "We want Willkie," "We want Willkie," "We want Willkie." Chairman Martin proclaimed, "The chair must remind the occupants of the galleries that they are guests of the convention. I trust as such they will not interfere with our program." "We want Willkie," "We want Willkie," they responded. Martin continued, "The chair must recognize delegates for seconding speeches. If you desire to hear them I suggest you come to order." "We want Willkie," "We want Willkie," the spectators responded. Martin said, "Those selected to make seconding speeches are entitled to be heard."

When finally a semblance of order descended, Congressman Bruce Barton, who represented the upper East Side of Manhattan in New York City, made the first seconding speech for Willkie. Barton began, "Perhaps I do not hear quite as well as I used to but I got the impression as I came up here that there were quite a goodly number of people in the Convention Hall who want to see Wendell Willkie nominated for President." Again the wave of applause swept the hall.

The former advertising executive observed, "For a good many years I have made my living in an occupation that depends in large part on the study and understanding of public opinion. I think I can differentiate between a created enthusiasm and one that is self-generated; between a sentiment that has been carefully let down from the top, and an instinctive liking that springs up from the bottom; between propaganda and the authentic voice of the people. And with these credentials, if they are worth anything, I think I understand what has happened in the springing up or creation of this spontaneous enthusiasm for Mr. Willkie." Now boos from the threatened campaigns of Dewey and Taft were heard against the chorus of Willkie cheers. "I do not mind the boos," said Barton who that month had broken from the Dewey forces. "You will be in the parade next January when he is inaugurated President." Applause and boos fought for dominance. "And if anyone else is nominated he will be there and you will too." At that, the entire convention united in applause.

Congressman Barton then pointed out, "I think this sudden and to me amazing interest in this man springs from two or three very simple factors. In the first place, people like his looks.... He has a big head, a big brain, a big body, a big smile, a big hearty laugh. He is just a genuine, likeable, companionable American. The second thing that I think has given Wendell Willkie this public interest is the fact that the people like to listen to him." He then recounted how Willkie had "made mincemeat" of the popular radio personality, New Dealer Robert Jackson, host of "Town Meeting of the Air." "I am wondering whether we have any other man in the Republican party who could turn a trick like that," Barton inquired. "I know this, he is not afraid of anybody, not even the radio champion of the world."

Barton's third reason was more serious, Willkie was popular "because the American people are greatly disturbed, and they have a right to be disturbed. Only those of you who have been in Washington within the last few weeks can have any idea of the chaos and confusion that exists there today. The capital of our country is a city that is afraid, terrifically afraid. The New Dealers, almost too late, have waked up to the fact that there is a new kind of war loose in the world, a war in which brave men are murdered before they ever have a chance to fight, murdered by planes, tanks, and so forth. The New Dealers are now realizing this, and it has almost stupefied them.... More than at any time in all our history the overwhelming need is for a man who can organize, coordinate, and administer." When Barton finished his seconding speech, Miss Ann Stuart, of Minnesota, and Connecticut Governor Raymond E. Baldwin followed. Thereupon, at 11:08 P.M., the convention recessed in a state of euphoria and consternation until Thursday morning.

The convention's fourth day, June 27, 1940, began at 10 A.M. when nominations for President continued. Verne Marshall, of Iowa, who was neither a delegate nor alternate, gained unanimous consent to nominate a man he thought could meet the European crisis, Hanford MacNider, of Iowa, "one of the greatest battle commanders in the history of American armed forces when he was in France 22 and 23 years ago." Marshall recounted MacNider's career which culminated as national commander of the American Legion. MacNider was seconded by Governor Frank F. Merriam, of California, Mrs. Fred P. Mann, Sr., of North Dakota, and Sherman Grindstaff, of Tennessee, who called him a national hero, a farmer, an industrialist, and life-long Republican (a swipe at Willkie).

When the roll call of states resumed with Michigan, Congressman Roy O. Woodruff, chairman of the House Republican caucus, placed into nomination Senator Arthur H. Vandenberg, of Michigan, who had been an early favorite before falling to Dewey in the primaries. "There has been too much talk here in Philadelphia this week about stopping this candidate or that candidate," Woodruff began, referring to the last minute panic about Willkie. "We seem to lose sight of the fact that the candidate we really have got to stop next November lives in Washington. And my man can do that job. And let me warn you and all the people of the United States that if next November you vote for the third term you may never vote again."

Then, having witnessed the enthusiasm shown toward Willkie, Woodruff cleverly asked that no demonstration be made during his speech "in view of the solemnity of this occasion, in view of the tragic conditions facing this country and world...." Nonetheless, his request drew applause. And he reiterated that whoever the nominee of the convention was, he "must become the next President of the United States. We owe it to the spirit of the Republic, yesterday, today, tomorrow!... The Liberty Bell must ring again."

Why nominate Vandenberg? he asked. "Every issue which we shall take to the country is personified and dramatized in his record. Indeed his record is substantially his party's platform. The country, in this campaign," Woodruff reasoned, "will look at the man rather than the platform. The man will be the platform. Therefore, we vastly simplify our approach to the popular conscience if, in the person of our nominee, we can point to deeds rather than mere words as the national reliance.

"Suppose the voter wants to know where we stand in respect to foreign contacts? Here is a nominee who has served 12 long years on the Senate Committee on Foreign Relations: who knows this desperate problem intimately in all of its developing jeopardies; who has spent a life-time defending George Washington's Farewell Address with its injunctions against alien entanglements and alliances; who believes that America must keep out of this war and out of any policies tending to pull us in, unless the war comes to our homeland or its essential outposts; who takes the Monroe Doctrine literally and insists that this western world shall survive as the impregnable citadel of republican institutions; who long since ceased to be an 'isolationist' in the sense that we can be immune to great events in this fore-shortened world, but who long since became an unchangeable 'insulationst' in the sense that we must think, speak, dream, hope, and plan for 'America first and America last' in dealing with the forces of disintegration and destruction which plague the victims of power politics in other lands.

"Suppose the voter wants to know where we stand in respect to the national defense? Here is a nominee who has lived through the congressional failures upon this score for the past seven years and knows at first hand the national need; who has preached preparedness for decades, not for war, unless war comes to our shores; who has supported every dollar sought for national defense in this emergency....

"Suppose the voter wants to know where we stand in respect to the dynastic danger of a third-term President in violation of every republican tradition upon which our free democracy rests? Here is a nominee who not only battles every inch of the way against the tragic notion that America has at last become a one-man country, but also who throws this whole burning question of the Presidential tenure into bold relief by asserting that America's 1940 need is a Republican chief executive prepledged to one term so that he and his party and the Jeffersonian allies may be wholly free of any incentive save the one, great, transcendent purpose to produce an all-American administration that will save the Republic. No other man can make this third-term issue quite so crystal clear.

"Suppose the voter wants to know where we stand in respect to American business and its release from the tyranny which has throttled progress and prosperity during these seven socialistic years? Here is a nominee who has fought the battles of free enterprise every inch of the way in the highest legislative forum of the land.... Suppose the voter wants to know where we stand in respect to economy in government and the need to save the American taxpayer from every needless drain upon his hard-pressed purse? Here is a nominee who has been the greatest, single economist in Congress....

"Suppose the voter wants to know where we stand in social vision? Here is a nominee who has drawn the sharp line between social-mindedness and socialism in a long legislative record which is as notable for its practical and constructive liberalism as for its fidelity to the great fundamentals of economic law. Social vision? He wrote the amendment to the Banking Act of 1933 under which Federal Bank Deposit Insurance was inaugurated in January, 1934.... Social vision? He led the battle which recently stripped the Social Security Act of its utterly indefensible reserve provisions which robbed its beneficiaries of many of their rights.... Social vision? He sponsored the Senate's inquiry into profit-sharing as a means for the larger and more equitable distribution of the fruits of labor among those who toil.

"Suppose the voters want to know where we stand in respect to tariff protection and the larger development of American markets? Here is a nominee who has been a faithful 'protectionist' all his life.... America's economic aspirations are written in his record.

"Ladies and gentlemen of the convention, here is the seasoned champion of every purpose to which the Republican party dedicates itself.... By instruction of the United Republicanism of Michigan and with the prayers of millions of our fellow countrymen from coast to coast, I invite you to the vanguard which shall lead to victory. I nominate United States Senator Arthur Hendrick Vandenberg for President of the United States."

Vandenberg's nomination sparked a modest but spirited demonstration. Then he was seconded by Thomas M. McCabe, of Minnesota, William L. Hutcheson, of Indiana, F. Henri Henriod, of Utah, and Jake F. Newell, of North Carolina.

When the roll call of states picked up once more with New Hampshire, one of its congressman, Foster Stearns, nominated its favorite son, Senator Styles Bridges, who had been left at age nine to support a farm and family, had worked his way through college milking cows, had become executive secretary of the State Farm Bureau Federation, and at age 36 had been elected New Hampshire's youngest governor, before balancing the state's budget, establishing a minimum wage, placing a maximum on working hours, and improving working conditions. "I submit that this is a record of intelligent liberalism," Stearns asserted. "It reflects a philosophy which recognizes that there are less fortunate people among us, and accepts the obligations to assist them. But it is also a philosophy that permits the free flow of the energies of the able, the development of initiative and self-reliance, a philosophy as durable and as elemental as the rocks of the Granite State."

In 1936, Bridges had avoided the New Deal rout to be elected to the United States Senate and had exposed corruption in the Democratic administration. Bridges was seconded by Worth Brown, of California, John Locke Green, of Virginia, Thomas J. Downs, of Illinois, and Senator George H. Moses, of New Hampshire.

Before the roll call of states continued, the great Hall of Fame pitcher, Walter Johnson, a convention delegate from Maryland, was introduced and photographed wearing a blue baseball cap, with Chairman Martin. Then Judge William A. Ekwall, of Oregon, nominated its favorite son, Senator Charles Linza McNary, whose "grandparents arrived in Oregon in 1845 in the typical covered wagon, from their former home in the State of Tennessee." Judge Ekwall noted that, "Charles L. McNary is typically a self-made man... educated in the public schools near his ranch home." He worked his way through Stanford University "not too proud to take what some would consider menial labor" and studied law. "His reputation for sound legal judgment brought him an appointment to the Supreme Court of the State of Oregon by a Democratic governor" and later appointment to fill out the term of Senator Harry Lane.

In 1918, McNary was first elected to a full term as U.S. Senator. During his 23 years of service, Senator McNary had risen to leadership in the Republican minority. Judge Ekwall called his judgment "universally respected because it is always mature and always progressive," a friend of labor and pioneer of farm legislation." And as a political strategist, the judge labeled him "second to none" whose "wise counsel had much to do with the defeat of the so-called Supreme Court packing bill several years ago." He was also credited as "a strong advocate of reclamation projects in the western states" because it meant work for migratory workers who had been driven from their homes in the dust bowl states. And the judge crowned him "perhaps the most beloved Senator of the present day." Senator McNary was seconded by E. C. Duncanson, of Minnesota.

Again the roll call of states resumed and Senator James J. Davis of Pennsylvania rose to nominate its favorite son, Governor Arthur H. James; governor of the second largest state in the Union. Son of an immigrant coal miner and a teacher, James had worked the anthracite mines as a nipper, brakeman, bratticeman, and mule driver, struggled for an education, and been elected district attorney, served as lieutenant governor, and was elected Superior Court Judge during the Roosevelt sweep of 1932, before receiving the largest majority ever for a Republican governor in 1938. "Arthur James speaks for the people because he is one of them," Senator Davis bellowed. "I present to you

Pennsylvania's native son, a man of courage and will, experience, pluck and skill, an administrator who understands government and freedom... the distinguished governor of the great state of Pennsylvania."

As the Senator stepped back from the rostrum, the Pennsylvania standard was raised on the floor and a procession of miners in overalls with miners' lamps in their caps mounted the platform and sang "Fight On, Pennsylvania." Delegates and local spectators took up the chant, "We want James," "We want James," "We want James." Then the governor was seconded by Frank C. Hilton, Andrew Hourigan, and Mrs. Worthington Scranton, a Republican national chairwoman, all of Pennsylvania.

Again the roll call of states rolled on and former U.S. Senator Gladys Pyle, of South Dakota, walked across the platform to nominate her governor, Harlan J. Bushfield. The pioneer in women's rights said, "We are a small state. Our delegation here is one of the smallest. But we have a large investment in the Republican party, and the Republican party in us.... What state was the spearhead of Republican renaissance in America in 1936? Yes, in 1936, a year of Democratic governors and congressmen. It was South Dakota.... Harlan J. Bushfield is the governor of South Dakota. He was the state chairman of the Republican party when this phenomenal victory in 1936 was won. His organizing ability in that campaign that he directed was conducted with the frugality of his Scotch ancestry, and ended without a deficit."

Bushfield himself was elected to head the state in 1938, and now stood as "an able member of the legal profession, 58 years old, a father and grandfather. He has always supported the principles of clean American manhood and womanhood, which produce fine American homes." She recommended him as the "candidate who would rid America of the political termites who are eating out the stability of our governmental foundations."

With the conclusion of the former Senator's speech, the nominations at last came to an end, and at 2:49 P.M., the convention was recessed. Then promptly at 4:30 P.M., June 27, 1940, the delegates reassembled to begin the balloting and the roll call of states for selection of a nominee for President began. This lasted over eight exhausting hours. At the end of the first ballot, with 1,000 delegates voting and a majority of 501 needed to secure victory, Thomas Dewey took the quick lead that he had predicted with 360 votes, but well below his claim of 400. Senator Taft surged into second place with 189 votes, but also below his prediction, followed by Willkie with 105; Vandenberg with 76; James with 74; Chairman Martin received 34, mostly from his home state of Massachusetts; MacNider also with 34; Gannett with 33; Bridges with 28; Senator Arthur Capper, of Kansas, (who had coauthored the Capper-Volstead Act that established Prohibition), 18; former President Hoover with 17; Bushfield with 9; and McNary with 13.

A protest in the Georgia delegation caused a delay during which its delegates were polled. All the while, the chorus of Willkie chants continued. Afterwards, Mr. George H. Moses, of New Hampshire, rose to protest, "Mr. Chairman, the delegates in this convention are unable to follow the proceedings. The confusion is so great that we do not know what is really being accomplished." Governor Dwight H. Green, of Illinois, called for help in allowing his delegates to find their seats. Chairman Martin banged away with his gavel and ordered the assistant sergeant at arms to clear the aisles. Mr. Moses again protested that delegates could not hear the proceedings because guests in the galleries were chanting so loudly and persistently, "We want Willkie," "We want Willkie" and so many people who had no right to be on the floor were in the aisles "buttonholing delegates."

The permanent chairman then declared, "No candidate having received a majority of the votes of the convention and therefore no nomination of a candidate for the Presidency having been made, the secretary will call the roll of the states for a second ballot." Again a chaotic count proceeded. Dewey had made a tactical error by not listening to his pollster's recommendation that he hold back a few votes so he could gain on each ballot. So on the second ballot, Dewey fell back to 338; Taft gained to 203; Willkie gained to 171; Vandenberg lost 3 votes to 73; former President Hoover gained to 21; Bridges faded to 9; Capper held at 18; Gannett recorded 30; James, 66; McNary, 10; MacNider, 34; Martin, 26; and New York Mayor LaGuardia polled 1. Again a dispute broke out in the Georgia delegation which required special polling of delegates. The secretary read the official tally and when he reached Willkie's 171, the galleries broke into loud and sustained applause. But Chairman Martin recessed the convention at 6:55 P.M. for dinner.

A frantic struggle to convince delegates to switch ensued. Dewey backers sought to convince Taft to take second place behind the New Yorker. But Taft counted on Dewey fading by the third ballot and neither candidate was willing to take a back seat. Connecticut Governor Raymond Baldwin had committed his delegates to Willkie. So had Massachusetts Governor Leverett Saltonstall, after it voted on the first ballots for its favorite son, the convention's Permanent Chairman Martin. Halleck, Kenneth Simpson, of New York, Baldwin, Saltonstall, and Wyoming Congressman Frank Horton were all working delegates for Willkie. Governor William H. Vanderbilt, of Rhode Island, abandoned Dewey for Willkie. Colorado Governor Ralph Carr turned from Vandenberg to Willkie. But several isolationist congressmen were actively working to overturn Willkie's bandwagon. Pennsylvania's 72 voters were under the control of Joseph Newton Pew, who had made his millions in oil, and they remained committed to Governor James.

At 8:30 p.m. on June 27, 1940, the delegates again gathered to resume balloting. Millions of Americans sat beside their radios listening to the dramatic political struggle. Dewey, Taft, Vandenberg, and Willkie all listened to the proceedings from their hotel headquarters, each talking on a bank of phones to their operatives at Convention Hall.

Again the proceedings were unruly, but at the end of the third ballot, the stalemate had not broken. Georgia again was polled. But disputes were breaking out in other delegations as well. Maryland and New York both demanded an official poll, while delegates shouted "Why waste time?" "Let us get along." Then Governor Saltonstall, changed the count of Massachusetts. The upshot at the end of three ballots, with 999 cast, was 1 for Bridges; Dewey fell back to 315; Gannett slid to 11; Hoover gained to 32; James slipped to 59; MacNider retreated to 28; Taft gained to 212; McNary held at 10; Vandenberg lost 1 vote to 72, and Willkie picked up steam with 259. The galleries were ecstatic.

Now hope was lost in the Dewey camp and the rebellion for Willkie in a number of delegations led Dewey' brain trust to tell their candidate to call it quits. But Dewey was not ready to give up. After the tally, Willkie joked to reporters, "Boys, I think I'm in." But his judgment was premature. The fourth ballot began with a frenzied rush on the floor to induce delegates to change their votes to support one of the leaders. But the favorite sons were holding onto their votes, either out of respect for their candidates or in hopes of a better deal as tensions rose. While he still had the lead, Dewey's floor managers contacted Taft's managers trying to work a deal. But Taft had Dewey where he wanted him and declined.

As the fourth ballot began, California passed, so did Illinois. Florida's vote was challenged, so was Oregon's. A California delegate called for a poll. Kentucky changed its tally. At the end of the fourth ballot, the total stood at Bridges 1; Dewey's support was collapsing at 250; Gannett faded to 4; Hoover lost to 31; James slid to 56; McNary dropped to 8; MacNider lost to 26; Taft gained momentum with 254; Vandenberg slipped to 61; while Willkie surged with 306; and 3 were absent. At the official announcement, the galleries were in a state of hysteria, relentlessly chanting their refrain, "We want Willkie."

Before the fifth ballot, in private phone conversations with Taft delegates, Willkie turned down their demands for a cabinet post and the Vice Presidency in exchange for more votes. Taft was trailing but coming on strong and Willkie heard rumors that Pennsylvania was about to go for the Ohio Senator. Willkie's optimism broke. He heard that a bitter Dewey was throwing his support to Taft. Willkie hung up the phone in his headquarters and turned to a confidant, saying, "Apparently Taft is going to be nominated on the next ballot and we have lost. It has been a grand fight and I would rather lose the nomination than win it by making any deal." But again, Willkie was premature in his judgment.

Chairman Martin called for order, but there was none to be had, and he ordered the fifth ballot. Before the voting began, Dewey had tried to make his way to the convention floor to urge support for Taft, but the count started before he arrived. Dewey's effort to get Hoover to support Taft failed as well. Amid the polling disorder, the secretary reached Kansas, and Alf Landon rose to switch all 18 of its ballots to Wendell Willkie and great cheering swept through the delirious galleries which felt the bandwagon breaking away for their candidate. Willkie who was ready to leave his headquarters out the back door sat down and listened.

But Kentucky countered, casting "her entire 22 votes for that lifelong Republican, Senator Bob Taft." Great applause on the floor greeted this none-too subtle slur against Willkie. Louisiana followed by casting all its 12 votes for Taft. But Robinson Verrill rose to throw 13 Maine votes to Willkie, which again set off the galleries. Then Michigan, North Carolina, Oregon, Washington, and Wisconsin, all passed while a frantic battle for their delegates was fought out among Taft and Willkie floor managers. Oklahoma cast 22 votes for Taft, but the tally was challenged, and in the end Willkie picked up 4 of the 22.

Then Nat Brown of Washington cast "16 votes for a real Republican, Robert Taft" to sustained floor applause. But Martin reprimanded him. "The chairman feels it is his duty to say to the delegate that characterizations of this kind are quite out of place here. This is a Republican convention, and all of the candidates before this body are Republican." And the galleries cheered for Willkie. Then an Iowa delegate called for a poll that yielded 2 for MacNider, 13 for Taft, and 7 for Willkie.

The fifth ballot total stood, with 998 voting, at just 57 for Dewey; Gannett, 1; Hoover, 20; James, 59; McNary, 9; MacNider, 4; Taft's votes swelled to 377; Vandenberg, 42; and Willkie took a commanding lead at 429 and his delegates and galleries created a furor with cries of "We want Willkie," "We want Willkie," "We want Willkie."

A sixth ballot immediately followed. California called for a poll that resulted in just 4 for Hoover, 22 for Taft, and 17 for Willkie. Connecticut cast all 16 of its votes for Willkie to great applause. Delaware followed with 6 for Willkie. Governor Green, of Illinois, threw 33 to Taft, 24 for Willkie, 1 for Dewey. Mr. Bobbitt, of Indiana, cast 23 for its native son, 5 for Taft. Among the five was the conservative former Senator James E. Watson. On the Saturday before the convention Willkie had run into him in the lobby of the Benjamin Franklin. Watson had served as President Taft's floor manager in the 1912 Chicago convention. He told Willkie, "You know Wendell that back in Indiana it's all right if the town whore joins the church, but they don't let her lead the choir on the first night." Willkie had laughed. Now he was laughing again.

Then Howard C. Lawrence, manager for Senator Vandenberg rose to applause full of anticipation. "Ladies and gentlemen of the convention: I would like just one moment of your time for the purpose of thanking those who stood so loyally in their support of Senator Vandenberg. In fairness to all of you I want to say that Senator Vandenberg has authorized me to release the Michigan delegation, and subject to that release the Michigan delegation has taken a poll. The chairman of the delegation has asked me to announce the result of that poll, as follows: For Hoover, 1; Taft, 2; Willkie, 35." The flood gates had broken open.

Chairman Martin responded, "Let us have quiet so we may proceed. The galleries will please act as guests and not interfere with the proceedings of the convention. The secretary will resume the roll call of the states on the sixth ballot."

Missouri cast 4 for Taft and 26 for Willkie who was edging toward victory. Then Mr. Bleakley, of New York, stood. "New York casts her 92 votes as follows: For Hoover, 1; Dewey, 6; Taft, 7; Willkie, 78." Again a madness swept the galleries. By the time Oregon was called, Senator McNary had released his delegates, and they cast all 10 for Willkie. Mr. Creager, of Texas, vainly sought to stop the Willkie bandwagon with 26 votes for Taft.

Finally, after a quick Pennsylvania caucus, former Senator David A. Reed took the microphone from Governor James who was still holding out and was greeted by a tremendous wave of cheers. The chairman banged his gavel for order, and then Pennsylvania cast its 72 votes for Wendell Willkie. (After the convention there were accusations within the Pennsylvania delegation that they had waited too long to make a difference and had thus squandered their leverage with the candidate.)

Governor Bricker, of Ohio, then rose to move "that the nomination of Wendell Willkie for President be made unanimous." The convention had worked its will with Willkie, but the chairman only allowed Ohio to change its 52 votes from Taft to Willkie, and the roll call was completed as states jumped on the bandwagon switching votes to the victor. Then the secretary read the revised results of the sixth and final ballot: For Willkie 998; absent 2, and a great demonstration followed in both the galleries and on the floor. Finally Governor Bricker was again recognized for his motion to make the nomination unanimous, and as the convention recessed at 1:57 A.M., one of the darkest dark horses since Lincoln or Garfield had been nominated as the Republican party candidate for President of the United States, in what was soon called the "Miracle in Philadelphia."

Willkie turned to his wife and associates and said, "I'm very, very appreciative, very humble, and very proud." He was also very tired but joked, "I guess the first thing I'll have to do is change my registration from Democrat to Republican." Then he waded into the mass of well wishers in the Benjamin Franklin lobby, before he retreated to the Warwick for a private party that lasted until nearly dawn.

On the fifth and final day of the convention, June 28, 1940, nominations for Vice President were presented, including one for Congressman Dewey Short, of Missouri, whom Homer B. Mann, of his home state, in seconding him said, wanted to "embalm and cremate the New Deal." But the delegates, learning of Wendell Lewis Willkie's desire to make Oregon Senator Charles Linza McNary his running mate, unanimously endorsed the senior Senator whose nomination was seconded by several of his Senate colleagues, including Arthur H. Vandenberg, Henry Cabot Lodge, Jr., and former Senator David A. Reed.

Then at 4:35 P.M., breaking with tradition, the Presidential nominee made an impromptu appearance at the convention to make a brief address. Franklin Delano Roosevelt had addressed the 1932 and 1936 Democratic conventions. Now Willkie made it a Republican tradition. Mr. and Mrs. Willkie strolled down the center aisle, the candidate waving and bowing to delegates as they walked up to the platform, escorted by former Governor Alf M. Landon, of Kansas, Russel Sprague, of New York, Governor Bricker, of Ohio, Howard C. Lawrence, of Michigan, and Governor Stassen, of Minnesota, who had served as Willkie's floor manager after delivering his keynote address. A torrent of cheers greeted him as the band played the new Walt Disney "Snow White and the Seven Dwarfs" tune that became Willkie's campaign song, "Heigh-ho, Heigh-ho. It's Back to Work We Go." When the entourage reached the platform, Willkie and his wife, Edith, were presented to the delegates by Chairman Martin.

A buoyant Willkie told them "that as your nominee I stand before you without a single pledge or promise or understanding of any kind except for the advancement of your cause and the preservation of American democracy." The tousle-haired Willkie exclaimed, "It is a moving and appealing and almost overwhelming thing to be the nominee of a great free convention of this kind.... I wanted to come here to you this afternoon not to discuss policies or principles, but merely to thank you and express my appreciation and tell you of the deep sense of dedication I feel to the cause you have asked me to lead. Democracy in our way of life is facing the most crucial test that it has ever faced in all its long history, and we meet not as Republicans alone, but as Americans, to dedicate ourselves to the preservation of the democratic way of life in the United States, because here stands the last firm, untouched foothold of freedom in all the world.

"And as your nominee I expect to conduct a crusading, aggressive, fighting campaign; to bring unity to America, to bring unity to labor, capital, and agriculture, and farmer and worker and all classes, to this great cause of preservation of freedom.... Only 48 days ago, I started out to preach to the American people the doctrine of unity, the doctrine of the destiny of America, and the fact that I am the nominee of this convention at this time proves conclusively how appealing these simple doctrines are to the American people. And so, you Republicans, I call upon you to join me, help me. The cause is great. We must win. We cannot fail if we stand together in one united fight." He added, "And now, I'm going to sleep for a week."

At his conclusion, Convention Hall resounded with cheers of the gathered multitude as Mr. and Mrs. Willkie made their way back down the center aisle, shaking hands and waving, the candidate bowing right and left, the cheering reaching a crescendo not even attained during the astounding hours of voting the previous evening. And at 4:55 P.M., John Hamilton, who had opened the convention, ordered that it adjourn.

The Willkie phenomenon represented one of the most exciting candidate victories in American history. Besides the considerable charisma of the man himself, who defied party labels and spoke from the natural appeal of homespun personality, Willkie's triumph was rooted in the world emergency of the moment. He alone among the major candidates was an internationalist at a time when America feared it could not turn its back on world affairs. Willkie also had the enthusiastic backing of important image makers at magazines like *Fortune, Time, Life*, and *Look*, who were attracted by his personal dynamism and shared his views on world affairs. Though he had no formal campaign or funding, persistent rumors held that the House of Morgan and other large corporate powers contributed freely to his spring drive to capture the nomination.

But above all, unlike Dewey, Willkie was natural and likeable, and his charm was reflected in his relentless rise in the polls all the way through campaign week. An unreleased Gallup Poll taken as the convention convened indicated that Willkie had overtaken Dewey by 44 to 29 percent, with Taft trailing far behind with just 13 percent. While George Gallup refused to release the results for fear he would be accused of trying to influence the convention's outcome, the results leaked out to the press and confirmed the Willkie boom with Republican voters for the delegates who made the decision. After the convention, Gallup called Willkie's charge to the nomination "the most astonishing" in the brief history of political polling. H. L. Mencken, the famed journalist who had attended almost every convention during the century, later proclaimed, "I am thoroughly convinced that the nomination of Willkie was managed by the Holy Ghost in person." But polling interviews with the Republican delegates later confirmed that at least half of those delegates who voted for Willkie had been directly influenced by their talks with the candidate before or during the convention. Another third of the delegates were persuaded to vote for him after the bombardment of mail and telegram support from voters around the nation. But an amazing 20 percent were swayed by the Willkie boosters in the balconies who kept the pressure on during the voting.

Willkie's extraordinary luck did not extend to election day, however. He may have surprised the big names of the Republican party, but he was not able to topple the incumbent President, a master politician who had held the hearts of the majority of the American people during the darkest days of the Depression.

FDR called Willkie the toughest opponent of his long political career. "He's grassroots stuff.... The people like him very much. His sincerity comes through with terrific impact," the President told reporter Walter Winchell. But Roosevelt had a simple strategy that worked perfectly. "Events move so fast in other parts of the world that it has become my duty to remain either in the White House itself or at some nearby point where I can reach Washington and even Europe and Asia by direct telephone, if need be, where I can be back at my desk in the space of a very few hours," he told delegates to the 1940 Democratic National Convention in Chicago by phone in his acceptance speech after it nominated him for a third term in mid-July. "... I shall not have the time or the inclination to engage in purely political debate." He added, "But I shall never be loath to call the attention of the nation to deliberate or unwitting falsifications of fact, which are sometimes made by political candidates." The strategy, which was the White House equivalent of the old "front porch campaign" had worked for FDR in 1936 and it would put him on the front page of newspapers across the nation when he conducted "inspection tours" of defense plants and military installations as the nation prepared to defend itself in a world at war.

On August 8, the lethal Nazi Luftwaffe attacked England by air with over 1,400 aircraft. The island nation resisted with all its might and the heroic Battle of Britain lasted into early October when Hitler finally postponed his invasion plans to the next spring, an invasion which never came. The American public watched in horror from a safe distance, and all domestic political issues paled in comparison. Allied leaders in Europe were relieved that no matter who won the U.S. election, at least they would have an ally in the White House.

Willkie's own campaign lost momentum during the summer months while the candidate vacationed in Colorado and then spent a month at his Rushville, Indiana, farms where he tried to shed his image as a Wall Street lawyer and utilities executive. It wasn't until August 17 that Willkie formally accepted the Republican nomination in his boyhood town of Elwood, Indiana, in what was to that date the largest political rally in U.S. history. The political carnival started with a flag-waving parade down Indiana Route 13 through the center of the little town of

10,000. Willkie waved wildly at the home crowd from the back seat of a convertible. His picture was captured on the cover of *Life* in what editors of the magazine called the greatest campaign photo ever.

With the temperature soaring to 103 degrees, 150,000 supporters showed up at Callaway Park on the outskirts of town to hear Willkie formally accept the nomination and outline his political philosophy. The band from his alma mater, Indiana University, played "Back Home In Indiana," and the crowd extended him a ten-minute ovation before he began his sentimental and surprising speech. Willkie had actually forgotten the text of the speech back in Rushville and it had to be rushed to him by state police. The event was broadcast by radio to voters across the nation.

Willkie was introduced by the man he had selected to be the new Republican National Chairman, the permanent chairman of the Philadelphia convention, Congressman Joseph W. Martin, Jr. Martin began, "We are here to carry out an old American custom, to notify you officially that you were chosen by the Republican party in its national convention in Philadelphia on June 28th as its candidate for the Presidency of the United States. I hope it will not come as too great a surprise," he chuckled.

Wiping the perspiration from his brow, Willkie said he intended his speech to give the nation "an outline of the political philosophy that is in my heart." He began by declaring, "We are here to represent a sacred cause, the preservation of American democracy." After a recollection of his boyhood days in Elwood, in which he confessed to many faults, he revealed "three steadfast convictions" which had remained with him ever since: a commitment to "the ideal of individual liberty," a "hatred of all special privileges and forms of oppression," and a belief that "without any doubt the greatest country on earth was the United States of America."

The new nominee also spoke of his ancestors "because the United States gave to my family their first chance for a free life... like the ancestors of millions of Americans." One, he said, had been exiled for his religion, another because he believed in the principles of the French revolution, yet another was jailed for insisting on the right of free speech. "As their descendent, I have fought from boyhood against all those restrictions, discriminations, and tyrannies. I am still fighting."

He added, "How familiar that sounds! Today, also people are being oppressed in Europe. The story of the barbarous and worse than medieval persecution of the Jews, a race that has done so much to improve the culture of these countries and our own, is the most tragic in human history. Today there are millions of refugees who desire sanctuary and opportunity in America, just like in my grandparents' time.... But their misery and suffering make us resolve to preserve our country as a land free of hate and bitterness, of racial and class distinction. I pledge you that kind of America."

After praising the values of his parents, Willkie again turned to the question of Europe. "Today we meet in a typical American town. The quiet streets, the pleasant fields that lie outside, the people casually about their business, seem far removed from the shattered cities, the gutted buildings, and the stricken people of Europe. It is hard for us to realize that the war in Europe can affect our daily lives. Instinctively we turn aside from the recurring conflicts over there, the diplomatic intrigue, the shifts of power that the last war failed to end.

"Yet, instinctively also, we know that we are not isolated from those suffering people. We live in the same world as they, and we are created in the same image. In all the democracies that have recently fallen, the people were living the same peaceful lives that we live. They had similar ideals of human freedom. Their methods of trade and exchange were similar to ours. Try as we will, we cannot brush the pitiless picture of their destructions from our vision, or escape the profound effects of it upon the world in which we live.

"No man is so wise as to foresee what the future holds or to lay out a plan for it. No man can guarantee to maintain peace. Peace is not something that a nation can achieve by itself. It also depends on what some other country does. It is neither practical, nor desirable, to adopt a foreign program committing the United States to future action under unknown circumstances. The best we can do is decide what principle shall guide us. For me that principle can be simply defined. In the foreign policy of the United States, as in its domestic policy, I would do everything to defend American democracy and I would refrain from doing anything that would injure it. We must not permit our emotions, our sympathies or hatreds, to move us from that fixed principle."

Then, in opposition to the position of many in his party, he declared that "some form of selective service is the only democratic way in which to secure the trained and competent man-power we need for national defense" and he called for help to aid Great Britain. "But I cannot follow the President in his conduct of foreign affairs in this critical time. There have been occasions when many of us have wondered if he is deliberately inciting us to war. I trust that I have made it plain that in the defense of America, and of our liberties, I should not hesitate to stand for war. But like a great many other Americans I saw what war was like at first hand in 1917. I know what war can do to demoralize civil liberties at home. And I believe it to be the first duty of a President to try to maintain peace.

"But Mr. Roosevelt has not done this. He has dabbled in inflammatory statements and manufactured panics.... The President's attacks on foreign powers have been useless and dangerous. He has courted a war for which the country is hopelessly unprepared, and which it emphatically does not want. He has secretly meddled in the affairs of Europe, and he has even unscrupulously encouraged other countries to hope for more help than we are able to give."

Then Willkie turned his guns on the New Deal. "The promises of the present administration cannot lead you to victory against Hitler, or against anyone else. The administration stands for principles exactly opposite to mine. It does not preach the doctrine of growth. It preaches the doctrine of division.... Why that is exactly the course France followed to her destruction!...

"Of course, if you start like the New Deal with the idea that we shall never have many more automobiles or radios, that we cannot develop many new inventions of importance, that our standard of living must remain about what it is, the rest of the argument is easy.... But this can only make the poor poorer and the rich less rich. It does not really distribute wealth. It distributes poverty.

"Because I am a business man, formerly connected with a large company, the doctrinaires of the opposition have attacked me as an opponent of liberalism. But I was a liberal before many of those men had heard the word, and I fought for many of the reforms of the elder LaFollette, Theodore Roosevelt, and Woodrow Wilson before another Roosevelt adopted, and distorted liberalism.... We know from our own experience that the less fortunate or less skillful among us must be protected from encroachment.

"That is why we support what is known as the liberal point of view. That is why we believe in reform.... I believe that the forces of free enterprise must be regulated. I am opposed to business monopolies. I believe in collective bargaining.... I believe in the maintenance of minimum standards for wages and maximum standards for hours. I believe such standards should constantly improve. I believe in the federal regulation of interstate utilities, of securities markets, and of banking. I believe in federal pensions, in adequate old age benefits, and in unemployment allowances. I believe the federal government has a responsibility to equalize the lot of the farmer with that of the manufacturer....

"But I do not base my claim to liberalism solely on my faith in such reforms. American liberalism does not consist merely in reforming things. It consists also in making things. The ability to grow, the ability to make things, is the measure of man's welfare on this earth. To be free, man must be creative. I am a liberal because I believe that in this industrial age there is no limit to the productive capacity of any man. And so I believe that there is no limit to the horizon of the United States...."

And Willkie challenged President Roosevelt to face-to-face

debates on these and other issues in all sections of the nation, a challenge that was quickly dismissed by the administration. Finally, Willkie approached his conclusion. "I accept the nomination of the Republican party for President of the United States. I accept it in the spirit in which I know it was given at our convention in Philadelphia, the spirit of dedication. I herein dedicate myself with all my heart and with all my mind and with all my soul to making this nation strong....

"In Europe those rights of person and property, the civil liberties, which your ancestors fought for, and which you still enjoy, are virtually extinct. And it is my profound conviction that even here in this country, the Democratic party, under its present leadership, will prove incapable of protecting those liberties of yours. The Democratic party today stands for division among our people; for the struggle of class against class and faction against faction; for the power of political machines and the exploitation of pressure groups. Liberty does not thrive in such soil. The only soil in which liberty can grow is that of a united people. We must have faith that the welfare of one is the welfare of all. We must know that the truth can only be reached by the expression of our free opinions, without fear and without rancor. We must acknowledge that all are equal before God and before the law. And we must learn to abhor those disruptive pressures, whether religious, political, or economic, that the enemies of liberty employ.... With the help of Almighty Providence, with unyielding determination and ceaseless effort, we must and shall make that American promise come true."

Willkie had wilted in the blistering heat and given a poor delivery of his speech. His energy was spent by the day's events leading up to appearance on stage, although he was revived near the middle of the speech by a soft drink. More important, the content of the speech alienated many conservatives and isolationists in his own party with its litany of liberal commitments. At the same time, Roosevelt's allies charged that Willkie's embrace of social improvements of the New Deal simply made him a "Me-too" candidate. He lost isolationist support by backing FDR on military conscription. That made it politically possible for nearly a million young men to be drafted by election time. He also silently supported Roosevelt's deal to send naval destroyers to Britain. But he later denounced Roosevelt's end run around Congress as "the most dictatorial action ever taken by any President," a comment he later regretted.

In the months that followed the large rally, the Republican candidate gave hundreds of speeches as he traveled nearly 19,000 miles across 31 states in a train called the "Willkie Special." His "crusade" to save democracy was the most exhausting effort since William Jennings Bryan's epic losing campaign against William McKinley in 1896. And like Bryan, Willkie's campaign style was evangelical. The "Willkie

Special" was packed with a staff of 30 and nearly 50 reporters who covered the candidate's every utterance. Large and not always friendly crowds met every whistle stop. He was cheered by huge throngs in cities like Los Angeles, Salt Lake City, and New York, but booed in low-income industrial neighborhoods wedded to the benefits of the New Deal. He even became target for tomatoes, bottles, ash trays, rocks, cantaloupes, telephone books. In Chicago Willkie was struck in the temple by a frozen egg.

Willkie's initial strategy was to split the Democratic vote over the issue of the third term and dissent within the Democratic party about FDR's selection for Vice President of Henry A. Wallace, a whimsical reformer, farmer, and former Republican. He made hundreds of phone calls seeking converts to "Democrats for Willkie." Former New York Governor Al Smith, long a Roosevelt foe, led the committee. Willkie also courted the black vote and got important endorsements from major African-American newspapers and personalities such as Joe Louis. He was passionately committed to civil rights, while Roosevelt valued his white Southern Democratic support.

Because he refused to use microphones, Willkie's throat gave out early in the campaign and he delivered his speeches in a low raspy voice despite help from doctors, whom he usually ignored. With no campaign manager or press secretary, Willkie made all important decisions and announcements himself. He threw aside schedules and caused headaches for his staff, which was often in open rebellion against one another. Reporters called it one of the most chaotic campaigns ever. Willkie, a master of one-liners, quipped, "The amateurs won the nomination, and they can win the election." He called his volunteers "fellow amateurs."

But by early September Willkie was trailing FDR in the polls by ten points. His attacks against Roosevelt's third term and New Deal failures to put people back to work had no resonance with voters as defense plants began hiring thousands of workers and business boomed anew. And Roosevelt refused to accept Willkie's challenge to directly debate, instead letting Willkie punch himself out. When he was pressed about Willkie's attacks, FDR coyly replied, "I don't know nothin' about politics." Willkie's frustration grew as Roosevelt continued to ignore him and ran instead against Hitler and Republican isolationists in Congress.

By October, Willkie was still seeking a message that could hurt the President. He found it in America's apparent rush to war. FDR didn't trust the polls and expected the race to tighten by election day. He was right. Willkie intensified his attacks on Roosevelt by changing tactics and shifting from calling Roosevelt an appeaser to tagging him as a warmonger. "If his promise to keep our boys out of foreign wars is no better than his promise to balance the budget, they're already almost on the transports," he charged. Willkie turned his back on the internationalists and catered to the isolationists whom he had alienated earlier in his campaign. His tactic worked and he began to rise again in the public opinion polls. He especially rebounded in the Midwest and along the eastern seaboard.

Roosevelt noted a backlash in the German-American and Italian-American communities, as well as among Irish-Americans who were not at all enthusiastic about aid to England. As Willkie gained in the polls, the Democratic campaign suddenly panicked and kicked into action. On October 18, Roosevelt who was "fighting mad" said he would answer Willkie's "deliberate falsification of fact" with five campaign speeches, and as always, the radio became his most effective tool. FDR's first address came from Philadelphia on October 23rd when he sternly said, "I give to you and to the people of this country this most solemn assurance: There is no secret understanding in any shape or form, direct or indirect, with any other government, or any other nation in any part of the world, to involve this nation in any war or for any other purpose." The President went on to defend the achievements of the New Deal for working men and women of the nation against the Republican "crocodile tears."

On October 28th, after a 14-hour driving tour of New York City, FDR told a packed Madison Square Garden rally that the Republicans were "playing politics with national defense." He attacked the isolationist records of Hoover, Taft, McNary, and Vandenberg. Then he added a lyrical twist that caught on with the huge and devoted crowd, and became a popular refrain during the remainder of the campaign. Who was responsible for America's unpreparedness? he asked. None other than the Republican isolationists in Congress, "Martin, Barton, and Fish." The crowd joined in several recitations of the catchy rhyme "Martin, Barton, and Fish" as FDR wagged his finger in rhythm.

On October 30, in the Boston Garden, FDR went further. "I have said this before but I shall say it again and again and again. Your boys are not going to be sent into any foreign wars." His statement left out the clause he had used before and that was part of the Democratic platform, "except in the case of attack." The crowd roared its approval. Willkie listening by radio, conceded, "This is going to beat me." FDR later told his aides the "in case of attack" clause was academic since if the United States was attacked, it was no longer a foreign war.

On November 1, in Brooklyn, FDR charged, "There is something very ominous in this combination that has been forming within the Republican party between the extreme reactionary and the extreme radical elements in this country." And he mentioned that Robert T. McCraken, Willkie's Philadelphia manager had asserted that FDR's only supporters were "paupers, those who earn less than $1,200 and aren't worth that, and the Roosevelt family." "Paupers not worth their salt," the President added for emphasis. "There speaks the true sentiment of the Republican leadership in this year of grace.... That, my friends, is what I am fighting against with all my heart and soul...." Since more than half the nation earned less than $1,200, his attack had bite. During the remaining days of the campaign, Democrats sent out workers shabbily dressed in "stovepipe" hats wearing buttons that read "I'm a pauper for Roosevelt."

FDR's next speech was in Cleveland, where the President said, "Seven years ago I started with loyal helpers and with the trust and faith and support of millions of ordinary Americans.... The way was difficult, the path was dark, but we have moved steadily toward the open fields and the glowing light that shines ahead."

On election eve, Roosevelt broadcast a "non-partisan" address urging citizens of the nation to vote and ended with a simple prayer. "... Bless our land with honorable industry, sound learning, and pure manners.... Defend our liberties, and fashion into one united people the multitudes brought hither out of many kindreds and tongues...."

On the night before the election, Willkie packed Madison Square Garden with 22,000 screaming supporters and warned that FDR's reelection might mean the "destruction of our democratic way of life.... Help me, Help me, help me save it," he implored in a voice that was steadily improving.

Down the stretch, *The New York Times* endorsed Willkie, as did most national magazines. Willkie also got a valuable election eve labor endorsement from C.I.O. chieftain John L. Lewis, who in a live radio broadcast said he would resign if FDR was reelected. The final pre-election polls showed Roosevelt at 52 percent, Willkie closing in with 48 percent. The experts were calling the match a tossup.

On election night, FDR nervously locked himself in his study along the Hudson River while the race teetered back and forth, with the outcome undecided until early morning. But after midnight the results became clear. FDR had another landslide Electoral College victory, narrowly taking all the major states. FDR polled over 27 million votes to Willkie's 22 million, the most votes in Republican history, and five million more than four years before. But Roosevelt swept 38 states and piled up 449 Electoral Votes to Willkie's 82. FDR also took Philadelphia for the second time with 532,149 votes to Willkie's 354,878 votes. The national race was not as lopsided as it appeared on paper. *The New York Times* reported that had 600,000 votes shifted sides in ten states, Willkie would have won. But the New Deal coalition had held.

In New York City's Commodore Hotel ballroom at 12:20 A.M., Willkie conceded, saying, "I never felt better in my life," and urging his supporters who yelled, "We'll elect you in '44" not to "be afraid and never quit." In the end, the likeable Willkie pledged his support to the commander-in-chief and during the war became FDR's personal diplomatic representative, traveling the world from Europe to Asia, and writing a best-selling book about post-war reconstruction entitled, *One World*. But before FDR was elected to his fourth term in 1944, Wendell L. Willkie had died at age 52 of a heart attack.

Willkie parades down Indiana Route 13, Main Street of his hometown of Elwood, before giving his acceptance speech to perhaps 150,000 people on August 17, 1940.

1948: Triple Convention Year
The Twenty-Fourth Republican National Convention

Convention-at-a-Glance

Event: Twenty-Fourth Republican National Convention
Date: June 21-25, 1948
Location: Municipal Auditorium/Convention Hall, Thirty-fourth Street and Civic Center Boulevard
Philadelphia Mayor: Bernard Samuel, Republican
Philadelphia's Population: 2,071,605 (1950)
Convention Permanent Chairman: Speaker of the House of Representatives, Joseph W. Martin Jr., Massachusetts
Number of Delegates: 1,094
Number Needed to Nominate: A majority
Candidates for Nomination: Senator Raymond E. Baldwin, Connecticut; Governor Thomas Edmund Dewey, New York; General Douglas MacArthur, Arkansas; Former Governor Harold Edward Stassen, Minnesota; Senator Robert Alphonso Taft, Ohio; Senator Arthur Hendrick Vandenberg, Michigan
Presidential Nominee: Governor Thomas Edmund Dewey, New York
Age at Nomination: 46
Number of Ballots: Three
Vice Presidential Nominee: Governor Earl Warren, California
Largest Audience: 16,500
Platform Positions: Support for achievements of the Eightieth Congress; promotion of civil rights, abolition of the poll tax, integration of the armed forces, passage of anti-lynching legislation; encouragement of more private housing at lower costs; aid to states for slum clearance and low-rental housing only where they cannot be done by private enterprise or by the states and localities; support of the Eightieth Congress' labor relations legislation (Taft-Hartley); passage of an equal rights amendment to the Constitution for women and equal pay for equal work regardless of sex; vigorous enforcement of existing laws against communists and new legislation where needed to expose the treasonable activities of communists; support for the United Nations and collective security against aggression and in behalf of justice and freedom, and support of a U.N. armed forces; support of Israel as a new member of the family of nations
Campaign Slogan: "Win With Dewey"
Campaign Song: "Date in '48"

Governor Thomas Edmund Dewey
1948 Republican Presidential
Nominee

Governor Earl Warren
1948 Republican Vice Presidential
Nominee

1948

Triple Convention Year
The Twenty-Fourth Republican National Convention

    Four-time Democratic President, Franklin Delano Roosevelt, was dead. The Allied military forces he had worked tirelessly in his last terms to mobilize and arm had defeated the Nazis in Europe. His successor, President Harry S Truman had dropped two atomic bombs on Japan and forced its unconditional surrender. In the wake of World War II, the world's two largest military powers—the U.S. and the U.S.S.R.—stood armed against one another in a new war: the "Cold War."

    The U.S. domestic landscape was in disarray. The New Deal political coalition had seemingly died with Roosevelt. Inflation was rampant. Strikes were frequent. Housing was in short supply. Most Americans wanted to turn away from world conflict and enjoy their family, friends, and get back to life as they knew it before the conflagration. Republicans were confident that 1948 would be their year to turn back 16 years of Democratic domination. With Roosevelt gone and Truman, the former haberdasher apparently over his head in White House responsibilities, the Grand Old Party was ready to steer a new course for America. In that spirit of optimism, Republicans returned to Philadelphia, the party's birthplace, during the last week of June 1948 to pick their candidate to lead the nation and the world. Most people assumed their nominee would become the next President of the United States.

    During World War I, Philadelphia had become known as the "Arsenal of Democracy" because of the war ships its workers built in the Navy Yard on the Delaware River and its related defense industries, a role that expanded during the second war. But soon after the end of World War II, Philadelphia began to rapidly decay and many of the 250,000 returning Philadelphia war veterans moved out of the old red brick city along with the middle-class exodus to the suburbs seeking a return to a more peaceful life. In 1947, the city responded by launching a post-war revitalization of its historic district and center city, with a new City Planning Commission, headed by Albert M. Greenfield, a former Republican turned Democrat, who was partially responsible for landing the three 1948 conventions in Philadelphia.

All during the week before the Republican convention opened, train after train rolled into the Pennsylvania Railroad's new Thirtieth Street Station along the banks of the Schuylkill River unloading delegates and political operatives by the thousands from all over the nation. (One of the first acts of Philadelphia's revitalization plan was to tear down the mammoth, old Broad Street Station, derogatorily known as the "Chinese Wall," to open up the center city for skyscrapers.) With the Cold War heating up, the Republican convention drew intense interest. Old William Penn's statue peered down from the tower of City Hall as brass bands marched on the streets below and glee clubs serenaded the banner-carrying crowds, hucksters peddled buttons, and partisans passed out pamphlets in front of hotels.

Inside the renovated Municipal Auditorium on Thirty-fourth Street, under the new asbestos-sprayed copper roof, electricians tested banks of high-powered lights and rows of new television cameras, and a 62-piece band and pipe organ practiced its repertoire of 600 tunes, including the convention theme song "Date in '48." This would the be the biggest musical event inside the auditorium since Frank Sinatra packed the hall in 1944 to kick off the War Chest Campaign. Auditorium renovations had cost the City of Brotherly Love some $600,000.

On Sunday, June 20, 1948, a confident Governor Thomas Edmund Dewey, of New York, with Mrs. Dewey at his side dressed in a black faille suit, pink blouse and string of pearls, was cheered by 1,500 delegates and supporters when they arrived at the governor's headquarters in the Bellevue-Stratford hotel the evening before the convention opened. On the hotel marquee stood a giant rubber elephant welcoming the guests. Dewey's convention headquarters was up on the hotel's eighth floor in the $1,000-a-day ballroom.

Dewey was still a young man at age 46. After his 1940 convention loss to Wendell Willkie (who had died in 1944 at age 52), Dewey had returned to New York to win a term as governor and then the 1944 Republican Presidential nomination on the first ballot. After losing that election to Franklin D. Roosevelt in his fourth-term bid, Dewey bounced back and was reelected New York governor in 1946 by the largest margin in the state's history. He had proved himself a sound administrator who had built large state surpluses and funded many postwar construction projects. He was moderately liberal, favoring collective bargaining and desegregation. After the war, Dewey became an internationalist who advocated a firm policy against Soviet Russia and financial assistance to Western Europe. In private, he was charming, but in public he was often seen as stiff, arrogant, and overly ambitious.

After meeting with the Women for Dewey Clubs, the always dapper governor held a press conference packed with 700 reporters, editors, photographers, television commentators, the biggest press conference he had ever attended, he said. Dewey predicted victory "on an early ballot." He also praised the work of the Republican-dominated Eightieth Congress, which was swept into power in the mid-term elections of 1946. He said it had "made a remarkable record in several major fields and I am proud of it." Among other achievements, the candidate noted that Congress had "made the greatest effort yet undertaken to shore up the free nations of the world" by extending reconstruction aid to the European democracies still devastated by the war, and had "prodded the administration into a more realistic and effective foreign policy." According to the New York governor, the Republican Congress also had stopped the administration from "wobbling" in its dealings with other nations and had rebuilt the nation's defense structure "which the administration had allowed to collapse." He also told the camera-toting assemblage that he had no preference for a running mate and would make that decision after he won the nomination. Mrs. Dewey, a former Broadway musical singer, said she was proud of her husband but refused to answer "any political questions" reporters put to her.

The Eightieth Congress was clearly going to be a campaign issue. It had come under attack by President Truman, and Senator J. Howard McGrath, the Democratic National Chairman, held a press conference as the Republicans met to brand the Eightieth Congress, the "privilege" Congress, charging it had taken care of the special interests, rather than the public. "The Congress has adjourned without doing anything to curb inflation," he stated, "without doing anything about the housing shortage." He suggested that the Republican platform should proclaim that Republicans "want prices to be high as long as profits are high."

Once he dispensed with the press, Dewey attended a reception in honor of Pennsylvania Governor James H. Duff and Senator Edward Martin at the suburban Rosemont estate of Martin W. Clement, president of the Pennsylvania Railroad. Also attending the bash was Dewey's main rival, Senator Robert Alphonso Taft, of Ohio, who ranked his prospects of victory as "very good," and Speaker of the House Joseph W. Martin, who was a dark, dark horse. Taft, who had driven himself from Washington in his 1946 Plymouth, had earlier told a cheering crowd of 1,500 at the Benjamin Franklin Hotel that, "I think the race is largely between Governor Dewey and myself, and I think I am in a better position."

Standing amid signs reading "To do the Job, Let's have Bob," Taft had told reporters he agreed with his campaign manager, Representative Clarence J. Brown, that he would attract "in the neighborhood of 312 votes on the first ballot." Then the band struck up his campaign song, "I'm Looking Over a Four-Leaf Clover." The Senator himself looked remarkably strong given that he had gotten only two or three hours sleep in the previous four days as Congress rushed to finish its business so it could adjourn for the summer.

Taft, who was the favorite of his congressional colleagues and of party regulars, hoped to pick up the second ballot votes of the numerous favorite sons to give him a majority. When reporters pressed him on the unresolved issues in Washington, Taft said he saw no reason for Congress to be called back into session. In his estimation, it had addressed the "must" legislation, and long deliberations would be required to complete work on other issues. Taft also said, "I never have felt that Russia would turn to military aggression." Taft's mascot was a live elephant, "Eva" from India, that was paraded outside the hotels. (Its sad eyes might have seemed to portend poorly for the Ohio Senator.)

All the contestants were smiling at Clement's lavish party, but behind this veneer a frantic "Stop Dewey" movement was being patched together by the camps of Taft and former Minnesota Governor Harold Edward Stassen, who had just picked up the preconvention support of Walter E. Edge, the former governor and Senator from New Jersey. Stassen, who represented many of the party's reform forces, was a favorite with young Republicans, and was a vocal internationalist. When he was 31, Stassen had been elected governor of Minnesota, and twice reelected. When the U.S. entered World War II, he resigned and joined the Navy and had seen considerable combat action. He represented the nation as a delegate to the founding of the United Nations in 1945. Tall, handsome, and ever-smiling, he had been campaigning for the Presidency since 1946. Stassen had shocked Dewey and MacArthur, the favorite, in the Wisconsin primary on April 6. Stassen then beat Dewey in Nebraska a week later on April 13. Dewey had won New Jersey on April 20.

But Stassen had beaten Dewey in Pennsylvania on April 27 and had won in West Virginia on May 11. The Oregon primary was seen as decisive and was hard-fought. In a debate, Stassen said he favored outlawing the Communist party. Dewey was opposed to such a move on civil libertarian grounds, and won a narrow victory. However, the vast majority of state delegations entered the 1948 Republican National Convention committed to favorite sons or uncommitted. A preconvention Gallup Poll showed Dewey favored by 33 percent of Republicans and Stassen by 26 percent. Other candidates, including Taft, trailed farther behind Dewey. The same poll showed Dewey beating Truman by 44 to 32 percent, while any of the other Republicans beat the President by 10 percent. But neither Taft nor Stassen was willing to step back and take the second spot on the ticket to further the "Stop Dewey" movement that was trying to gain steam as the convention opened. Stassen hoped that at around the ninth ballot, the convention would turn to him.

As he had done in 1940, Senator Arthur Hendrick Vandenberg,

of Michigan, announced his "availability" as a compromise candidate should the convention deadlock between Dewey and Taft. Senator Henry Cabot Lodge, Jr., of Massachusetts, was leading the Michigan Senator's effort. Most of Stassen's support was expected to drift toward the Michigan Senator, who arrived in Philadelphia on Monday. Stassen was expected to accept the Vice Presidency under Vandenberg.

Also in the mix of potential nominees was California Governor Earl Warren, who arrived in Philadelphia by train with his large delegation on Sunday. Warren held the solid support of his state's 53 delegates, whose chairman was Senator William F. Knowland, but the California governor was not actively recruiting other commitments, because he already had "a terrific job." Warren said, "I don't think any one candidate has enough votes to win... it's a wide open convention." He thought that under those conditions, he had "a fair opportunity" to become the nominee, but denied any interest in the Vice Presidency or "any deals" to stop Dewey.

Warren also argued, "If the Republican party is to capture the confidence of the American people and retain it, we must have a progressive, forward-looking program that will tackle every fundamental problem of the American people. We have to prove that we are not going back to isolation, that we will fulfill every fundamental commitment made since the cessation of hostilities." He also said he was opposed to legislation outlawing the Communist party. Warren and Stassen proved that the Republican party still had two wings, as it had had since Teddy Roosevelt's day, one of progressives and one of conservatives.

That evening, after the Clement party when the Pennsylvania delegation of 73 met in caucus to determine strategy, it avoided an open split by reaffirming its endorsement of favorite son Senator Edward Martin, on the first ballot. Governor Duff was a backer of Senator Vandenberg and expected the delegation to give him its eventual support, although many in the group favored Dewey.

The Twenty-Fourth Republican National Convention came to order at 11:27 A.M., Monday, June 21, 1948. Walter S. Hallanan, of West Virginia, chairman of the Committee on Arrangements, banged the gavel several times before the aisles were cleared. Then Hallanan recalled that the Republican party had gotten its start in Philadelphia 92 years earlier. Two huge crossed American flags, joined at the poles and spread in a giant "V" hung above him in the steamy hall, and red, white, and blue star-spangled bunting decorated the upper spectator decks. The convention floor was crowded, but the galleries were sparsely populated for the morning session.

Television cameramen and still photographers were perched in boxes high above the floor to provide the public with the first "full-scale" visual coverage of a convention. (Television cameras were first used to catch highlights of the 1940 Republican convention.) The candidates themselves followed the proceedings on television in their air-conditioned hotel suites. The public in distant locations, such as Zanesville, Ohio, saw the convention as a result of Westinghouse's "stratovision," a technique by which airplanes picked up the transmission from TV towers in urban locations and rebroadcast it to locations as far as 500 miles outside normal viewing areas. Most viewing areas were limited to 50 miles of a transmitter.

After the National Anthem was sung by Virginia Davis, of Philadelphia, delegates heard an invocation by the Reverend Fred Pierce Corson, Bishop of the Methodist Church, Philadelphia. Mrs. Dudley C. Hay, of Michigan, the first woman to act as secretary of the Republican party, read the convention call. The delegates were then welcomed by Philadelphia's Republican mayor, Bernard "Barney" Samuel, a likeable political operative for the Republican machine, who thanks to a change in state law was the first Philadelphia mayor eligible to succeed himself. Under his tenure, the city was plagued by constant financial troubles, as well as corruption prosecutions at the gas works, the rapid transit authority, the water and sewage department, the magistrates' court, and for mismanagement of city elections. The police were also the target of prosecution for their protection of gamblers and racketeers.

Then came Governor Duff, who proclaimed, "The eyes of the whole world are on this convention because what we will do here will affect the future of civilization." Cloverleaves of loudspeakers loomed overhead and his words were blasted throughout the meeting hall. On the floor, all the delegates from Missouri were carrying corncob pipes. Vandenberg delegates wore badges saying "The Bell Tolls Two," a sailor's reference to "All Is Safe."

Delegates next heard a "pep" talk from the national chairman, Carroll Reece, dressed in a white cotton suit, who asserted that there were only two powerful forces in the world, the "Republican party and the Communist party." The Democratic party, he said, had become "sterile" and futile and was "torn by philosophical and sectional differences." It was, he argued, no longer capable of resisting the "march of radical aggression." Reece said the problem went back to 1932 when voters had been deluded "by the most persuasive demagoguery of modern times." He also applauded the Eightieth Congress for its job in unraveling the "skein of New Deal encroachments" on personal liberty. And he promised that the rest of the job would be done "in 1949 when a Republican President moves into the White House."

Finally, committee assignments were made and Governor Dwight H. Green, of Illinois, was elected the convention's temporary chairman before the body, anxious to get to work, adjourned at 1:03 P. M., on the motion of motion picture actor George Murphy. The committees dispersed to the hotels and Convention Hall meeting rooms to conduct their business.

The initial convention fight for control took place in the Credentials Committee, where the Taft-Stassen coalition challenged 16 Dewey delegates from Georgia placed on the convention's temporary roll the previous week by the Republican National Committee. But Dewey's marginal strength was revealed when the Committee on Credentials voted 26 to 24 to seat the Georgia delegation. The committee also voted to seat the challenging, six-member Mississippi delegation, headed by African-American lawyer and national committeeman Perry Howard, over a "lily-white" delegation that had barred blacks from its deliberations. The Taft campaign abandoned its plan to fight the Georgia decision on the convention floor after it could muster no support among other delegates.

On Monday afternoon, Colonel Robert R. McCormick, publisher and editor of the conservative *Chicago Tribune*, who dominated the Illinois delegation of 56 votes, threw the first bucket of cold water on the unity veneer by publicly endorsing a "Stop Dewey" ticket of Taft-Stassen. "I am for Taft and I have no second choice," he said. "Vandenberg can't even carry Michigan. He only got back to the Senate by making a deal with Roosevelt, backing the Roosevelt foreign policy in return for which a stooge who was put up against him who really campaigned for Vandenberg, and the logical candidate, who stepped out of the way for the stooge, was rewarded for his treachery to the Democratic party by being appointed Governor of Austria." (He had actually been appointed Governor of Bavaria.)

Referring to Dewey's failed campaign of 1944, the fiery Chicago publisher, who was seeking to halt both the internationalists Dewey and Vandenberg in a single strategic move, continued, "Dewey ran 250,000 behind the ticket in Illinois and dragged a great many state and county candidates down with him. He wouldn't do any better this year. I don't think he can carry any more than 12 states again this year." Then he reasoned, "Stassen is strong with young people, but mature people think he lacks maturity. In 1900, McKinley was nominated for his prestige and Theodore Roosevelt for his personal popularity. Therefore, it seems reasonable to nominate Taft and Stassen for the same reasons."

Candidate Taft refused to comment on McCormick's recommendation, except to say that "any ticket with Taft at the head would not be beatable." Stassen's floor manager, Minnesota Governor Luther Youngdahl, expressed his disapproval of the idea, saying, "There's nothing to it. There'll never be anything of the kind." Herbert Brownell, one of Dewey's managers, told reporters, "I'm glad that the *Chicago Tribune* ticket is out in the open at last." But he insisted that Dewey would be nominated and elected, and would make "no deals." He pointed out that, "Every poll of public opinion shows that Tom Dewey will beat

President Truman." Dewey's campaign was hopeful that McCormick's isolationist statements would push Stassen's internationalist delegates into the New York governor's camp.

That evening, at 9 P.M., when the convention reassembled, there was considerable tension on the floor over who would become the party's eventual nominee and what the platform would look like, internationalist or isolationist, progressive or conservative. Governor Dwight H. Green, of Illinois, delivered a keynote address that was interrupted with only intermittent bursts of applause. Green had been picked by the Dewey men who controlled the convention in hopes that he could deliver the Illinois delegation out of the grip of *Chicago Tribune* publisher McCormick. The perspiring delegates were not boisterous, but serious about the work before them, as a shifting spotlight cast its beam across the convention floor.

Governor Green began, "We are here to nominate the thirty-fourth President of the United States," a line that roused the delegates to cheers. "Here in Philadelphia, the Declaration of Independence proclaimed the freedom of America. We in this convention reaffirm American freedom and independence." Although Green asserted, "this is no place for narrow partisanship," he delivered a frontal attack on the Democratic record of "bosses, boodle, bunkum, and blarney." He called the gathering "a people's convention" that belonged "to the 145 million Americans in 48 states" who were following the proceedings on radio and television, and promised to "keep the faith with you wherever you are." Green proclaimed that the Republican party was the party that had "faith in the individual American," while the "New Deal party can have no real program, because it is no longer a real party. It musters its majorities from a fantastic partnership of reaction and radicalism."

Green charged the New Deal's "offspring was the sorriest series of broken promises in the history of our nation. It promised economy and gave us unproductive spending, unbalanced budgets, oppressive taxes, and massive debt.... It promised peace again and again and again, when it knew war was inevitable." The crowd applauded. The Illinois governor called President Truman a "great flop" and the New Dealers "crackpots" and "lunatics" unfit for public office and contrasted them with the Republican party which began its return to power after 16 years by "giving clean government to small cities and communities." But he added that "the Republican party was not founded to elect sheriffs. It was founded to elect Presidents." It had "recaptured the governorships of many states ten years ago, and because it gave competent government, it won repeated reelection in those states." Then two years ago the American people had restored the Republican party to power in Congress. Now "it has earned the right to greater things."

Green applauded the work of the Eightieth Congress which he

234

said had redeemed Republican election pledges. Green asserted it had freed the national economy of "regimentation." It had balanced the budget. It had promised to cut taxes and it had done so. It had corrected a "chaotic" condition in labor relations "which were paralyzing American production" by passing the Taft-Hartley Act, which abolished the closed shop, required a majority vote to establish labor unions in a work site, and outlawed secondary boycotts.

Green also charged that America was "losing the peace." He declared that, "The blood and treasure which we so willingly gave are being wasted by confused and incompetent foreign policy. We fought for justice and freedom, but almost a dozen nations have been despoiled of their property, robbed of their liberty, driven from their homes or murdered in cold blood. In a rich world, Europeans and Asiatics are facing starvation." He said, "The truth is that New Deal diplomacy threw away victory long before our fighters had won it. It permitted the Russians to take Berlin. At Teheran and Yalta one New Deal President agreed to Russia's domination of Poland and much of China. At Potsdam another New Deal President confirmed the Soviet's domination of the satellite countries and their sole right to occupy Eastern Germany and Eastern Austria...."

"The cold war we face today is the lusty child of the New Deal's rendezvous with communism," Green shouted. "That rendezvous began with recognition of the Soviets in 1933. It continued with the socialistic compromises with communism preached by Harry Hopkins. It reached its tragic climax in those years when we supinely suffered communism to master half of Europe." Green pledged that Republicans would reverse that trend. "A Republican President will man the State Department with personnel who will make our diplomacy respected in every corner of the world. It is an old and tried Republican tradition that American influence shall be felt wherever America has a legitimate duty in the world outside our gates." Then Green outlined the achievements of Republican Secretaries of State Seward, Blaine, Hay, Root, Hughes, and Kellogg. "Merely to recall them is to blast the New Deal falsehood that the Republican party is timid or provincial in its foreign policy. It is the New Deal party's retreat before the Iron Curtain in Europe and Asia which threatens to isolate America...." In this, he was also rebuking Colonel McCormick's and the pre-war Republican party's isolationist beliefs.

"With our best will and our best skill we must meet the challenge of communism. Communism is a world-wide infection of false doctrine. It grows upon darkness and poverty and hunger. Our defense at home and abroad is not in arms alone, but in every means that builds for freedom and human welfare, or that propagates the truth concerning economic well-being and personal freedom under our republican form of government. Our best answer to communism will be a sound America, in which all the people shall enjoy the prosperity produced by our free economy, and which shall offer effective cooperation to free men throughout the world." Governor Green promised a strong America under Republican leadership.

And he insisted, "We shall ferret out and drive out every red and pink on the federal payrolls... we shall expose every subversive individual and organization. We shall change the social climate which has permitted foreign exponents of Marxism to bask in the profitable sunshine of publicity while they abuse our American hospitality." The Illinois governor vowed that Republicans would bring the world a lasting peace based on justice and freedom and would preserve the nation's strength. Green concluded, "May God grant that this convention meet this challenge with truth and vision. By God's grace may we choose wisely and well."

Despite the rousing presentation, delegate response was tepid in the steamy auditorium. When the Illinois governor finished, the large pipe organ played vibrant renditions of "America the Beautiful," the "Battle Hymn of the Republic," and "God Bless America." Then the lovely former congresswoman from Connecticut, Mrs. Clare Boothe Luce, the first woman to deliver a formal address to a Republican convention when she appeared at the 1944 convention in Chicago, walked to the rostrum and dazzled the delegates with her verbal wizardry. Her short, loose, blond hair and string of white pearls flashed in the spotlight as she threw a kiss to the delegates and photographers. Then she launched into a speech which caught the fascination of the sweat-drenched crowd.

First, Mrs. Luce assured the partisan assembly that the next President of the United States would be a Republican. "Why is everyone so certain?" she asked. "For three reasons: Our people want a competent President: our people want a truthful President: our people want a Constitution-minded President." The crowd applauded in agreement when she asserted that even Democrats "know" that they cannot produce such a man. "That's why so many of them are hoping against hope that they may be able at their convention to draft a Republican." The crowd laughed at this reference to General Eisenhower, whom several Democrats were aggressively courting.

As for President Truman, Mrs. Luce said, he was "a gone goose." But, she exclaimed, "We should be grateful to Mr. Truman that he tried to be President in 1944, and that he was the gallant aid of the big city bosses Kelly, Pendergast, and Hague, and that he didn't fail. If he had failed, our President today would be Mr. Henry Wallace." The crowd booed Wallace. So fate had worked its way when "the Pendergast machine gave us a colorless Harry Truman, instead of the Red Hank Wallace." The convention roared its agreement.

Analyzing the Democratic opposition, Mrs. Luce called it, "less

Demonstration for Thomas Dewey inside Convention Hall. *Philadelphia Record.* The Historical Society of Pennsylvania (HSP).

a party than a podge and mismatch of die-hard warring factions" composed of the extreme right, Jim Crow wing; the left or "Moscow wing" containing most of the nation's political "bubble heads" and a "dangerous core of labor racketeers, native and imported communists, and foreign agents of the Kremlin"; and the center or Pendergast wing (referring to the Kansas City mayor) run by the "wampum and boodle boys, the same big city bosses who gave us Harry Truman in one of their more pixilated moments." She added, these bosses were the "same boys who are ready to stuff a ballot box or steal an election before you can say Missouri." The crowd laughed uproariously at their golden girl's witty delivery.

The Democrats were, Mrs. Luce contended, the party of "political bedlam." It was held together with a three-pronged formula of padding the public payroll; creating confusion and crisis; and of arousing extravagant hopes. The wife of *Time* magazine's publisher Henry Luce charged that every government employee delivered five family votes and therefore, "the feeding of countless hordes of bureaucrats at the public trough is less an ideological principle with the party than a practical vote-getting necessity." She also declared that, "Democratic Presidents are always troubadours of trouble and crooners of catastrophe," and asserted that, "They cannot win elections except in the climate of crisis. So the party, by its very composition, has a vested interest in depression at home and war abroad." In contrast, she said, Republicans "will not promise heaven on earth... but to do our level, honest, commonsensical best to keep you out of those hells on earth, constant domestic crises and a third world war."

"We Republicans believe," she said, "that peace can be brought to a great section of the world by electing a President who will show the ample courage of saying what he means and meaning what he says." Then Mrs. Luce set off the first convention demonstration for a Presidential candidate when she said that Senator Arthur Vandenberg had stopped two New Deal Presidents from giving away all of Europe to "Joe Stalin." At the mention of Vandenberg's name, the Michigan delegation jumped to its feet and paraded around behind its state standard to the applause of delegates and the galleries. Senator Vandenberg was seated in a box behind the speaker's platform. As an after-thought, Luce added that Governor Dewey and Senator Taft would do the same, but their names elicited only mild responses.

The former congresswoman gracefully concluded in her clarion voice, "Let's recall the words of President Theodore Roosevelt. They are durable words, therefore, they are prophetic words. They were written 38 years ago and are strangely timely to our ears as we gather here to choose the next President of the United States." The beautiful Mrs. Luce opened her hands as though she were pleading. "Said T. R., 'Our country, this great Republic, means nothing unless it means the triumph of a real democracy.' The world has set itself hopefully towards our democracy," she observed. "And oh, my fellow citizens, said T.R. across 40 years to you men and women here. Each of you carries on your shoulders the burden of doing well not just for the sake of seeing that our own country does well, but the burden of doing well and seeing that this nation does well for the sake of all mankind." As she stepped away from the microphone, the convention burst into deafening applause. Amid the stir she had caused, the convention adjourned at 11 P.M.

Later that Monday night, the Connecticut delegation met in a 90-minute closed caucus to give its support to U.S. Senator Raymond E. Baldwin, its favorite son, until he released them. Mrs. Clare Boothe Luce, a member of the delegation, who favored the candidacy of Senator Arthur Vandenberg, indicated that she would go "right down the line for Baldwin." Meanwhile the 35 delegates from Massachusetts, in a caucus at the Sylvania Hotel on Locust Street decided to vote for its favorite son, Senator Leverett Saltonstall, on the first and second ballots. The decision of these and other favorite sons was putting a road block in front of the potential Dewey juggernaut.

On Tuesday, June 22, 1948, Temporary Chairman Green brought the convention to order at 11 A.M. During the morning session, party members listened first to a spirited addresses by Senator Kenneth S. Wherry, of Nebraska, the Senate's Republican whip, who denounced Truman's domestic and foreign policy, saying, "Let the record show that there has been and will continue to be cooperation by the Republican majority in Congress with all Americans of good will in a fair and reasonable foreign policy.... But the Republican party and its leadership have never been the appeasers of Soviet Russia." He said no clique of alien-minded radicals had ever captured the Republican party. Then Wherry added that President Truman "has fired the boilers of inflation. In November, he will face the gray ashes of defeat."

Representative Frances P. Bolton, of Ohio, began her address saluting her colleague, Representative Margaret Chase Smith. Republican women at the convention were celebrating Smith's Senate primary victory 700 miles away in Maine, by a two-to-one margin, beating three men. Her victory virtually assured that she would become the first elected Republican female member of the U.S. Senate. Mrs. Smith had begun her political career filling out the term of her deceased husband, Congressman Clyde H. Smith. Senator Owen Brewster, of Maine, had declared, "Her victory is the most inspiring development for women everywhere."

Then Representative Bolton exclaimed, "The moment has come when we Republicans must provide the real leadership that will bring back sanity and balance to our economy, to our country, to every walk of life including the home, that center of our whole way of life." She added, "We who are women must assume our whole share of the burden. When have we ever refused, we who hold title to most of the land, who control the major holdings?" Then she asked, "As it is the women of America who have to make ends meet, who have to stay within budgets, it is the women of America who should rise up in November and give the country relief from the spending spree of these last long years."

Senator Raymond E. Baldwin, of Connecticut, then spoke and was followed by Magistrate Hobson Reynolds, an African American from Philadelphia. The judge predicted that if the Republicans of 1948 did as much for "his race as Abraham Lincoln had done," there was no fear that communism would find a breeding ground in that quarter. He was loudly applauded. Then reports were presented by the Credentials Committee, the Rules Committee, and the Committee on Organization. Next the convention elected its permanent officers, including Speaker of the House Joseph W. Martin, Jr., as permanent chairman. Its business completed, the body adjourned at 2:20 P.M. until that evening.

While the proceedings labored forward on Tuesday morning, the Dewey campaign received a decisive boost that would prove key to the outcome. Pennsylvania Senator Edward Martin dramatically announced that he would not stand as a favorite son from his state and that he would lead 35 to 50 of the state's 73 votes into the camp of Governor Dewey, thereby practically assuring the New York governor of an early ballot victory as the GOP's 1948 nominee. "Anything which would protract this convention would tend to intensify factionalism," Senator Martin told the press. "Therefore it is my belief that every effort should be made by the party to close ranks promptly and strive for the common good. In my heart, I am convinced that the Republican victory is of paramount importance to our nation and the world. We should not permit this convention to continue to the point where prejudice or hatred or selfishness might color any phase of it."

Governor Duff had tried hard to keep the Pennsylvania delegation together as a unit until it could make a united decision and have the greatest strategic impact on the outcome, something it had failed to do with the 1940 nomination of Wendell Willkie when the Keystone delegation waited too long and the maverick was all but nominated. The current Pennsylvania Governor was known to oppose Dewey and back Vandenberg. Standing before the flashing cameras, Duff grimly said, "This is not my idea of harmony or of fair treatment of our delegation." He noted that Senator Martin acted "without even consulting the delegation." In exchange for his endorsement, the Dewey camp had given Senator Martin the privilege of putting Governor Dewey's name into nomination.

Former Governor Stassen immediately attacked the Martin deal as "a desperate admission of weakness." A deep gloom settled into the

Taft headquarters. Others denounced the Dewey "blitz" and warned that if Dewey failed on the first ballot, as he had in 1940, he would not be nominated. Yet others complained of the behind-the-scenes influence of Pennsylvania millionaire Joseph R. Grundy, head of the Pennsylvania Manufacturers Association. But word of Senator Martin's decision set off jubilation at the Dewey headquarters. Herbert Brownell stood on a table and announced to reporters that the Martin decision would have the "force of a new, improved atomic bomb." Governor Warren also decried the deal, saying there was "so much talk about deals it would be a wholesome thing if after the nominating speeches, we could have one roll-call so that these deals and double deals could be brought into the open and let the delegates sleep over them."

The Martin decision stimulated a stream of other favorite sons who relinquished their formalities to join the Dewey camp. Indiana, which came to the convention intending to nominate Representative Charles A. Halleck, the Republican House floor leader, was considering the same move.

Dewey later told 800 reporters that he felt "swell," and was "very grateful" for the endorsement and called Martin one of his oldest friends in public life. He spent most of his day courting delegates in room 807, his Victorian suite at the Bellevue-Stratford. A steady stream of delegates, delegation heads, governors, and other elected officials dropped in for chats. Most were interested in some patronage position for someone in their delegation in exchange for votes. While Dewey never made deals, he was often encouraging about their prospects.

All day, Senator Taft was also working hard to find support, visiting delegations from Utah, Missouri, Kansas, Washington state, Nevada, Vermont, Colorado, Tennessee, Iowa, Wisconsin, Hawaii, Idaho, and North and South Carolina. He reiterated that he had entered into no agreement with former Governor Stassen. Meanwhile, Stassen, who had served on a navy flagship in the Pacific during the war, was trying to send signals to delegates from his Hotel Warwick headquarters. He insisted that the Dewey camp was over-claiming first-ballot votes. To show his seriousness, he publicly eliminated himself from any Vice Presidential talks as well as for Senator from Minnesota. He was a Presidential contender and nothing less, he said, and was buoyed by the decision of seven Colorado delegates to join his cause.

At 9 P.M., Temporary Chairman Green introduced Permanent Chairman Martin, who gave his address to the body. The conservative Speaker of the House of Representatives began, "For the third time you have honored me with this gavel as your permanent chairman." He had previously managed the 1940 and 1944 conventions. Martin told the delegates that their party was ready to lead again and had been tested by both its victories and its defeats. He then congratulated the nation for resisting old world philosophies of statism. But he warned, "No longer may we relax in youthful faith in our own invincibility; no longer may we rely on the security which our natural borders once offered. When America acts today, it acts as the keeper of the world's peace.... Never has the need for sound executive leadership and firm policy in Washington been of such far-reaching importance."

Martin listed three problems that had faced Congress and would confront the new President. "First, the New Deal, over a period of 15 years of experimenting with statism had permitted hundreds of enemies of America to infiltrate into official positions. In the belief that no nation can continue to exist half free and half statist, we decided to go after these disciples of alien philosophies.... At first the administration protested that there were no communists in the government. Can you imagine that!...

"Second, it was evident to all that a free economy could not long last with taxes taking more than one-fourth of the national income.... Third, it was clear to all of us who dared to face the facts that no country could call itself free when organized labor was being forced to run, hat in hand, to the White House for pay increases; when management and labor alike were being denied, through government interference, their fundamental right of bargaining...." Martin said that the Eightieth Congress had begun to deal with all three problems, but needed a Republican President to finish the job and to lead the world in a time of international crisis.

Afterwards, former President Hoover, the nation's only living former President, was presented to tumultuous cheers. A 16-minute demonstration followed his arrival on the platform and the "Battle Hymn of the Republic" lifted the level of emotion. President Hoover, who had become friends with Harry Truman because the Missourian had invited him to visit the White House from which he had been exiled during FDR's tenure, delivered a major policy address which he said was not a partisan speech but one of principle. He told the convention that it must "generate a spirit which will rekindle in every American a love not only for his country, but for American civilization." He called on delegates to "feed the reviving fires of spiritual fervor which once made the word, 'American,' a stirring description of a man who lived and died for human liberty, who knew no private interest, no personal ambition, no popular acclaim, no advantage of price or place which overshadows the burning love for the freedom of man."

The former President then outlined the role the nation should take if it was to check the advance of collectivism. He stressed the need for foreign aid, but warned against "non-essentials, profligacy, or inefficiency" that hurt the national economy. He warned the party that it must not dwell in "platitudes." He concluded, "If you produce no leadership here, no virile fighter for the right, you will have done nothing of historic significance.... If you temporize with collectivism you will stimulate its growth and the defeat of free men.... And so I bespeak to you tonight to make yourselves worthy of the victory."

Finally that night, the convention heard from Representative Katharine St. George, of New York, who told delegates that, "The people of this nation, especially the women, are weary of wars and rumors of wars. They are going to turn the war party out and return to the Republican ideal of peace with honor." She added, that the American people "are beginning to realize that their government has gradually been taken from them by trickery and chicanery and that they are being led in a direction not of their own choosing. We can achieve peace only by having in office a President who will not try to stay in power by trotting a new crisis out of his propaganda barn every time his political fortunes look dim, and who will not, when it comes to the worse, save his political fortunes by plunging us into another war."

Then she charged that the Democrats "have many in the higher ranks who are tinged with communism and are fellow travelers. They honeycomb the departments of government and cry out to high heaven about their constitutional rights, the same Constitution that they are bent on destroying." She concluded that the Republican party was the only party not tainted by communism.

Late Tuesday, Representative Halleck visited with Governor Dewey, while the Massachusetts delegation deliberated hopping on the Dewey bandwagon. At the same time, the forces of the "Stop Dewey" movement met at the Union League Club on South Broad Street behind closed doors until 1:30 A.M. Wednesday morning seeking a strategy to halt the growing Dewey momentum. Most of the bargainers understood that it would take a heroic effort to reach their objective. Taft and Stassen both declared they were still in the race, and both had refused to yield to Vandenberg, who was staying out of the limelight at 250 Eighteenth Street overlooking Rittenhouse Square, a location known only to his close friends.

On Wednesday morning, June 23, 1948, the convention reconvened at 11 A.M. After an invocation, the body listened to addresses by Representative Charles A. Halleck, of Indiana, the House Majority Leader, who said, "The American people next November are not going back to disastrous New Dealism"; Mrs. Robert W. Macauley, assistant chairman of the Republican National Committee; Ralph Becker, president of the Young Republican Federation; and Senator Harry P. Cain, of Washington. Mrs. Margaret Chase Smith, who had been invited to the convention by several of its officers, was introduced to a cheering audience.

Then Senator Henry Cabot Lodge, Jr., of Massachusetts, who

served as chairman of the Resolutions Committee, presented the platform, which ran 2,400 words, 900 words longer than the original draft Lodge had brought to Philadelphia. The committee work had been contentious. Southern delegates had complained about the bold civil rights plank, even though similar words had appeared in almost every Republican platform since the party's founding in 1856. A group of "isolationists" who were not in agreement with the document's broad international scope had kept the committee in session until after midnight on Monday and Tuesday. But the convention unanimously adopted the platform without debate, assuring the world that it would continue support for the United Nations and the European Recovery Program. The party pledged it intended to keep foreign policy out of the Presidential campaign. The foreign affairs plank was seen as a victory for Senator Vandenberg and those who followed his leadership and a defeat for "Nationalist" Republicans who had fought the plank. Conservative Senator C. Wayland Brooks, of Illinois, had won limitations on the commitment to European reconstruction and any sharing of atomic technology. The platform also had watered down promises of reciprocal free trade agreements.

The twenty-fourth Republican national platform celebrated the nation's competitive system, which "furnishes vital opportunity for youth and all enterprising citizens." It called America's "productive power" a "unique weapon of our national defense and is the mainspring of material well-being and political freedom." The platform declared that, "Government, as the servant of such a system, should take all needed steps to strengthen and develop public health, to promote scientific research, to provide security for the aged, and to promote a stable economy so that men and women need not fear the loss of their jobs or the threat of economic hardships through no fault of their own." Thus the GOP seemed to have adopted the most positive lessons of the New Deal as articles of faith for the American people.

The platform also heralded the achievements of the Republican-dominated Eightieth Congress, including a balanced budget, tax reduction, assistance to veterans, assistance to agriculture, elimination of the poll tax for black soldiers who wanted to vote, reform of the labor laws (Taft-Hartley and the outlawing of strikes in industries vital to the nation's welfare), a military draft, support of the United Nations, "the most far-reaching measures in history adopted to aid the recovery of the free world on a basis of self help," all done "in the face of frequent obstruction from the executive branch."

The 1948 Republicans pledged to "protect labor's rights," against "coercion and exploitation of employers... and whatever quarter..." and upheld the right of collective bargaining. On civil rights, Republicans affirmed their historic commitment to people of color and said, "Lynching, or any other form of mob violence anywhere, is a disgrace to any civilized state and we favor prompt enactment of legislation to end this infamy." The Republican party promised to end the "poll tax as a requisite to voting" and was "opposed to the idea of racial segregation in the Armed Forces of the United States," although the Republican Congress had not yet acted on these issues.

Additionally, Republicans promised a "fight" against inflation. And they pledged, "vigorous enforcement of existing laws against communists and enactment of such new legislation as may be necessary to expose the treasonable activities of communists and defeat of their objective of establishing here a Godless dictatorship controlled from abroad."

Republicans, as they had in the past, called for "a Constitutional Amendment providing equal rights for women. We favor equal pay for equal work, regardless of sex." They also favored "the elimination of unnecessary federal bureaus and of the duplication of the functions of necessary governmental agencies." And they favored "equality of educational opportunity for all and the promotion of education and educational facilities." States' rightists were appeased by the call for "restoration to the states of their historic rights to the tide and submerged lands, territorial waters, lakes, and streams." Republicans also went on record for statehood for Alaska, Hawaii, and Puerto Rico, as well as "self-government for the residents of the nation's capital."

The Republican platform asked for "peace with all nations" and pledged a foreign policy dedicated to "the preservation of a free America in a free world of free men." And Republicans declared, "We support the United Nations as the world's best hope in this direction...." The party welcomed Israel into "the family of nations," and pointed out that the "Republican party was the first to call for the establishment of a free and independent Jewish commonwealth."

The platform proved popular with the party. It was a combined collection of traditional rhetorical positions on labor and civil rights, and of more recently held progressive positions on women and internationalism. In the case of labor relations, the document glossed over the tough Congressional fight over Taft-Hartley and the party's actual antagonism to most of the nation's labor unions. On foreign affairs and anti-communism it reflected the party's fervent beliefs. Lodge's reading of the document elicited only occasional bursts of applause, in part because it had been released the day before. But Governor Dewey told reporters it was "a mighty fine statement of the principles of the Republican party."

While the convention proceeded, talk of the Vice Presidential nomination was beginning to creep onto the floor. A leading candidate at the beginning of the day was Governor Green. Many delegates had been impressed by his hard-hitting address. But before the evening was out he made it clear he was for Taft and would not accept a Vice Presidential bid with Governor Dewey, disappointing the Dewey strategists who made him the keynoter. Earl Warren's name was also being circulated, as was that of Ohio Senator John Bricker, who had run with Dewey in the failed 1944 campaign. Others were talking about Senator Kenneth S. Wherry. Neither Senator Taft nor Harold Stassen were given much chance because of the animosity they had built up in the Dewey camp. Others possible V.P.s were Senator Edward Martin, Senator Henry Cabot Lodge, Jr., Senator Leverett Saltonstall, Senator Raymond Baldwin, and Pennsylvania Governor Duff. But by the end of the session, Representative Charles A. Halleck, of Indiana, was the hot name.

That evening at 9:20 P.M., the roll call of the states for nominations for President of the United States finally began. By 3:10 A.M. the names Dewey, Taft, Warren, Stassen, Baldwin, Vandenberg, had all been placed into nomination and seconded in elaborate speeches that set off noisy demonstrations. Many were the same candidates who had been nominated, and defeated by Wendell Willkie in Philadelphia in 1940, and who had been brought to the floor of the Chicago convention in 1944 before Governor Dewey claimed rapid victory.

In the 1948 roll call of states, Alabama yielded to Pennsylvania, and Dewey was indeed nominated by Senator Edward Martin, who first extolled the critical role of Philadelphia and nearby Valley Forge in the nation's formation and the founding of the Republican party. "Once more we meet to save America," the Pennsylvania Senator declared. "Fortunately our party is prepared." Martin described the leadership his party offered. "By every test, there is one man who towers above the others. Every man and woman who hears my voice knows who I mean.... He has the fighting vigor to wage a winning campaign. He can carry the crushing burdens of the Presidency."

Martin spoke of Dewey's qualifications. "For many years, the biggest state of the Union was controlled by an alliance of Tammany Hall corruption and left-wing radicalism. It became the spawning place of the New Deal. Then, in the darkest days of the 1930s, there arose in New York City, a young man born and raised in Michigan, in our great Midwest. He gave stirring leadership to the fight against organized crime and corruption. He gave Tammany Hall the worst beating it ever had in its whole history. His name and fame were on the lips of all the nation....

"Then in 1942 the years of effort were rewarded. The people of New York elected him the state's first Republican governor in 20 years.... Two years ago, he was reelected Governor of New York by nearly 700,000 votes, the greatest majority ever given any governor." Finally, Martin described the problems awaiting the next President and the qualifications he needed to confront them. "This candidate has all these qualities so necessary for the next President of the United States. It is the greatest honor of my life to present to this convention a man who for years has belonged to all America, tried, tested, and true, America's next President, Thomas E, Dewey." The nomination set off a broad demonstration. With 400 portraits of Dewey fastened to poles, delegates marched across the convention floor blowing small horns and kazoos. However, numerous "boos" could also be heard. The demonstration lasted 25 minutes, though it lacked spontaneity and was slow in gaining momentum. Some observers said the celebrants seemed to "have lead in their pants."

When the roll call continued, Arizona yielded to Ohio and Senator John W. Bricker, Dewey's running mate in 1944, nominated his colleague, Senator Taft. Bricker praised Taft's work as chairman of the Republican Policy Committee of the Senate, chairman of the Joint Committee on the Economic Report, and chairman of the Labor Committee. He added, "The nation and the world are indebted to his superb leadership. The magnificent record of the Eightieth Congress is his record; upon it he stands." Bricker lauded Taft's courage in authoring the Taft-Hartley Act, which was passed over President Truman's veto. And Bricker said, "There is in him no guile or deceit. He will lift the curtain of secrecy from the many manipulations of the New Deal. He believes in the truth and knows the truth will keep the people free." The heat-exhausted delegates cheered modestly.

California's Governor Earl Warren was nominated by Dr. Robert Gordon Sproul, president of the University of California, who called him "a liberal, an administrator, and a popular leader." He then outlined Warren's 25-year career of "government by goodwill, confidence, and cooperation." And Sproul claimed that Warren was "neither an isolationist nor an internationalist. He is a modern American who is intelligently aware of a world in which space and time have been almost eliminated."

Harold Stassen was nominated by Congressman Walter H. Judd, of Minnesota, who said that Stassen had "taken his message to the people and won it with the people, has won their overwhelming support wherever, in primary elections or polls, all of the people, independents as well as Republicans [voted]..." He said the polls showed that Stassen would win the November election by five million votes more than any other Republican candidate. "He knows war first-hand," Judd added. "For 30 months he lived with America's young men in fierce battle and in lonely isolation. He understands their needs and their problems as no other candidate can. He understands the grave problems of trying to make and maintain a just and enduring peace."

Judd pointed out that Stassen "was called back from naval service to serve as one of our delegates to the United Nations conference at San Francisco and was rated there by hard-boiled newspaper men as one of the two most outstanding statesmen at that conference, not just from the

United States, but from the world." Judd concluded that Stassen had "done more to revitalize our Republican party throughout the whole country than any other person in our generation." The demonstration staged for Stassen was by far the largest and noisiest of all the nominees' parades, reminiscent of the Willkie hullabaloo of 1940. Balloons streamed down 90 feet onto the celebrants who carried 32 of the state standards and waved flags on the floor and in the galleries as sirens wailed, stirring the delegates and spectators out of their wilted, late-night stupors. The outburst lasted 25 minutes. Delegates were on the very edge of total heat exhaustion.

Connecticut's favorite son, Senator Raymond E. Baldwin, was nominated by the secretary of that state, Mrs. Frances Burke Redick, at 2:40 A.M., who called him, "a warm human being, skilled and practiced in the complicated science of government, a statesman beloved by the people, a responsible and patriotic American."

Michigan Governor Kim Sigler nominated Vandenberg, and noted the people of the nation had observed that "he has not sought this office; that he has made no attempt to gather or pledge delegates. The people have observed that he has subordinated any and all personal aspirations in a determination to develop for America a foreign policy recognized for its breadth and vision throughout the world" and that he was an expert on domestic issues as well.

Just after 3:30 A.M., Thursday June 24, General Douglas MacArthur was nominated by Harlan Kelley, of Wisconsin, a former school mate of Dewey's. MacArthur had been sidetracked after finishing second in the Wisconsin primary and was the one candidate few people had been talking about during the week. Kelley was accurate when he said, "We average American citizens are horribly confused. We do not know if we have just finished a war, whether we are now engaged in a war, hot or cold, or whether we are about to plunge into a war. We are swimming around hopelessly in a post-Roosevelt New Deal sea, without a pilot, without a compass, and without a rudder. We need a leader in fact as well as in name." He said everyone knew that sooner or later there had to be a "showdown" with Russia, and that hopefully it would be a peaceful one.

"When this showdown takes place, Stalin and Molotov, or their successors, will be on one side of the table." On the other side, Kelley said, must be a leader who commands their respect. "Deep down in your hearts fellow delegates, regardless of whether you came to this convention pledged or unpledged, who in all America is best qualified to occupy that chair? We need as President today a man whose experience is world-wide, not just state-wide, or even nation-wide. We need a man of global stature.... We need a man who in his dealings with Soviet Russia will make us proud, instead of apologetic or ashamed of being an

248

American. We need a man whose very name commands respect throughout the entire world.... We need Douglas MacArthur."

Then the convention adjourned with voting scheduled for later Thursday. In the interim, Governor Green released the Illinois delegates from voting for him and the bulk of them, under Colonel McCormick's influence, were going to Taft. Green was no longer considered a Vice Presidential contender. Charles Halleck also released Indiana's 29 delegates, who were transferring their allegiance to Dewey. That move increased the speculation that Halleck would get the second spot.

Early Wednesday evening, the Pennsylvania caucus had finally decided to give 41 first ballot votes to the New York governor and 27 to Senator Taft. Governor Duff was joined by Joseph N. Pew and state chairman M. Harvey Taylor in supporting Taft. Joseph Grundy, Mrs. Scranton, and chief justice of the Pennsylvania supreme court, George W. Maxey, said they would cast their votes for Dewey. Senator Martin told the caucus he made his endorsement because he did not want Pennsylvania to suffer a "debacle like we had eight years ago" when Wendell Willkie all but sewed up the nomination without Pennsylvania's help, before it put him over the top.

Governor Alfred E. Driscoll, of New Jersey, who favored Dewey, also promised to release his state's 35 delegates after the first ballot. Dewey called the New Jersey governor "a great and progressive leader and administrator of a great state." The majority of Missouri delegates declared for Dewey. Massachusetts said that after the first ballot, the majority of its delegation would vote for Dewey.

All day a stream of individuals and groups of delegates came to the Dewey headquarters, accompanied by liaisons assigned to their states, and were taken for interviews with Herbert Brownell, Jr., J. Russel Sprague, or Edwin F. Jaeckle, Dewey's convention managers, who had a background card for each delegate and gave each personal attention. The most important met directly with the candidate himself. The confident Dewey bandwagon was speeding toward victory.

But Senator Taft continued to insist, "I think he has to be nominated on the second ballot or not at all." Some anti-Dewey operatives were turning to Governor Warren as a last-ditch compromise candidate who had not been scarred by the week's battles. Even General Eisenhower's name was being bandied about. But because the Stop Dewey movement had little else in common than its opposition to the New York governor, its hopes were rapidly fading. And neither Stassen nor Taft had given up hopes of winning the nomination outright. Insiders were saying if Taft could hold his Southern delegates, his candidacy still had viability. But by 3 A.M. Thursday, Stassen shifted from promoting his own candidacy to advancing that of Senator Vandenberg. It was too late.

Thursday afternoon, at 2:25 P.M., June 24, 1948, Republican delegates gathered to make their final decision on the hottest day of the year. The Dewey "blitzkrieg" was about to show its devastating effects. On the first ballot, with 548 votes needed to win, Dewey took a commanding lead of 434 votes to Taft's 224. Stassen attracted 157 votes, Senator Vandenberg received 62 votes, Governor Warren picked up 59 votes, Governor Green 56, Governor Driscoll received 35, Speaker Martin 18, National Chairman Carroll Reece attracted 15 votes, General MacArthur fielded only 11, and Representative Everett M. Dirksen, of Illinois, a future star of the party, attracted 1.

Immediately, the chair called for the second ballot. Dewey gained 81 votes to 515, just 33 fewer than he needed for victory. Taft climbed to 274, Stassen slipped to 149, and Vandenberg held at 62. Governor Warren received 57, Senator Baldwin 19, Speaker Martin 10, General MacArthur 7, and Chairman Reece 1. The Dewey bandwagon had turned into a steamroller. Pennsylvania Governor James H. Duff, who had taken the public role of leading the anti-Dewey coalition, called for a temporary recess at 4:55 P.M. Senator William F. Knowland, of California, seconded the motion. "The New York delegation has no objection to a recess," said a confident William F. Bleakley, the delegation's chairman, while the packed galleries shouted in protest.

Finally, at 7:30 P.M., before the third ballot, the other nominees withdrew their names and pledged support in November to their rival. Outside, the heat broke with a sudden, violent rain storm moving in from the southwest. Power lines outside Convention Hall snapped with a flash of blue-arced flame. But inside the humidity just grew thicker in the hall that delegates were calling the "steamheated iron lung." Former Governor Stassen and Senator Baldwin personally went to the podium to urge the Dewey nomination. Then at 8:48 P.M., Governor Thomas Edmund Dewey was unanimously nominated by the Twenty-Fourth Republican National Convention, receiving all of the 1,094 votes.

One of those votes was an Illinois alternate. Rather than cast his ballot for the liberal, internationalist Dewey, *Chicago Tribune* publisher Robert McCormick walked out of Convention Hall. He said he left rather than embarrass his delegation by voting against the New York governor. "But it might have been worse. It could have been Vandenberg," he bitterly remarked.

The New York governor and his wife came into the auditorium at 9:17 P.M. as the band played "Michigan" and then "Hail, Hail, The Gang's All Here." His managers, Herbert Brownell, Jr., Edwin F. Jaeckle, and Russel Sprague walked closely behind. Dewey was the only person in Republican history to that point to be nominated after losing a Presidential contest. And never before had a candidate who had lost the first important primary, Wisconsin in 1948, gone on to win the nomination. Had Stassen won the Oregon primary, he might have been the nominee. But Dewey's managers had waged an effective psychological war in Philadelphia, making it appear as though their candidate were invincible. Then the bandwagon began rolling. Senator Martin and Pennsylvania had put the last wheel on the old wagon so it could roll to victory.

Governor Dewey stood before the hot and enthusiastic delegates to deliver his acceptance speech. "You, the elected representatives of our Republican party have again given to me the highest honor you can bestow; your nomination for President of the United States." The crowd warmly applauded him. "I thank you with all my heart for your friendship and confidence. I am profoundly sensible of the responsibility that goes with it. I accept your nomination. In all humility, I pray God that I may deserve this opportunity to serve our country," the new nominee began in his deep, calm, sophisticated voice.

"I come to you unfettered by a single obligation, or promise to any living person, free to join you in selecting to serve our nation, the finest men and women in the nation, free to unite our party and our country in meeting the grave challenge of our time," he assured them. "United we can match this challenge with depth of understanding and largeness of spirit; with unity which is above recrimination; above partisanship; above self-interest. These are articles of faith from which the greatness of America has been fashioned. Our people are eager to know again the upsurging power of that faith. They are turning to us to put such a faith at the heart of our national life...."

Dewey congratulated his opponents and called the convention "a stirring demonstration of the life and vitality and ideals of our Republican party. There has been honest contention, spirited disagreement, hot argument." The delegates laughed. "But let no one be misled. You have given moving and dramatic proof of how Americans, who honestly differ, close ranks and move forward, for the nation's well-being, shoulder to shoulder....

"We are a united party. Our nation stands tragically in need of that same unity. Our people are turning away from the meaner things that divide us. They yearn to move to higher ground, to find a common purpose in the finer things that unite us. We must be the instrument of that aspiration. We must be the means by which America's full powers are released and this uncertain future filled again with opportunity. That is our pledge. That will be the fruit of our victory....

"The next Presidential term will see the completion of the first half of the twentieth century. So far it has been a century of amazing progress and of terrible tragedy. We have seen the world transformed. We have seen mankind's age-long struggle against nature crowned by extraordinary success. Yet our triumphs have been darkened by bitter defeats in the equally ancient struggle of men to live together in peace, security, and understanding....

"We must learn to do better. The period that is drawing to a close has been one of scientific achievement. The era that is opening before us must be a period of human and spiritual achievement.... We must solve the problem of establishing a just and lasting peace in the world, and of securing to our own and other like-minded people the blessings of freedom and opportunity. To me, to be a Republican in this hour, is to dedicate one's life to the freedom of men. As long as the world is half free and half slave, we must peacefully labor to help men everywhere achieve liberty.... When these rights are secure in the world, the permanent ideals of the Republican party shall have been realized.

"The ideals of the American people are the ideals of the Republican party. We have lighted a beacon here in Philadelphia, in this cradle of our own independence. We have lighted a beacon to give eternal hope that men may live in liberty with human dignity and before God and loving Him, stand erect and free." The convention rose as one to its feet to herald the stirring speech of its national leader, certain that his serene and principled words would lead the party to victory. When Dewey finished, someone put garlands of flowers over his shoulder as if he were an ancient Olympic hero. He was 46 years old and had been in the public eye for 18 of those years. He was happy, smiled broadly, and waved to his admirers.

On Friday, June 25, 1948, the convention convened one last time to vote by acclamation to honor Governor Dewey's choice of Governor Earl Warren as his Vice Presidential nominee. Charles Halleck had been Dewey's early choice, but several senior Republicans who remembered his role in nominating Willkie eight years earlier took their revenge and put a stop to him.

Meanwhile, half a world away in Berlin, where a Soviet blockade threatened starvation to half of the city, General Lucius D. Clay, U.S. Military Governor, warned that the U.S. would not leave short of war with Russia. In Washington, President Truman signed a draft bill that would induct 225,000 young men into the military before the end of the year. Thomas Dewey, who was an exponent of bipartisan foreign policy to contain communism, would be fighting his last political war on two fronts; against a sitting President and against world events over which he had no control.

1948: Triple Convention Year
The Thirtieth Democratic National Convention

Convention-at-a-Glance

Event: Thirtieth Democratic National Convention
Date: July 12-15, 1948
Location: Municipal Auditorium/Convention Hall, Thirty-fourth Street and Civic Center Boulevard
Philadelphia Mayor: Bernard Samuel, Republican
Philadelphia's Population: 2,071,605 (1950)
Convention Permanent Chairman: Representative Sam Rayburn, Texas
Number of Delegates: 1,592 delegates with 1,234 votes, since at-large delegates only had ½ votes; (1,210 ½ actually voted for a nominee after the Dixiecrat walk-out.)
Number Needed to Nominate: A majority
Candidates for Nomination: Senator Richard Brevard Russell, Georgia; President Harry S Truman, Missouri
Presidential Nominee: President Harry S Truman
Age at Nomination: 64
Number of Ballots: One
Vice Presidential Nominee: Senator Alben William Barkley, Kentucky
Largest Audience: 16,500
Platform Positions: Promotion of civil rights, including abolition of the poll tax as a condition for voting, an anti-lynching law, a fair employment practices commission, integration of the armed forces; repeal of the Taft-Hartley labor law; support of the United Nations, development of a U. N. armed force; support for the Marshall Plan and the Truman Doctrine; support of Israel; end to arms embargo in the Middle East; lifting the limit on the number of displaced people allowed to enter the U.S.; reaffirmation of New Deal domestic programs
Campaign Slogan: "Give 'em Hell, Harry"
Campaign Song: "I'm Just Wild About Harry"

President Harry S Truman
1948 Democratic Presidential
Nominee

Senator Alben William Barkley
1948 Democratic Vice Presidential
Nominee

1948

Triple Convention Year
The Thirtieth Democratic National Convention

Most Americans were convinced President Harry S Truman would be a loser if he ran in 1948. Polls predicted it. Republicans promised it. Democrats, who had already lost their hold on Congress in the 1946 mid-term election, believed it. Many progressive Democrats, disturbed by Truman's foreign and domestic policy, had already defected to Henry A. Wallace, Franklin D. Roosevelt's Secretary of Agriculture and Commerce and Vice President from 1941 to 1945. Several Southern delegations were threatening a revolt over civil rights versus states' rights at the Philadelphia convention. The New Deal coalition was apparently falling apart. So in the weeks leading up to the Thirtieth Democratic National Convention, many party bosses, afraid that their local and state tickets would go down to defeat with Truman, and liberal activists, as well as Southerners opposed to his policies, searched for an alternative to save the New Deal Democracy.

Two alternate candidates were courted by the disillusioned Democrats: General Dwight D. Eisenhower and Supreme Court Justice William O. Douglas. On July 3, 1948, 19 party leaders, including New York City Mayor William O'Dwyer, sent telegrams to the 1,592 delegates to the Democratic National Convention inviting them to a July 10 preconvention caucus to discuss alternatives to Truman. James Roosevelt, California Democratic State Chairman and son of President Franklin D. Roosevelt, one of the ringleaders, suggested the telegram idea. The majority of California delegates were reportedly ready to desert Truman. The meeting was scheduled for the headquarters of the Illinois delegation in the Bartram Hotel at the invitation of Jacob (Jack) M. Arvey, Cook County Democratic Chairman. Early respondents to the anti-Truman call included Senator Claude Pepper, of Florida, Lester H. Loble, Montana State chairman, and Thomas R. Mahoney, chairman of the Oregon delegation, which was already pledged to Truman on the first ballot. The national group was predicting a "knock-down and drag-out fight" for the nomination in Philadelphia. In the weeks leading up to the convention, pressure mounted on the plain-speaking man from Missouri to step aside and let someone else lead the party.

Over the course of the Republic, six Vice Presidents had succeeded a President who had died in office. Only two won renomination by their party: Theodore Roosevelt in 1904 and Calvin Coolidge in 1924. Four others failed to get renominated, including John Tyler, an anti-Jackson Democrat who succeeded Whig William Henry Harrison in 1841; Whig Millard Fillmore, who assumed the reigns of power from Zachary Taylor in 1850; Andrew Johnson, who filled out the term of the slain Abraham Lincoln in 1865; and Chester A. Arthur, who was elevated after James Garfield was assassinated in 1881. In the weeks before the 1948 Democratic convention, it was unclear which group Harry S Truman might follow.

The Georgia and Virginia delegations had already been instructed to support General Eisenhower for the nomination. Alabama, which was scheduled to lead off the roll call of the states, said it would yield to any state that would place Eisenhower's name in nomination. In a radio address, Alabama's Senator John J. Sparkman, a future Vice Presidential nominee, called on Eisenhower to answer the "call to duty." Barney L. Whatley, a Democratic National Committeeman from Colorado, said that Eisenhower boosters were trying to line up the first six states in the roll call for the popular general in a psychological effort to stampede the convention to their candidate. Delegates in most of the 48 states were reportedly reconsidering their commitments to Truman.

On July 4, Frank Hague, former mayor of Jersey City and vice chairman of the Democratic National Committee, hastily called New Jersey delegates and alternates into caucus to say he was withdrawing his recent endorsement of President Truman and was now urging a draft of General Eisenhower; "Every leader in this state has informed me that if Truman is a candidate there will be a complete Republican landslide." New York political leaders had told President Truman the same thing. The 100 New Jersey political leaders who gathered in the ballroom of the Monterey Hotel in Asbury Park cheered the general's name for three minutes before unanimously adopting a resolution to nominate Dwight D. Eisenhower, calling him "the people's choice" and pledging the state's 36 votes to his candidacy.

The five-star general, who had left active army service in 1947 and now served as president of Columbia University in New York City, was keeping his own counsel on the draft movement. Two years earlier, President Truman had hinted to the general that he would be willing to step aside and run as Vice President if Eisenhower wanted to run at the top of the Democratic ticket. In the interim, the President had grown to like his job and felt more confident he could perform it well. And if Eisenhower's name was placed into nomination, Truman felt he still had the votes to win. However, Eisenhower actually had wanted the Republican nomination in 1948 and had made his wish clear to a number of ranking GOP members. But other long-time party members such as Taft and Dewey had their own eyes on the crown and Eisenhower was left to wait his turn and play coy.

In a January 23, 1948, letter to Manchester, New Hampshire, publisher Leonard W. Finder, Eisenhower had already written, "The necessary and wise subordination of the military to civil power will be best sustained when lifelong professional soldiers, in the absence of some obvious and overriding reasons, abstain from seeking high political office." But Harry Carlson, National Democratic Committeeman from New Hampshire, who had talked more recently to the general said he was "satisfied" that Eisenhower would accept an "honest draft."

At the same time, a liberal group, the Committee of New York Democrats for Douglas, set up offices in Philadelphia's Sylvania Hotel. The group was headed by Maurice P. Davidson, former New York City Commissioner of Water Supply, Gas, and Electricity, and a founder of the Fusion party. He had already heard from several Democrats and vainly hoped that a Douglas nomination would draw Progressive party candidate Henry A. Wallace and his followers back to the Democratic party. He predicted that the 57-year-old Douglas, as a good New Dealer, would restore "order and a clear sense of direction" to the Democratic party. He hoped his group would coordinate the work of the Young Democrats for Douglas and student clubs for Douglas that had sprung up in 38 states. Other activists from the liberal Americans for Democratic Action (ADA), such as Minneapolis Mayor Hubert H. Humphrey, were stumping for either Douglas or Eisenhower as an alternative to Truman.

Meanwhile, a smiling and joking Harry Truman, traveling by train on a preconvention speaking tour taking him 9,000 miles across 18 western states, seemed unfazed by the Eisenhower boom and insisted that he would run again for President and refused to withdraw from seeking the nomination, even though pressure seemed to be building from every direction. But he was not helping himself with the local politicians, keeping them off of the train and not doing enough advance work to talk about local issues. Still, he was getting good crowd response to his new "off-the-cuff" delivery of speeches that allowed his infectious and good-natured personality to come across to listeners. As many as a million people turned out in Los Angeles to view the President. He confidently laughed at press inquiries about stepping aside, calling them "foolish question number one." He claimed to have enough pledged votes to win on the first ballot. With 618 votes needed to take the nomination, the President's private calculations gave him at least 809 of the 1234 votes, while just 425 were undecided or committed to the anti-Truman movement.

Asked if he would accept Mrs. Franklin D. Roosevelt or General Eisenhower as running mates, the President indicated that of course he would, but that was up to them. However, a spokeswoman for Eleanor Roosevelt, whom Truman had appointed to head the U.S. Delegation to the new United Nations, confirmed that she had "no intention of running for public office at any time whatsoever." Truman added that he was certain that he would beat the Dewey-Warren ticket in November. He privately told his friends that back in 1940, he had been informed that he could not win renomination or reelection to the U.S. Senate, but had done so, and that he intended to prove critics wrong again. Senator J. Howard McGrath, of Rhode Island, the Democratic National Chairman, later added that the America public would never turn out an incumbent when the country was enjoying the greatest economic prosperity in its history.

Finally, on July 5, the general spoke, through a spokesman. In a memorandum to Columbia University's Public Relations Office, Eisenhower reaffirmed his decision not to be a candidate or accept any draft for the Presidency. "I know that your office has for some days been overburdened with innumerable queries concerning my intentions in regard to the current political situation. My decisions and earnest convictions concerning possible personal connection with this year's political contest were given to the public several months ago, but it now appears that there has arisen a question as to whether or not I have changed my position. Profoundly touched by the renewed suggestion that I could satisfactorily fill high public office, my views with respect to my proper course of duty are still identical with those presented in the letter I wrote on January 23, 1948.... I shall continue, subject to the pleasure of the university trustees, to perform the important duties I have undertaken as president of Columbia. I will not, at this time, identify myself with any political party, and could not accept nomination for any public office or participate in a partisan political convention."

With General Eisenhower's announcement, most anti-Truman Democrats dourly admitted defeat in their efforts to find a viable alternative to draft at the Philadelphia convention. "I don't see how we can unite now behind any one candidate," said Senator Sparkman. Of Supreme Court Justice Douglas, Senator William J. Fulbright, of Arkansas, said, "He doesn't have the appeal to the South. He wouldn't fit at all like Eisenhower." Justice Douglas, on vacation in Oregon, refused comment on the draft movement, simply saying, "I'm not running for anything." Leon Henderson, chairman of the Americans for Democratic Action, said the general's statement did not "alter the fact that President Truman has repudiated the Democratic party." Henderson hoped the convention would ignore the general's statement and nominate him anyway as the "best man the country can provide."

James Roosevelt said Eisenhower's statement "confirms his desire not to accept partisan office" but urged the Democratic party to offer him as a "national candidate unfettered in these days of international crisis by the normal traffic of partisan politics. I hope and believe the Democratic party is equal to this challenge." Senator Claude Pepper urged the Democratic party to transform itself temporarily into a national movement to draft General Eisenhower, giving him the power to write his own platform and choose his own Vice President. "The country is in the kind of crisis that demands exceptional responses. The people are clearly troubled and with good reason. They will not be satisfied with any ordinary partisan candidate of either party. The international situation is acute, and there are so many causes of friction that at any moment World War III could break out. And we have seen the country go unchecked toward a disastrous inflation which, unless something is done to check it, will lead some day to economic collapse and another depression."

Frank Hague said he still hoped to convince Truman not to run. "If the President knew the real conditions and knew the disastrous results that confront the Democratic party in this campaign, I am sure he would hesitate to subject the party to such a disastrous defeat. It is the duty of Democratic leaders throughout the country not to sit idly by and deceive the President and their constituents but to advise him truthfully as to the real conditions in their respective states." Others in the anti-Truman chorus were simply gloomy over the seeming inevitability of the President's renomination and likely defeat in November. They predicted local and state support for the national ticket would be marginal.

When he was informed of Eisenhower's statement, Truman, who was traveling back to Washington by train, simply commented, "General Eisenhower is an honorable man." Party officials and Presidential staff close to Truman were now confident, as Truman had been all along, that he could easily hold onto the nomination. The preconvention anti-Truman caucus fell apart and the draft Eisenhower movement subsided to a whisper. The big-city bosses who had pushed for Truman to replace Henry A. Wallace as Roosevelt's Vice President in 1944 were now unable to remove him from the top of the ticket four years later.

But on July 7, 1948, 5,000 New Yorkers held a vigil outside Eisenhower's Columbia University residence at 60 Morningside Drive, chanting "We want Eisenhower." From his second floor balcony, the general again refused, saying. "I am of course, very honored and flattered.... Thank you and good night." Meanwhile on the train to Philadelphia from California, James Roosevelt was berated by members of his own delegation for turning on Truman. "This train is smeared with Eisenhower stuff," said one upset California delegate. Reporters were reminded that John Shelley, of San Francisco, not James Roosevelt, was chair of the California delegation.

By the time the California train reached William Penn's settlement, Eisenhower had made his last and most emphatic rebuff to the Democrats. He followed in the military tradition of General William

Tecumseh Sherman, who wrote the 1884 Republican convention, "If nominated, I will not run. If elected I will not serve." In a telegram to Claude Pepper, Eisenhower reiterated that he would not accept the Democratic nomination "no matter on what terms, conditions, or premises a proposal might be couched." The same day, Justice Douglas put the final nail in the anti-Truman movement. "I am not a candidate, have never been a candidate, and don't plan on becoming a candidate. And I would not accept the nomination if drafted," Douglas added for finality. New York Mayor William O'Dwyer and Chicago's Jacob Arvey issued a joint statement endorsing the President. The anti-Truman boom collapsed.

The sole survivor was President Harry S Truman. Born on a farm near Lamar, Missouri, on May 8, 1884, Truman had graduated from high school in Independence, Missouri. He left the farm to become a partner in a small haberdashery business, but with the outbreak of World War I, he was commissioned as a lieutenant in the U.S. Army in 1917, and saw plenty of action commanding an artillery unit. The future President was mustered out of the Army in 1919, and married his high school sweetheart, Bess Wallace, later that year.

Truman's rise to the top of the political heap had been a combination of skill and pure luck. One of the soldiers under his command during World War I was a nephew of Kansas City political boss Tom Pendergast. At age 37, after Truman's haberdashery business failed, a chance meeting with the nephew led to a political job with the uncle instead of a pair of overalls back on the Truman family farm. Truman's large network of friends was valuable to the political machine. After winning an election in 1922 to become Jackson County judge, Truman wanted to run for tax collector in 1934 and collect its big salary of $25,000. Pendergast replied, "That office is promised. The best I can do for you is U.S. Senator." It was a post with little graft potential, and therefore of little machine interest, where local problems almost always took precedence.

Truman took the chance in 1934 and ended up in Washington. But his political sponsor ended up in jail after pleading guilty to income tax evasion for not reporting a bribe. Several members of his machine were sent away along with him. Truman was not implicated but was tarnished. "I am sorry it happened. But I am not going to desert a sinking ship," he responded. The future President had to fight to get renominated and elected on his own in 1940, campaigning hard on the dusty roads of the state. When World War II began, Truman, who was a reserve colonel, tried to re-enlist. He was rejected because of his age. But that luckily led him to his position as chairman of the Senate committee investigating war contracts. He uncovered and exposed inefficiency and corruption and greatly speeded up the war production effort while saving money for taxpayers. He was in the national spotlight.

When the big-city bosses and Southerners in the party who resented Henry A. Wallace and his reformer and integrationist philosophy, made plans to get rid of him at the 1944 Chicago convention, they turned to Truman as a replacement, thinking he couldn't do any harm behind Roosevelt: the Vice Presidency would also get him out of a position where he had done much harm to the profits of war suppliers. Truman resisted overtures. "I have the best job a man could have and want to stick to it," he protested. But President Roosevelt, who was indifferent to his running mate despite his ill health, made it clear that Truman was to do his duty to his party and country. Less than three months after the 1945 inauguration, President Roosevelt was dead, and Harry S Truman, a former haberdasher from Missouri, was President of the United States in the midst of a savage world war.

"I don't know whether any of you fellows ever had a load of hay or a bull fall on you," he told reporters. "But last night the whole weight of the moon and the stars and all of the planets fell on me. I feel tremendous responsibility. Please pray for me. I mean that." The President's first few months were an unqualified success. The Allies won the war against Germany and then, after his decision to drop two atomic bombs on Japan, the empire of the rising sun capitulated. Next came the founding of the United Nations and the hopes for world peace that it inspired. When post-war cooperation broke down with the Soviet Union, the new President issued the "Truman Doctrine" promising to stop communist aggression and promoting free governments for all nations and the Marshall Plan to reconstruct a war-devastated western Europe.

Truman got tough with the Soviets and an atomic World War III seemed to hover ominously over the world. But domestic problems came to the fore and wore at the President's credibility and popularity. Truman had trouble with an outbreak of labor strikes. In the mid-term, 1946 congressional elections, Truman favored continued price controls. The Republicans opposed them. He opposed tax cuts. The Republicans campaigned upon them. Truman opposed labor law reform. The Republicans were adamant in their desire to break labor. In November, Republicans swept to victory and control of the House and Senate for the first time since the 1920s. The House of Representatives went 246 Republicans to 188 Democrats; the Senate, 51 Republicans to 45 Democrats. Truman seemed dazed and weary. The burdens of the office were telling on him. One administration insider explained, "People are restless, dissatisfied, and fearful. Truman is just a man, a likable, courageous, stubborn man. So away with him."

Threatened by defeat, Truman was a fighter. When party regulars advised him to step aside for some other candidate who could hold the party together and beat the Republicans in 1948, Truman replied, "I'm not a quitter." Indeed, he was ready to take the battle right to the Republican Congress and to the American people. And his poll numbers appeared to be getting better. Dr. George Gallup's public opinion charts said 36 percent of the public thought he was doing a good job in April. By early June, the number had risen to 39 percent.

But as the delegates headed for Philadelphia, the world was still on red alert. The latest flash point was in Germany, where the Soviets were tightening their blockade of Berlin in response to Allied economic unification of their sectors. The Russian authorities cut off electricity and ordered that no automobile traffic leave the city for the western zones. Truman, in turn, ordered Allied planes to fly in tons of supplies to break the blockade. The question of when to use or not use atomic weapons was being discussed in the White House and at Allied command posts. "We'll stay in Berlin, come what may...," Truman said, and ordered three more squadrons of B-29 bombers to Europe. At the same time, in Palestine, fighting again flared between the new Israeli state and Arab resistance forces and was spreading. Egyptian planes had just bombed Tel Aviv. In eastern Europe, Yugoslavia was breaking away from Russian domination after Russia's failed attempt to overthrow Marshal Tito. And in the United States, nine leftist labor union officials were held in contempt of Congress for refusing to say whether they had ever been communists. As had been the case at the last two Democratic national conventions, menacing world affairs were hovering over the proceedings.

During the week before the convention, Senator McGrath, who had succeeded Robert Hannegan as party boss, set up Truman's Philadelphia headquarters in the Bellevue-Stratford hotel on South Broad Street. An oversized Democrat in a laughing donkey suit posed with the party chairman as he entered the grand old building. McGrath had just come from a White House strategy meeting which included Kenneth Royall, Secretary of the Army; John L. Sullivan, Secretary of the Navy; former Justice Samuel I. Rosenman, of New York; Charles Brennan, Secretary of Agriculture; Charles Sawyer, who had replaced Henry A. Wallace as Secretary of Commerce; Oscar R. Ewing, Administrator of the Federal Security Agency; Oscar Chapman, Under-Secretary of Agriculture; Matthew Connelly, secretary to the President, Leslie L. Biffle, Director of the Democratic Senate Policy Committee, and Charles S. Murphy, who had been doing campaign planning for the President for the past two years. In addition to making sure no uncontrollable stampede for someone beside Truman got started, they discussed the civil rights plank of the 1948 platform which could cause problems, and the question of the Vice Presidency.

Justice William O. Douglas' statement seemed to take him out of the picture for the second spot, at least Senator McGrath believed it did. A day later Douglas said he would not "quit the bench" for either the

Presidential or Vice Presidential nominations. Still Truman courted him as a way to bring a younger New Dealer onto the ticket. His reluctance put a damper on ADA members carrying around Douglas signs reading, "Turn Gloom to Bloom." James A. Farley, the former head of the party, opposed Douglas, and chided party members for undercutting Truman. "It's disgusting," the once powerful chairman snarled. The apparent refusal of Justice Douglas catapulted Senator Alben William Barkley, of Kentucky, near the top of a long list of potential seconds that included Senator Joseph C. Mahoney, of Wyoming, Governor Mon C. Wallgren, of Washington, Millard Tydings, of Maryland, Senator Scott W. Lucas, of Illinois, and former Speaker of the House, Sam Rayburn, of Texas. Inclusion of a Southerner might do much to salve the wounds that Southern delegates felt inflicted on them by the party they had fostered with Thomas Jefferson, of Virginia, and Andrew Jackson, of Tennessee. But the Truman forces now had firm control of the convention, they thought. They would name the President, the Vice President, and write the platform.

As the delegates arrived in Philadelphia the weekend before the convention opened, they were engulfed with defeatism. Cabbies greeted passengers at the new Thirtieth Street train station, invited them into their "hearse" and joked, "Welcome to Hannegan's wake," a literary allusion to James Joyce's *Finnegan's Wake* and former party director Robert Hannegan, who had been part of the group that convinced Roosevelt to dump Wallace for Truman four years earlier. Even ENIAC, the world's first computer, built a few blocks away on the campus of the University of Pennsylvania, couldn't have given Truman very good odds of survival. Revolt was in the air from both the left and the right factions of the party, and sectional division, mostly absent during the days of FDR was splitting the party into North and South. Senator Olin D. Johnston, of South Carolina, one of the ring leaders of the growing Southern revolt, reported that seven Southern states: Texas, Louisiana, Arkansas, Mississippi, Alabama, Florida, and South Carolina, would shift their attention from stopping Truman to stopping any strong civil rights plank of the platform that the convention might chose to impose upon them. They were also trying to persuade Senator Richard Russell, of Georgia, to stand as their favorite son candidate, so at least they could make their position on civil rights clear in their nominating speeches.

Liberal Senator Claude Pepper promoted his own nomination, without much success. Looking for a cause, he decided to fight along with other Southern delegations to put the old Democratic "two-thirds" nomination rule back in effect for the first three ballots of future conventions to stop any future Trumans. Others like New York Mayor O'Dwyer wanted to fight for Truman's civil rights program "to the hilt," and show no "compromise with bigotry." He said New York also wanted repeal of the Taft-Hartley Act, extension of the Marshall Plan, a strong United Nations, aid for Israel, and lifting of the arms embargo to the Middle East. He said Democrats had to unite behind "a hard hitting, sincere, dynamic and progressive program" unless they wished "to hand the future of the world over to reactionaries of both the right and left."

On the evening before the convention came to life, Pennsylvania's 74 delegates, the second largest contingent, voted to unite for Truman. Said Philip Mathews, the state's Democratic chairman, "Where can we go?" By the time the convention was gaveled to order, Frank Hague, and other anti-Truman regulars, sheepishly climbed back onto the Truman bandwagon. The pro-Truman Michigan delegation retaliated against insurgents by not reelecting E. Cyril Bevan as national committeeman because he had supported Eisenhower. It then voted unanimously to back Truman.

The old Quaker City had barely recovered from the Republican festivities when Democrats began pouring into town for their quadrennial gathering. With 3,192 delegates and alternates, Democrats were more numerous and noisier than the 2,188 Republican delegates and alternatives who had just left town. They were also known as heavier drinkers. To keep Democrats cooler, two dozen extra fans had been installed in the Municipal Auditorium since the Republican blast furnace had been shut down. Flags representing every state were scattered about the auditorium. Early-arriving delegates were taken on a pilgrimage to Valley Forge and Independence Hall.

Then on Monday, July 12, at 12:45 P.M., party chairman, Senator J. Howard McGrath, of Rhode Island, gaveled the Thirtieth Democratic National Convention to order. Hanging 40 feet above the speakers' platform were portraits of Presidents Roosevelt and Truman. The seal of the President of the United States graced the front of the rostrum. A portrait of General Eisenhower suddenly appeared further down on the front of the platform, stuck there by an anti-Truman delegate. The floor was crowded and noisy, but the galleries were sparsely occupied. Five former Democratic National Chairman sat on the platform; James A. Farley, Frank Walker, and Edward J. Flynn, all of New York, Homer S. Cummings, of Connecticut, and Robert E. Hannegan, of Missouri.

After Dennis Cardinal Dougherty delivered his invocation, Pittsburgh Mayor David Lawrence brought cheers by reminding the crowd that they were in the same hall that nominated FDR in 1936. In his welcoming address, Mayor Lawrence brought the convention home to Pennsylvania by accusing Philadelphia's high-tariff, millionaire, Republican industrialist Joseph R. Grundy of manipulating the deal by Senator Edward Martin and the Pennsylvania delegation to support Dewey three weeks earlier at the Republican convention. "Joseph Grundy watched the snarling pack of candidates with amused and cynical eyes and selected the Republican nominee from among them...." He implicated Philadelphia's Republican Congressman, Hugh D. Scott Jr., of brokering the Martin agreement to end his favorite son candidacy in exchange for protecting Grundy's economic interests in a Dewey administration. "He will protect the high-tariff, special privilege, beat-the-taxes, beat-down-labor, forget-the-world Republicans, the dominant element of the Republican party," Lawrence charged. "That deal doesn't sit well on Pennsylvania's stomachs.... It should defeat Dewey two to one," the mayor predicted.

McGrath took over the verbal bombast and berated the Republican Eightieth Congress for "being more occupied in opposing, condemning, and obstructing than in creating, constructing, or enlightening...." It had "one of the most dismal records of stultification, reaction, and retrogression in our annals." Then Pennsylvania Senator Francis J. Myers promised the next four years of the Truman administration would please every one, except "the gimme boys, the grab boys, the me-first boys, the American patriots, junior grade, who set out two years ago to stuff America into their own pockets." But the Pennsylvanian pledged, "We'll be back in the Eighty-first Congress in full strength, full control once again of America's destiny. We'll be back at the old stand, back at the Roosevelt New Deal stand under Harry S Truman." Noting that the Republicans had chosen the same defeated candidate of 1944, he promised, "We'll lick him again with a different standard bearer of our own this time. But with the same weapon, the weapon of the truth and decency in American political and economic democracy."

Philadelphia's Bernard Samuel, who would be last of the Republican mayors of the century, welcomed the delegates with Toquevillean praise, "Here, we feel, is being demonstrated the process of government by a free people. And Philadelphia, rich in traditions of the past, rejoices that it is still the scene of national history in the making."

The high-flown rhetoric was doing little to lift the depression and lethargy on the floor where many delegates felt as though they were attending an overheated funeral. The morning session had little left to do but appoint temporary officers and make committee assignments before it recessed until evening. Then the committees got down to serious work. Representative Mary T. Norton, of New Jersey, was appointed chairman of the Credentials Committee, the first woman to hold the spot. Senator Herbert R. O'Conor was named to lead the Rules and Order of Business Committee, along with Katherine M. Hickson, of Maine, co-chairman of the Democratic National Committee. Former Speaker of the House, Representative Sam Rayburn was appointed the convention's permanent chairman. Oratory, the chief currency of the first day, would wait until darkness and the national radio and television audience that sat in their living room chairs of decision on the Truman Democracy. But Democrats got more bad news that day when it was learned that a *Boston Globe* poll showed Dewey leading Truman by a 56 to 28 percent margin in Massachusetts, a state that hadn't voted Republican since the days of its former governor, Calvin Coolidge.

The most important meeting of the afternoon was of the Resolutions Committee. Senator Francis J. Myers, of Pennsylvania, chairman of the committee, had been holding talks since the previous Wednesday before the convention officially opened. On Sunday evening, the president's legal counsel, Clark M. Clifford, had delivered the President's version of a platform to Senator Myers and the committee at the Drake Hotel. The debate that followed lasted until 2:30 A.M. Truman emphatically endorsed a strong civil rights plank, Clifford confirmed, and did not think he could run on anything less. But Clifford pointed out the party had to be held together to win the election. He did not bring a specific version of the civil rights plank. Truman left that to the committee. He had made clear his views on civil rights to the nation in his January 7, 1948, State of the Union address when he called for a ten-point civil rights program. He had introduced it to Congress on February 2, 1948, but the Eightieth Congress failed to act on his legislative program. Ever since his poll numbers had been low, especially in the South. Truman's poll approval rating in October 1947 was 55 percent. By April 1948, it had slid to 36 percent. Civil rights reform was long overdue, but it wasn't all that popular.

Southerners on the Resolutions Committee were upset by platform drafts which included a strong civil rights plank. South Carolina Governor Strom Thurman, who had been a Truman supporter, was now a leader in the revolt. Senior party officials, who had negotiated with him, predicted a convention floor fight that could wreck the convention and further erode unity. Governor Fielding Wright, of Mississippi, was hinting that Southern delegates might walk out of the convention altogether if their views were not respected. In fact on June 22, 1948, Mississippi states' righters elected 30 national convention delegates who were obligated to walk out of the Philadelphia convention "if President Truman is nominated or if his civil rights program is not repudiated."

Also meeting before the convention, in Minneapolis on the fourth of July, 50 Democratic leaders brought together by the Americans for Democratic Action which was formed in January 1947, many involved in the anti-Truman movement, had announced that they would fight to have the President's civil rights program explicitly included in the 1948 Democratic Platform, despite opposition of Southern delegates. Leading that group were Hubert H. Humphrey, the host city's young mayor, Congressman James Roosevelt, Cook County, Illinois, Democratic leader Jacob Arvey, as well as former New York governor Herbert H.

Lehman, Edward J. Flynn, and Emma Guffey Miller, of Pennsylvania, who had not joined the anti-Truman movement. The group's statement called the President's Committee on Civil Rights "one of the most important measures of moral strategy devised by the United States in modern times." The activists added with flawed historical memory, "The issue of civil rights is in the worthiest tradition of our party," but correctly noted, "It is as a measure contributing to the moral strength of America as a free nation that we uphold the President's civil rights policy." Other signatories included New York Senator Robert F. Wagner, Henry Morgenthau Jr., Chester Bowles, who was running for Connecticut governor, Pittsburgh mayor David L. Lawrence, and Will Rogers, Jr.

Aware of the growing Southern revolt, several party officials and Presidential aides were trying to hold the party together by seeking to find a platform compromise that would mollify both civil rights boosters and Southern states' right advocates. Through Clifford, the President indicated that perhaps one or two of the Southerner's demands could be met, perhaps by again using the generalized civil rights plank from the 1944 platform in the 1948 document. That plank had declared that religious and racial minorities should have "the right to live, vote, and enjoy the rights guaranteed by the Constitution equally with all citizens and that those rights ought to be enforced by Congress." This might comfort Southern politicians since for years they had been able to successfully filibuster civil rights legislation. Truman figured he would try to hold the party together through the convention and election, and then win his civil rights program in a Democratic Congress in 1949.

Perhaps a states' rights plank that reaffirmed the constitutional validity of state power also could be inserted, Clifford indicated, as long as that plank was not directly tied to the civil rights plank. Clearly the Democrats had to take a strong stand. The Republican platform had already declared for civil rights, including abolition of the poll tax used to discourage voting, integration of the armed forces, equal access to employment, and tough anti-lynching laws. The GOP was actively courting African-American voters in Northern urban centers. Dewey was in favor of civil rights and New York was way ahead of the South. Truman was from the border state of Missouri where Jim Crow still lived. Democrats had to hold the black vote up North.

At the Monday afternoon Resolutions Committee meeting, Mayor Humphrey indicated his group would fight in the committee for inclusion of all ten of President Truman's civil rights points into the platform. If he lost, they would file a minority report, he threatened, which included specific support for an anti-lynching law, abolition of the poll tax, a fair employment practices commission, and an end to segregation in the armed forces. Democratic party officials kept pushing for adoption of the 1944 language. And the Southern governors kept insisting that states' rights must be protected. "Now if these boys [his colleagues on the Platform Committee] are wised up here," said Governor Sparks, they'll give something to the South. We want a strong pledge for state sovereignty, and with it, Mr. Truman might get some of his support back in the South." Senator John Stennis, of Mississippi, simply decried the Truman civil rights program as destructive of Southern civilization. The Resolutions Committee would continue to fight in meetings that lasted almost all night, and that fight could spill onto the floor of the convention, and some feared, fatally poison Truman's hopes for reelection.

Monday evening, a few minutes before the second session began, Senator Millard Tydings made it known he was withdrawing his name from Vice Presidential consideration. Kentucky Senator Alben W. Barkley, the convention's temporary chairman, then delivered the 1948 keynote address, as he had been doing since the convention that first nominated Franklin Roosevelt in Chicago in 1932. Barkley was the convention's favorite for the Vice Presidency and he suspected that the post might be his by week's end. But he knew Truman wasn't enthusiastic. Barkley went for broke and eloquently laid out for the listening and viewing nation the Democratic campaign theme for the fall. Democrats would reverse the work of a "reactionary " Congress, drawled Barkley, a big man, who was one of the last great Southern orators of a bygone era. The affable Kentucky Senator could blister his opponent for over an hour without tiring his listeners. But in 1948, he shortened this keynote for the national audience, giving it even more impact than usual. The 70-year-old Kentucky Senator, who served as Majority Leader of the United States Senate under Roosevelt, delivered an old-fashioned, spell-binding, bare-knuckled attack on the record of the Republican's Eightieth Congress.

"My fellow Americans.... We have assembled for a great purpose. We have assembled to give to millions of American men and women an accounting of our stewardship for 16 eventful years, for not one of which we apologize to anyone." His defense of the New Deal set off a 28-minute demonstration of delegates waiting for something to celebrate. Standards from a dozen states followed Kentucky's banner around the big hall and through the crowded aisles in a spontaneous outburst. Delegates were on their feet as the Kentucky Senator set out the Democratic record of Roosevelt and Truman and denounced the Republican Eightieth Congress that had been praised from the same platform three weeks earlier by Republican orators.

Hinting at the civil rights issue, the Kentuckian continued, "But, in a broader sense, we have assembled here in the name not only of American democracy but in the name of democracy for all mankind without regard to race, creed, color, or condition. Our claim upon the confidence of the American people is based on an untiring record of devotion to their welfare, a record which rescued the American economy and the free enterprise system from collapse which we did not foster, and a record which has been four times overwhelmingly endorsed by the American people."

Searching a way out of the North-South stand-off, he said, "There has never been greater need in the world than now for the kind of leadership which the Democratic party from its origin has given in the development of American democracy. That leadership has not been sectional; it has been national. It has undertaken to serve the American people without regard to class or distinction and without undue detriment to any section of our people. The unprecedented challenge that beckons us to service in these uncertain times demands that we look beyond the boundaries of states or nations or political parties and search for the wider opportunity by which we may implement our democracy with the democracy of the world for which we have fought time and time again."

Barkley was just getting warmed up. "What is the record of which I speak?... They call it the New Deal. At every Republican convention since 1932 and on every political rostrum, Republican politicians hurled their anathemas at this New Deal as if it were some blight or plague that had poisoned their lives and consumed the liberties of our people. What is this thing they denounce with their tongues and imitate in their platforms? In the first place, it was recovery. The new administration of Franklin D. Roosevelt breathed life into the nostrils of every worthy American enterprise, new birth and new life, and new hope and new determination and put the agencies of government where they existed, and created new ones where they did not exist, in order that we might demonstrate that our government even in the midst of depression and disaster can be made to serve the American people." The delegates proudly applauded their history.

Then Barkley rattled off the New Deal record, of which he was a part, for half an hour. "It was an agricultural and price support program, which, in 16 years, has increased the income of the American farmer by 800 percent.... It is a rural electrification program.... It is a program for the development of our great waterways.... It is a Labor Relations Act.... It is a reciprocal trade program fathered by one of America's greatest Secretaries of State, Cordell Hull....

"What is this whipping boy they doubt every four years and on every stump and which was placed on exhibit here in this very hall three short weeks ago?" Barkley mocked. "It was a reorganized and strengthened banking system and a Federal Deposit Insurance Corporation by which bank failures in the United States have been reduced from 4,004 15 years ago to only six in 1947.... It is the gainful employment in this year of more than 61 million of America workers compared to 15

269

million unemployed 15 years ago.... It is corporate profits to the corporations of the United States after taxes of more than $17 billion.... It means a prosperity under which the American people have been able to indulge in the luxury of personal savings of more than $100 billion since 1939 and has allowed the Secretary of the Treasury of the United States in little more than two years to discharge $27 billion of the national debt which we inherited from the great war out of which we have just fought.... It has meant these things and more to the American people...."

Senator Barkley put that record up against the recently recessed Eightieth Congress. On the most important issue of them all, the newly acquired and feared atomic power, Barkley said, "The Eightieth Congress refused to confirm the reappointment of this atomic commission for the allotted terms, but reduced their term to two years in the hope that if they gain power, they may be able to use the commission and its functions for political purposes. That is part of the record of the Eightieth Congress....

"The Eightieth Congress refused to enact minimum wage legislation repeatedly recommended by the President...." Barkley added to his complaint the things the Republicans had failed to do: "You do not see a housing bill in that visible record.... What happened to the President's recommendation for legislation to improve and conserve the health of the American people? What became of the recommendations to give further facilities to our educational institutions of this country and hospitalization for the American people?... And if I may quote a very distinguished authority on that subject which was on display here at the Republican convention, I would say these measures are all 'gone geese'...." The Democratic convention laughed at the witty Kentuckian's reference to Republican orator, Mrs. Clare Boothe Luce, who had called Truman "a gone goose."

Why didn't they pass? Barkley wanted to know: "... it may be interesting to recall that there were more lobbyists in Washington during the Eightieth Congress than ever before in the history of American legislation.... In the Seventy-ninth Congress, which was Democratic, there were 360 lobbyists and lobbying organizations registered with the Department of Justice. But during the Eightieth Congress, which was Republican, more than 1,400 lobbyists and lobbying organizations were registered... more than three lobbyists for every member in the House of Representatives and in the Senate... and they spent $8 million dollars.... These recitals my friends scarcely scratch the surface of Republican failures of the Eightieth Congress...."

That brought Barkley to what he called, the "question of inflation." He noted, "Today the retail food price index in the United States has climbed to 211 percent, compared to the average of 1935-1939. It is higher than it has ever been in the United States. Food prices are 12

½ percent higher than they were a year ago.... The consumer price index covering food, clothing, rent, fuel, electricity, ice, house furnishing, and other necessities now stands at 171 percent than in 1935-1939.... But the Eightieth Congress refused to take further steps during its entire existence to deal with the question of inflation and the high cost of living...." The crowd emotionally responded to Barkley's assault.

Then he took on the Eightieth Congress's record on labor before he systematically argued with the entire Republican platform, giving his audience plenty of ammunition to use in the coming campaign. Barkley moved forward in defense of Truman's military defense record. "It is not our fault the world is not enjoying peace which it undertakes to have and fought for during five years of brutal and bloody war." He saluted the efforts of his Republican colleagues Senator Vandenberg and Congressman Eaton and others who built a bipartisan foreign policy. He knew his praise would tend to divide Republicans. Then he turned on the isolationists. "I need not repeat here the efforts of the Republican majority in the House of Representatives to sabotage the Marshall Plan, the Economy Recovery Agency... but, my friends, these same men will be in charge of the House of Representatives if the Republican party should win in November." He pointed out, "...the American people must decide for themselves on the second of November whether they desire to take the chance of having all their efforts to bring about recovery and peace, of economic and political stability in the world go for naught because of partisan politics...." Barkley was not about to let Truman run on his own. The shadow of FDR and all of the emotional connections to the New Deal would be his companions.

Roosevelt's Senate Majority Leader then gave the assembly his studied interpretations of the "Jeffersonian philosophy" on which the old Democracy had developed over the years and the document Jefferson had written in a house in Philadelphia's High Street in 1776. Jefferson "was the founder of American democracy to which we have devoted ourselves and our cause for more than 150 years." Barkley said the Declaration of Independence meant what it said, "All men are created equal." The old wise Southerner counseled the convention, "No genuine believer in the Jeffersonian philosophy was at liberty to deny the worldwide application of this pronouncement.... No true follower of Jefferson is at liberty to withhold it from our own people.... Surely the great Democratic party assembled here in the midst of a great crisis that confronts mankind... in the midst of a world upheaval unprecedented in the annals of history, assembled here in the shadow of the historic hall where Jefferson wrote these things, then surely, in these conditions neither the great Democratic party nor the American people can forswear their obligation to march forward on the highway of human advancement, both here and throughout the world." An old Southerner was appealing to old

Southerners, telling them it was time to lift and cleanse their vision on the issue of race.

Barkley got a strong response from the restless convention crowd trying to make it clear he was its preference for the number two spot on their national ticket. The band played passionately and conventioneers sang along in a heart-felt version of "My Old Kentucky Home." Signs urging, "Barkley for Vice President," appeared throughout the hall to the cheers of the delegates. Some had the "Vice" crossed out. But White House operatives were worried about the Senate Minority Leader's age, and that Kentucky's proximity to Missouri gave no geographic balance to the ticket. Nonetheless, the convention loved Barkley and so did the party. He had been FDR's confidant and truly believed in New Deal Democracy. Senator Tydings immediately threw his support behind Barkley and said the nomination "would be in the nature of a well deserved promotion after years of unselfish and untiring, constructive effort to promote prosperity and security at home and peace and good will abroad." Still, Truman was somewhat reluctant to accept Barkley. The White House put out feelers to Maryland governor, William Preston Lane, who declined.

The convention delegates were beginning to feel the heat of the night mount in the auditorium which was hotter than it was outside because the interior was illuminated with high-intensity Klieg lights. Delegates next heard from Mrs. India Edwards, Director of the Women's Division of the Democratic National Committee and Francis Perkins, Roosevelt's Secretary of Labor. Mrs. Edwards carried along props to help make her point about inflation. "Here in front of me I have a large box," she said. "The lid on this box is like the lid the Democrats kept on prices. We knew then that it was dangerous to lift the lid and we refused to tamper with it. We knew the evils of inflation and refused to take a chance. We held prices down under this lid." But as she uncovered the lid, she said Republican politicians, "the henchmen of big business," had lifted the lid. A balloon flew out and upward. While retrieving the balloon by pulling down a string, she explained how Democrats would bring prices back under control, because, "The Democratic party is the friend of millions, not millionaires."

Miss Perkins brought the session to a close with recollections of her President. "No one in this room tonight can forget or wants to forget a great and beloved man whose smiling face, whose nerve in the face of disaster, gave hope and encouragement first to a prostated nation and later to a harassed and terrified world." The evening session adjourned, delegates satisfied with the day's events, at 1 A.M.

On Tuesday, July 13, delegates and guests were blessed by Reverend Felix Kloman, rector of Christ Church, Philadelphia; listened

Municipal Auditorium/Convention Hall (right), site of the 1936, 1940, and 1948 conventions, dwarfs the Exposition Auditorium (left), site of the 1900 Republican Convention. The Library Company of Philadelphia.

to the National Anthem sung by Miss Carol Brice; and heard speeches from Democratic activists such as Roy Baker, president of the Young Democratic Clubs of America; Oscar R. Ewing, Federal Security Administrator, Representative Michael J. Kirwin, of Ohio, Mrs. Charles W. Tillet, vice chairman of the Democratic National Committee, and Senator Brien McMahon, of Connecticut. More women were participating in this Democratic convention than ever before; 512 female delegates and alternates were on the floor.

When the Credentials Committee issued its report, an effort to expel the Mississippi delegation for its strident denunciations of President Truman and threats to bolt the convention was defeated on the floor in a voice vote. But George L. Vaughn, an African-American delegate from Missouri, was booed by Southern delegates who yelled, "Shut up," when he rose to speak on the issue. Permanent Chairman Barkley pounded his gavel for order. An argument broke out around the Florida standard. Then two challenges were made against Governor Strom Thurman's South Carolina delegation because it excluded blacks from all delegate selection meetings. The challenges overwhelmingly failed. Some on the floor demanded a statement of loyalty from the Virginia delegation, headed by Senator Harry F. Byrd, but the Rules Committee recommended no such action. Senator Claude Pepper, hoping to hold the party together, publicly renounced his own candidacy and said he would support the party's nominee over the "ruthless forces" who controlled the Republican party. His unity thesis fell flat.

By late afternoon, temperatures on the convention floor had topped 100 degrees and delegates were sweltering in the heat of the hall and the tedium of the speeches. Party leadership was trying to speed up proceedings so the convention could end by Wednesday night. To spirited cheers, party chairman McGrath announced that the convention would run continuously on Wednesday until the 1948 platform was adopted, the ticket was nominated, and the acceptance speeches were delivered.

At 7:30 P.M. Philadelphia's Mummers paraded down Broad Street. The local police and fire department bands stopped in front of the Bellvue-Stratford and Ritz-Carlton hotels to serenade conventioneers. Men and women watched from hotel balconies and windows and sent confetti down on their heads. Back at the auditorium, the evening was dedicated to a special and emotional memorial program honoring Franklin D. Roosevelt and servicemen killed in World War II.

That evening, word finally reached delegates that President Truman would honor their wishes; "Old Man" Barkley, as Truman called him, would become his running-mate. The President yielded to overwhelming sentiment for Barkley after his triumphant keynote speech. The President placed a series of telephone calls to his convention lieutenants and put out the word. He then called Barkley, but only to